CHILD DEVELOPMENT
FROM BIRTH TO 8 YEARS

Sara Miller McCune founded SAGE Publishing in 1965 to support the dissemination of usable knowledge and educate a global community. SAGE publishes more than 1000 journals and over 800 new books each year, spanning a wide range of subject areas. Our growing selection of library products includes archives, data, case studies and video. SAGE remains majority owned by our founder and after her lifetime will become owned by a charitable trust that secures the company's continued independence.

Los Angeles | London | New Delhi | Singapore | Washington DC | Melbourne

CHILD DEVELOPMENT
FROM BIRTH TO 8 YEARS
AN INTERDISCIPLINARY APPROACH

AMANDA THOMAS
& ALYSON LEWIS

Los Angeles | London | New Delhi
Singapore | Washington DC | Melbourne

Los Angeles | London | New Delhi
Singapore | Washington DC | Melbourne

SAGE Publications Ltd
1 Oliver's Yard
55 City Road
London EC1Y 1SP

SAGE Publications Inc.
2455 Teller Road
Thousand Oaks, California 91320

SAGE Publications India Pvt Ltd
B 1/I 1 Mohan Cooperative Industrial Area
Mathura Road
New Delhi 110 044

SAGE Publications Asia-Pacific Pte Ltd
3 Church Street
#10-04 Samsung Hub
Singapore 049483

Editor: Delayna Spencer
Editorial assistant: Bali Birch-Lee
Production editor: Sarah Sewell
Copyeditor: Diana Chambers
Proofreader: Bryan Campbell
Indexer: Silvia Benvenuto
Marketing manager: Lorna Patkai
Cover design: Sheila Tong
Typeset by: C&M Digitals (P) Ltd, Chennai, India
Printed in the UK

Library of Congress Control Number: 2022939615

British Library Cataloguing in Publication data

A catalogue record for this book is available from the British Library

ISBN 978-1-5297-4260-2
ISBN 978-1-5297-4259-6 (pbk)

At SAGE we take sustainability seriously. Most of our products are printed in the UK using responsibly sourced papers and boards. When we print overseas we ensure sustainable papers are used as measured by the PREPS grading system. We undertake an annual audit to monitor our sustainability.

CONTENTS

ABOUT THE AUTHORS

Dr Amanda Thomas is a Senior Lecturer in early years education at USW and teaches on the Early Years Education degree and the Working with Children and Families degree. She has taught in both primary and further education before taking up her role in higher education in 2011. Amanda currently teaches on a range of education modules, including play, child development, pedagogy, and leading and managing others. She competed her PhD in 2018 exploring children's schemas in the Foundation Phase. She has had books and research published on early years education, schemas and transitions within education. Amanda has just completed a suite of materials for the Welsh Government on schemas. In her spare time, Amanda is a trustee of a charity trying to restore the former miners' institute in her local village.

Dr Alyson Lewis has worked in a range of sectors including early years/primary education, further and higher education and Government Social Research (GSR). In further education she led two foundation degrees and a top-up degree, and was award leader at Bath Spa University for the BA (Hons) Early Childhood Studies and delivered modules to students in China studying a transnational education programme. She is currently lecturer in education development at Cardiff University teaching on the Advance HE fellowship programme. She completed her PhD in 2017, which examined the concept and practices of well-being in the early years curriculum. She co-authored *An Introduction to the Foundation Phase in Wales* with Amanda Thomas, and has published articles relating to well-being and children's rights.

ACKNOWLEDGEMENTS

I would like to acknowledge and thank Dr Kevin Crowley who was a colleague and one of my PhD supervisors. Kevin sadly passed away in 2018, but he had written several books on child development published by SAGE which I found invaluable while writing this book. I would also like to thank Tina Bruce for allowing me to adapt one of her case studies for use in this book. Finally, thank you to my family and colleagues who have supported and encouraged me in writing this book and, of course, Alyson, my co-author, and the publishers for all their help and guidance.

Amanda Thomas

I would like to thank my family and friends for their continued support in writing this book and to the publishers for their advice and guidance. Lastly, I would like to thank my co-author, Amanda, for being easy to work with and always being motivated!

Alyson Lewis

ONE
INTRODUCTION

This chapter explains the rationale and importance of the book, who will benefit from reading it, some useful key terms, chapter features to support your knowledge and understanding, and a structure of the book with brief chapter overviews. The chapter concludes with a *thoughtful pause* task which can be revisited in the conclusion chapter.

Why is this book needed?

There are many child development books and good quality ones which are informative and rich in theory, but they usually only focus on a specific discipline such as psychology. While this is important, we feel that it can limit what we know about young children's development and their lives. It can also send out a message to readers that other disciplines are not as important or worthwhile. We try to show in this book how different disciplines complement one another and the value of discussing them together, rather than privileging or singling out psychology, for example, which has been the case for many years. It is important to remember that all disciplines have their strengths and limitations, and it is not the aim of this book to take sides, but instead we want the book to raise awareness of the debates that surround early childhood development. It is important to be open-minded about any discipline in order to avoid making assumptions about certain subjects (Ingleby and Oliver, 2008).

Why is this book important?

This book is important because we examine child development through seven disciplines – psychology, sociology, economics, anthropology, philosophy, neuroscience and finally education, and explore the main debates that are taking place. The book challenges dominant discourses within the field of early child development and raises global awareness of children's lived experiences. There are competing models of thought within each discipline, and reading and knowing about them will enrich your understanding of young children as well as social science in general (Ingleby and Oliver, 2008).

This book is also unique because it includes creative and spiritual development, and gives them the space they deserve as they tend to appear less frequently in child development texts; the book also includes the more common child development domains such as social, emotional, cognitive, physical and language development that appear in so many child development texts. Our aim was not to reproduce another child development book like the many that are available, but instead to offer an alternative, interdisciplinary approach.

Who will find this book useful?

On entering university at Level 4, we often find that students have difficulty in understanding theory, including the notion of disciplines and what they have to offer. Students can get confused with terminology and concepts underpinning child development and practice; depending on what they have studied previously, they are generally familiar with theorists such as Piaget, Freud, Skinner and Vygotsky – arguably, a narrow understanding of child development. This book will first help students to broaden their understanding of child development and second will help them understand how these interdisciplinary approaches apply to the domains of child development and practice.

This will be an essential book for undergraduate students studying early childhood degrees and education-related degrees that adopt an interdisciplinary focus to their programme. Students studying joint honours degrees – for example, psychology and education, or philosophy and education – will also find the book valuable. We envisage the book being useful throughout Year 1 to Year 3 where students can revisit Part 1 to refresh their understanding of the key concepts of different disciplines. The book will also be beneficial for experienced professionals who work with young children in early childhood education contexts, particularly if they want to refresh, reflect or engage with continuing professional development.

What key terms are included and what do they mean?

Discipline   A subject that has a particular focus and its own boundaries.

Discourse   A way of thinking and communicating an idea or theory; the language used within a discipline or profession.

Interdisciplinary   Different disciplines (subjects) working together which have many theories and ideas that overlap.

Paradigm   A dominant school of thought/way of thinking (e.g., about children, childhood, development) in a discipline/in society at a particular time in history.

Praxis Critical reflection that leads to action. It involves professionals going beyond critical reflection and applying theoretical knowledge and seeing it in practice to take action, and involves deeper/higher level thinking.

Theories Claims, statements, assumptions and tested ideas that help to frame our understanding.

What does each chapter have to support your knowledge and understanding of early childhood development and practice?

Each chapter has the following:

- clear objectives to inform you about how your knowledge and understanding will be developed and enhanced;
- case studies that provide opportunities for you to apply your understanding of theory, and make links to practice and real-life contexts;
- reflective questions embedded throughout to encourage you to think more deeply about the concepts, theories and ideas being explored;
- succinct summaries to help reinforce the key messages of the chapter;
- end-of-chapter questions that aim to stimulate your thinking beyond your current knowledge and understanding;
- suggestions for further reading, with a brief description of how the reading will extend your knowledge and understanding;

What is included in the book?

The book is organised into three parts, each with a clearly defined aim and purpose.

- **Part 1** (Chapters 2 to 8) aims to introduce you to seven disciplines and discusses their related concepts, ideas and principles. We have not included or discussed politics, history or biology as separate chapters because they are embedded and implicit throughout the book. By the end of Part 1 you will have developed an understanding of the importance of an interdisciplinary/holistic focus on child development.
- **Part 2** (Chapters 9 to 15) aims to examine seven child development domains, but explains them through an interdisciplinary lens (i.e., perspective) which helps you extend your understanding from Part 1.

- **Part 3** (Chapters 16 to 20) aims to explore five different contemporary aspects of early childhood practice which enables you to deepen your understanding of the disciplines and child development domains explored in Parts 1 and 2 and apply this learning to other contexts.

Chapter 21, the final chapter, is titled 'Opportunities to recap and reflect (the conclusion)'. Brief chapter overviews are described next.

Part 1 Understanding interdisciplinary approaches to child development

Chapter 2 The psychology of child development

Chapter 2 opens Part 1 of the book and considers perhaps the most well-known discipline of child development, that of psychology. This chapter explains the different discourses within psychology and the critical debates surrounding each of them. It considers the reliance on developmental milestones or norms, and the advantages and disadvantages of this approach to child development.

Chapter 3 The sociology of child development

Chapter 3 focuses on three sociological perspectives such as functionalism, interactionism and conflict theory. It discusses the new sociology of childhood movement that started to emerge from the 1980s and explores how various social factors influence child development.

Chapter 4 The economics of child development

Chapter 4 allows the reader to develop a basic awareness of concepts relating to economics, such as neoliberalism and cost–benefit analysis. Further, it develops an understanding of the relationship between economics and early intervention. Through the case studies and thought-provoking questions, there is an opportunity to reflect upon the importance of community support and the impact of economics upon a child's life chances.

Chapter 5 The anthropology of child development

Chapter 5 highlights the importance of understanding concepts such as cultural relativism, enculturation, acculturation and ethnography in understanding child development. It debates the various ways that culture can impact on child development and considers how adults can help children develop positive identities. It also explores how development norms provide a limited view of a child's development, thus supporting the discussion started in Chapter 2.

Chapter 6   The philosophy of child development

Chapter 6 introduces the reader to concepts such as poststructuralism, discourse, ontology and epistemology. Moreover, this chapter helps the reader develop an appreciation of how philosophy can help develop critical thinking and support reflective practice. Within this chapter there is a timeline indicating key developments and improvements that have taken place in children's lives since the seventeenth century.

Chapter 7   The neuroscience of child development

Chapter 7 discusses the growing knowledge of the brain and what is meant by neuro-myths and neuro-hits, and how they can impact on people's perceptions of child development. It cites the importance of different professionals learning from each other to improve their knowledge and practice. This chapter also includes information on neurodevelopmental conditions and impairments, and their impact on child development.

Chapter 8   The education of child development

This is the final chapter of Part 1 which considers education as a separate discipline and explores how the history of education has shaped current curriculum policy and practice, including how stakeholders view children and child development. It explains what is meant by key concepts such as praxis, curriculum perspectives (progressive and sociocultural versus instrumental and vocational) and human capital theory. The chapter concludes Part 1 with a brief discussion about the importance of an interdisciplinary focus on child development.

Part 2   Exploring child development domains with an interdisciplinary lens

Chapter 9   Physical development and growth

Chapter 9 opens Part 2 of the book and discusses physical development by distinguishing between gross and fine motor skills, and the influences of both genetic and environmental factors, including culture on physical development and growth.

Chapter 10   Social development

Chapter 10 explores social development through the sense of self and the concept of socialisation with others. It examines the impact of maturation, learning and the interactions between genetic and environmental factors on social development.

Chapter 11 Emotional development

Chapter 11 examines what is meant by emotional development and how children's personalities and temperaments develop. It considers attachment theory and the causes of variations in patterns of attachment. This chapter also explores adverse childhood experiences (ACEs) and their impact on children.

Chapter 12 Creative development

Chapter 12 discusses how children's creativity can be nurtured and developed through the different disciplines discussed in Part 1. Theories and concepts such as symbolic representation underpinning creative development are debated, including the work of Gardner and other theories of creative intelligence.

Chapter 13 Spiritual development

Chapter 13 examines the meaning of spiritual development in the context of child development and the disciplines from Part 1. It further explains how spiritual development contributes to a holistic understanding of the needs and rights of children, families and communities.

Chapter 14 Cognitive development

Chapter 14 focuses on cognitive development and how it is viewed through the different disciplines, which makes it different from other child development books. The chapter closely links to Chapter 2 with its discussion of Piaget and Vygotsky and their role within understanding children's cognitive development. The chapter also discusses schemas and how they can nurture and nourish a child's cognition.

Chapter 15 Language development

Chapter 15 explores the theories of Chomsky and Skinner, and considers the biological and environmental aspects of language development. In addition, this chapter compares and contrasts the different theories of language development and how they are used within education. It explores language development through the different disciplinary lenses discussed in Part 1 and is the final chapter of Part 2.

Part 3 Understanding contemporary aspects of early childhood practice

Chapter 16 Understanding play through the disciplines and domains

Chapter 16 considers what is meant by play and playfulness, and the implications for practice. It looks at how different curricula interpret what is meant by play alongside the role of the adult. It considers both classical and contemporary theories of play, and the different stages and types of play seen with children. The links between play and child development are explored and the importance of outdoor play discussed.

Chapter 17   Understanding well-being through the disciplines and domains

Chapter 17 explores well-being within the context of child development and the importance of promoting and supporting well-being. It explains and defines different well-being discourses linked to the disciplines evidenced in Part 1 and key words associated with them. Perceptions of well-being are also discussed, as well as interventions that are targeted towards improving well-being.

Chapter 18   Understanding global curricula through the disciplines and domains

Chapter 18 explores global curricula, including both national and international curricula. Here the work of Froebel is discussed and his emphasis on learning outdoors and learning through play. This chapter also discusses the curricula of Sweden, America, China and New Zealand, and how they impact on child development within a global context.

Chapter 19   Understanding inclusivity through the disciplines and domains

Chapter 19 begins with an explanation of what is meant by inclusivity and models of disability and inclusion. The chapter also considers the impact of inequalities such as poverty on children's life chances and development. The importance of children's rights are discussed and relevant legislation explained.

Chapter 20   Understanding how shared spaces support child development and the role of the adult within this

Chapter 20 is the final chapter in Part 3 and discusses shared spaces (i.e., the environment). It explores the role of the adult and how spaces that are shared (i.e., between child and adult) facilitate child development. It revisits some of the theorists already written about in previous chapters and how their theories have shaped shared spaces within settings. It describes other approaches to shared spaces (e.g., sustained shared thinking) and how they support the different disciplines detailed in Part 1 and their impact on child development. It concludes with a consideration of how to nurture a child's sense of creativity and autonomy within settings and the crucial role of the adult within this.

Chapter 21   Opportunities to recap and reflect (the conclusion)

This chapter recaps the structure of the book and reflects on the key messages that run throughout the chapters. We also share in this concluding chapter what we have learnt from writing the book before encouraging the reader to think also about what they have learnt from reading it. Lastly, readers are encouraged to revisit the *thoughtful pause* task which is set out below.

II ━━━━━ THOUGHTFUL PAUSE ━━━━━━━━━━━━━━━━━━

Jot down your understanding of any disciplines and child development domains mentioned above and think about what they mean to you and early childhood education and care. You will have an opportunity to revisit this task in the conclusion in order to understand how your knowledge has changed/improved/refined/or been challenged from reading the book.

PART ONE

UNDERSTANDING INTERDISCIPLINARY APPROACHES TO CHILD DEVELOPMENT

TWO

THE PSYCHOLOGY OF CHILD DEVELOPMENT

This chapter will help you to

- understand the basic principles of developmental, humanistic and positive psychology relating to child development;
- become familiar with the criticisms relating to developmental, humanistic and positive psychology.

Introduction

There are many different branches/schools of psychology, such as clinical, forensic, health neuro-psychology, to name but a few. The British Psychological Society (BPS) recognises that there are nine mainstream branches and the American Psychological Association (APA) recognises 56 different branches (Hefferon and Boniwell, 2011), which makes psychology an interesting discipline. This chapter introduces you to the basic principles of developmental, humanistic and positive psychology. These three branches of psychology are helpful in relation to understanding how young children develop, and they have been chosen for the following reasons. First, they are frequently discussed in child development textbooks and therefore you might already be familiar with some of their principles and key concepts. Second, the theories and studies associated with them complement each other in terms of their historical trajectory. For example, developmental psychology is thought to have emerged around the nineteenth century, then humanistic psychology is believed to have emerged around the mid twentieth century, and more recently positive psychology is thought to have emerged around the late twentieth century. Third, developmental, humanistic and positive psychology have been chosen because they help to highlight one of the tensions in the field of early childhood, which is the positive and negative/deficit perspective of young children's development. The positive perspective focuses on a child's strengths and capabilities, whereas the deficit perspective focuses on a child's difficulties and deficiencies. Furthermore, the deficit perspective tends to focus on what children cannot do and compares their development, skills and/or abilities to developmental norms and/or their peers. Haworth and Hart (2007) suggest that a deficit perspective of young children has existed for a very long time and is still evident today.

Basic principles of developmental psychology

Developmental psychology is mainly interested in understanding the behavioural changes that take place as children develop and learn. In order to understand what influences behaviour, thoughts and feelings, there is the long-standing debate of nature (genetic inheritance) versus nurture (influence of the environment). However, Levine and Munsch (2016) highlight that a more contemporary way of thinking would be to consider nature *through* nurture. They define the latter as 'many genes, particularly those related to traits and behaviours, are expressed only through a process of constant interaction with their environment' (Levine and Munsch, 2016: 11). Those interested in examining the factors that influence the chemical reaction of a gene are known to be working in the field of epigenetics (Levine and Munsch, 2016). The field of epigenetics is an important one because it seeks to understand how a gene functions in response to a child's environment and has been useful in understanding attachment and aggression in children.

One of the basic principles associated with developmental psychology and young children is viewing development as linear (progressing in a line) with norms of expected behaviour that naturally lead to adulthood. Developmental charts or milestones with ages and stages are thought to be useful for adults in order to help them respond appropriately at each age and stage. Moreover, they can be used as a guide to assess whether a behaviour is age appropriate (Neaum, 2019). Knowing when to intervene early in order to help and support a child is important for them to develop and learn, and reach their full potential. Neaum (2019) explains that early intervention and targeted programmes are usually underpinned by developmental psychology. It is a useful school of thought because a developmental chart can show whether a child needs additional support and resources to help them reach their full potential. The approach is thought to be effective because it is accessible to many professionals such as educators, childcare workers or health professionals; it is easily understood and provides measurable ways of assessing children (Neaum, 2019). However, there are concerns as to whether developmental psychology by default normalises child development and privileges certain groups of children in society. There are also concerns that developmental psychology focuses too heavily on children's difficulties and deficiencies.

Case study: Using developmental norms

It soon became apparent that two practitioners, one with many years' experience (Pat) and the other who had just recently qualified with a degree in early childhood studies (Chloe), had different views about the use of developmental charts in their practice. Pat would regularly refer to the document used in England called 'Development Matters' to identify where a child was performing by using the descriptors in the document. Then Pat would identify what the child needed to work on in order to meet the next step/milestone. Chloe, who was newly qualified, was keen to ask Pat about her practice, but she was trying to find the right time and the conversation went something like this.

Pat: I find 'Development Matters' so helpful, don't you? It tells me what I should be looking out for.

Chloe: Um, sometimes… it's a bit narrow, though.

Pat: Narrow – what do you mean by narrow?

Chloe: Well, when I first saw it at uni, I thought 'this is great' and it would be so helpful. Then we started critiquing it. I say it's narrow because it only tells us part of the picture.

Pat: Part of a picture is better than none, surely?

Chloe: By narrow, I also mean the actual developmental norms. It means we only look out for them and miss other strengths and talents a child has. Did you know that, in the main, the development norms relate to certain groups of children in particular parts of the world?

Pat: Really? I wasn't aware of that. I've not really questioned documents produced by the government. That's not my place.

Chloe: My early childhood studies degree really made me think about wider contexts, global childhoods and diversity, and helped me understand the importance of sensitively challenging what is written about young children, and consider how this is used in practice to a child's advantage or disadvantage.

Pat: Okay, it sounds like we need to plan a meeting to rethink how we use developmental norms in our practice.

The case study above highlights three important aspects of practice. The first one relates to respecting each other's practice and understanding why adults do what they do. The second aspect relates to having the confidence to challenge/critique what is written about young children – for example, by the government, academics or other professionals. The third aspect relates to the importance of planning time to reflect on practice in order to engage with more contemporary understandings of early childhood.

Reflective question

To what extent is your understanding of child development underpinned by empirical evidence or cultural understandings?

Key theorists: Jean Piaget

The most well-known Western grand theorist of developmental psychology was Jean Piaget (Pound, 2011) and his theory of cognitive development which dominates what people expect from children on starting school (Hedegaard, 2009). From the mid to late twentieth century onwards, Piaget's work about understanding children's thinking was ground-breaking and very influential (Ford, 2018; Neaum, 2019; Woolfolk et al., 2013) and Smidt describes his findings as 'revolutionary at the time' (2013: 19).

Piaget championed ideas of discovery learning, child-centredness (MacBlain, 2018) and constructivism (Levine and Munsch, 2016). In other words, Piaget was interested in understanding how children made sense of their world and is well known for his four-stage theory of cognitive development which is described as being discontinuous in nature (Ford, 2018). In addition, Piaget (1970; cited in Woolfolk et al., 2013) found that a child's thinking process was influenced by four different factors: 1) biological maturation; 2) activity; 3) social experiences; and 4) equilibration.

However, critics argue that Piaget underestimated the ability of young children and suggest that the tasks he set for children were too difficult and the instructions far too complicated (Woolfolk et al., 2013). Margaret Donaldson (1978; cited in Neaum, 2019) challenged Piaget's findings and argued that children were not able to truly show their capabilities because his research was carried out under experimental conditions rather than within naturalistic settings. Martin Hughes (1978; cited in Neaum, 2019) also challenged Piaget's claim that children were egocentric (unable to see another person's point of view). Piaget's work also disregards a child's cultural and social context (Woolfolk et al., 2013) whereas Russian psychologist Lev Vygotksy argued for the importance of the social and cultural context in children's learning and development (Smidt, 2013), but he has been described as ethnocentric (Pound, 2011). Being ethnocentric means that you tend to believe that your own culture is superior to other people's. Moreover, it is important to note that cultural psychologist Michael Cole first translated Vygotsky's ideas into English and there is some debate as to whether Vygotsky's work has been mistranslated (Penn, 2014). MacBlain (2018) reiterates this point and states that questions have been raised about the accuracy of Vygotsky's ideas as a result of translating his work. It is also important to note that because Vygotsky died young, his work has not received as much criticism as Piaget's (Pound, 2011).

Key theorists: Lev Vygotsky

Vygotsky (1981; cited in Smidt, 2013) was interested in cultural and symbolic tools – for example, language, art, painting and signs – and investigated how various artefacts 'transform mental functioning and affect thinking' (2013: 34). Language was the most important tool for Vygotsky and he was a strong advocate of children engaging in meaningful, purposeful tasks that made sense to them (Woolfolk et al., 2013). He also acknowledged nature and nurture in children's development. In other words, babies are born with the ability to do many things, and with the help of others and their environment, basic functions become higher mental functions (Ford, 2018).

Like Piaget, Vygotsky was interested in how children construct knowledge and believed that internalising knowledge occurs on two levels – first, the social and second the psychological or personal level – whereas Piaget was mainly interested in the latter (Smidt, 2013). Barbara Rogoff (2003; cited in Smidt, 2013) has developed Vygotsky's ideas further and suggests that internalising knowledge takes place at three levels: first, the individual; second, the social; and third the sociocultural.

Language as a cultural and symbolic tool was important to Vygotsky (1978; cited in Smidt, 2013), but he was also famous for introducing the concept of the zone of proximal development (ZPD), which is described in more detail in Chapter 14. In sum, ZPD is the gap between what a child has mastered (their performance level) and what they can do with the help and support of someone else (their potential development). Vygotsky (1978; cited in Crowley, 2014) strongly believed that children develop with the help of others and development follows a continuous pattern. However, he did not explain how adults and children should work together. It was Jerome Bruner (1983; cited in Crowley, 2014) who extended his work and introduced the idea of scaffolding as the process of supporting children's ZPD. Nonetheless, MacBlain argues that Vygotsky's ZPD concept 'has become overly representative of his work to the exclusion of many of his other ideas' (2018: 58).

Like Vygotsky, American psychologist Urie Bronfenbrenner was interested in nature (bio) and nurture (ecological) and argued that when children are developing biologically, there is also a complex pattern of interactions occurring from the child's immediate environment (microsystem) through to their wider environment (macrosystem) (Neaum, 2019). Similar to Piaget, Bronfenbrenner's work in the 1970s was considered ground-breaking because it challenged the universal understanding of child development and highlighted the complex nature of development (Neaum, 2019).

Key theorists: Urie Bronfenbrenner

Bronfenbrenner (1979; cited in Crowley, 2014) hypothesised the influences upon a child's development and was interested in the child's immediate environment, which he called the microsystem (home/family), but he was also interested in environments beyond the child's microsystem. For example, the mesosystem is described as a child's early years setting, neighbourhood or community, whereas the exosystem is often described as being non-direct to the child, but having some kind of influence (the parents' job/work context). The macrosystem is furthest away from the child (who is at the centre of his model) and is described as being the wider political, social and cultural contexts that influence a child's development. The chronosystem is used to describe how historical events and dominant paradigms (such as children should be seen and not heard) can influence a child's development. Bronfenbrenner's bioecological model of understanding child development is usually presented as concentric circles with the child at the centre, and it aims to show how different systems interact. The model encourages adults to think more broadly beyond a child's microsystem. His model is sometimes described as a set of nested structures or like a set of Russian dolls (Marsh, 2018), and as a child grows and develops, their relationship between the systems also changes (Levine and Munsch, 2016). To summarise the bioecological model, the different systems have a direct and indirect impact on a child's development. However, Penn highlights that Bronfenbrenner 'made many scientific predictions' (2014: 50) and his work was far too wide to be tested.

Basic principles of humanistic psychology

Generally, humanistic psychology is underrepresented in explaining child development (DeRobertis, 2011). Even though child development textbooks rarely include humanistic psychology, there are humanistic themes in the work of Erikson, Vygotsky and Bronfenbrenner due to their holistic nature (DeRobertis, 2006, 2011). One of the basic principles of humanistic psychology involves focusing on the unique development of the whole child within their social world rather than on subdivisions of the self (DeRobertis, 2006). In other words, humanistic psychologists are interested in the healthy development of the self. However, it is important to note that the way in which the self is conceptualised varies.

Humanistic psychologists are interested in how individuals integrate and organise their experiences and are keen to understand someone's interpersonal relationships (external) rather than their intrapersonal (internal) communication. Moreover, humanistic psychology takes a positive perspective on human existence and focuses on understanding someone's subjective experience (Cardwell, 1996; DeRobertis, 2006). Dillon (2019: 1) states that 'inner nature, flourishing, freedom, and culture' are some of the most important principles of humanistic psychology, often referred to as 'the good life'. This raises interesting questions, such as what does it mean to flourish and what does a good life look like? Arguably, we would all answer differently.

Like Vygotsky and Bronfenbrenner, nature and nurture are both important to humanistic psychologists, and it is believed that with the appropriate love and nurture, a young child will develop a strong sense of belonging that will continue to develop into adulthood (DeRobertis, 2006). The key ideas of humanistic psychologists Maslow and Rogers are now briefly explored.

Human needs and the here and now

Abraham Maslow, American-born psychologist, was interested in motivation and developed a theory called the 'hierarchy of needs' and he hypothesised that when a human's need is satisfied, another one emerges (Gordon Biddle et al., 2014). His theory is presented as a pyramid, and human needs are described by Maslow as being physiological/biological (bottom of the pyramid) in nature, and social and psychological (top of the pyramid) in nature. However, there is limited empirical evidence to support his theory, as most of his predictions derived from his observations and intuitions (Gordon Biddle et al., 2014).

Carl Rogers (1961; cited in Hayes, 1994), another American psychologist, who was mainly interested in personality development, argued that humans have only two basic psychological needs – first, they need 'positive regard' (love, affection or respect from others) and second they need 'self-actualisation' where an individual explores their own potential and abilities. He believed that these needs are essential for psychological health. Rogers is often included in child development textbooks, even though his work did not involve observing children (DeRobertis, 2006).

Unlike developmental psychology, the main principle of humanistic psychology is that 'the child is not held to be the mere result or byproduct of material forces determining his or her development in advance of his or her active participation in the developmental process' (DeRobertis, 2006: 196). The focus in humanistic psychology is on the present and the here and now, whereas positive psychology (discussed next) focuses on understanding the experiences of the past, present and future (Hefferon and Boniwell, 2011).

Case study: Thinking and being holistically

Three-year-old Katie enjoys coming to nursery and happily waves goodbye to her father (Tom) when he leaves her at nursery. Katie is capable of carrying out tasks independently and enjoys taking part in many different activities. She loves to draw, paint and be creative with different items around the nursery. Katie has lots of friends and is caring and helpful. She also loves to play outdoors, climb and use the tricycles. One Friday afternoon, Tom approached the nursery staff to explain that she is not finding it easy to write her name at home and doesn't concentrate for long periods of time on the weekends. He asked them for advice about what to do. He also explained that other parents are talking about how their child can write a few letters of their name and he feels that something may be wrong. The nursery staff talk very positively about how Katie engages with tasks and is full of life at nursery. They explain to Tom that in order for Katie to engage with tasks, they need to be meaningful and purposeful. They also explain that the tasks need to be holistic in nature. They help Tom understand the importance of working in the present, in the here and now, rather than focusing on name writing, which is something that Katie will have experience of in the near future. The nursery staff explain that Katie always seems secure in herself, she knows her interests and has a strong sense of belonging and identity. They communicated to Tom how these characteristics far outweigh the child's ability to write their name. They reassured Tom that writing is a complex act and the way forward is to focus on all aspects of Katie's development, which in turn will help her with many other complex tasks as she grows and develops.

In the case study above, Katie's father is determining the development trajectory for his daughter, rather than thinking holistically, and concentrating on the here and now and what is important to her. The case study highlights that parents may compare their child to other children and feel that something may be wrong, but instead they should focus on their child's strengths and inner nature, and provide the appropriate conditions for them to flourish. The case study also shows the confidence among the practitioners in conveying the importance of Katie's strengths and focusing on characteristics relating to her inner nature.

Reflective question

What does a 'good quality life' look like for a child?

Basic principles of positive psychology

A more contemporary branch of psychology is positive psychology, where Martin Seligman (2011; cited in Dodge et al., 2012) has significantly contributed to developing this movement, but it was humanistic psychologist Maslow who first mentioned positive psychology (Hefferon and Boniwell, 2011).

Hence, there are many overlaps between humanistic and positive psychology (Robbins, 2008) – for example, they both focus on flourishing, happiness and values. Dillon (2019) highlights that Seligman provides a fresh, scientific perspective to the 'good life/full life' and the 'meaningful life'. The 'engaged life' is another important aspect of positive psychology which relates to the state of flow (Seligman et al., 2009) and the important work of Mihaly Csikszentmihalyi. Being in a state of flow (physically or mentally) is often described as being totally absorbed in something or being in the zone. Csikszentmihalyi's work (2002; Hefferon and Boniwell, 2011) focuses on addressing the following question: what is it like for someone when it's going well? It is believed that the following conditions are needed for 'flow' to take place – structured activities with goals and a sense of realistic accomplishment, an element of challenge, a sense of control, distortion of time (time flies when you're enjoying yourself) and, lastly, a desire to repeat the activity (Hefferon and Boniwell, 2011).

Case study: State of flow

After a long day in an early years classroom, two practitioners, Julie and Pete, started reflecting on their daily observations of 5-year-old Jacob. Jacob is a lively child who always enjoys interacting with others and concentrates on tasks for long periods of time and is not easily interrupted. Julie had noticed that on this particular day, Jacob was not spending long periods of time as usual on tasks and was slightly worried, so she mentioned this to Pete. Pete listened to Julie, but he had noticed something different, and he continued to explain that he too had noticed Jacob spending much shorter amounts of time on tasks, but when Pete stopped to observe what Jacob was doing, he was fully engaged, head slightly tilted to one side and chattering away to himself. Jacob was in the zone; he was in his element. Pete then went on to explain to Julie that he had recently read a book by Ken Robinson called *The Element: How Finding Your Passion Changes Everything* (see Further reading) and had applied what he had read from the book to his practice. Julie decided to borrow the book and when she returned it to Pete, she said, 'I get it now'.

The case study above highlights that the state of flow can vary in length and the amount of time that children spend *in the zone* is not necessarily important; it is what they experience during that time that is significant. Behaviour changes do not always have to be negative in nature and observation is key to understanding the detail. The case study also highlights how one practitioner has applied their reading to their practice to understand children's actions more carefully. It highlights the importance of professionals reflecting together.

Reflective question

When you are in your zone/element, how does this make you feel?

Robbins (2008) reminds us that many branches of psychology ignore the state of flow, apart from humanistic psychology. One of the main differences between the branches of psychology is the way they approach research – for example, humanistic psychologists tend to engage with qualitative research (people's thoughts and views) and positive psychologists tend to engage with quantitative research (generalisations and numbers) and test hypotheses. In sum, positive psychology is about understanding what factors contribute to someone thriving and it focuses on strengths rather than weaknesses (Hefferon and Boniwell, 2011).

Robbins (2008) states that humanistic psychologists refer to 'self-actualisation', whereas positive psychologists call this 'eudaimonic well-being'. The eudaimonic well-being discourse encompasses ideas of human functioning and development, autonomy, self-realisation and fulfilment, having a sense of purpose and meaning to life, living an authentic life, being true to oneself and fulfilling one's potential (Ryan and Deci, 2001). Some adults might not associate a eudaimonic discourse with young children because some of the broader components, such as purpose in life, being true to yourself and living authentically, are abstract ideas that younger children might find difficult to comprehend (Wigelsworth et al., 2010). These reasons might explain why a developmental psychology school of thought is so dominant for understanding child development.

In terms of measuring aspects of subjective well-being mentioned above, the majority of measures are aimed at 8-year-olds and above, so there is a tendency to adapt measures for use with younger children. An example of this is evident in the *Growing Up in Scotland* (GUS) study (Parkes et al., 2014). The report states: 'little is known about the importance of relationships, material and other influences on subjective well-being in children younger than ten years old' (Parkes et al., 2014: 4). Therefore, Parkes et al. (2014) adapted Huebner's multi-dimensional Life Satisfaction Scale for 7-year-olds in the GUS study. Objective indicator tools are more commonly associated with children younger than 8 years old. This is where children are conceptualised as 'objects', rather than as 'subjects' who are willing and capable of reflecting upon their experiences (Seland et al., 2015). Part 2 of this book sets out the capabilities and strengths of young children across the development domains.

At times, positive psychology has been called 'happiology' and criticised for polarising the positive and negative (Hefferon and Boniwell, 2011). Critics suggest that positive psychology needs more philosophical rigour concerning ethics and methods (Robbins, 2008). McLellan and Steward (2015) argue that positive psychologists focus too narrowly on feelings and functioning, and highlight the importance of sociology – for example, in understanding well-being. The next chapter explores the discipline of sociology and child development.

Reflective question

How important and relevant is it to focus on a young child's subjective experience of the world?

Summary of chapter

- There are numerous branches/schools of psychology, and developmental psychology is one of the most dominant branches used to explain and understand child development. Development is usually understood as being discontinuous (ages and stages) or continuous (gradual change) in nature.
- Critical reflection should be applied to the developmental milestones/charts that are in common use for young children because they are representative of children from North America and Europe, and lack cultural context.
- Nature and nurture are equally important in understanding how children grow, develop and learn. Child development should be understood in context because the pace of growth varies from one child to another.
- Developmental psychology focuses on the present and future. Humanistic psychology focuses on the present experience of children, whereas positive psychology focuses on the past, present and future.

End-of-chapter questions

1. What is your understanding of psychology and child development?
2. What are the advantages and disadvantages of having a dominant developmental psychology school of thought on child development in the twenty-first century?
3. Why is humanistic and positive psychology underrepresented in discussions about child development?

Further reading

Burman, E. (2018) 'Towards a posthuman developmental psychology of child, families and communities', in M. Fleer and B. Van Oers (eds), *International Handbook on Early Childhood Education and Development*. Netherlands: Springer Nature. pp. 1599–620.

This chapter, from an international handbook, provides an in-depth theoretical discussion about post-human perspectives to understand child development and will introduce you to new concepts.

Doherty, J. and Hughes, M. (2014) *Child Development: Theory and Practice 0–11*. London: Pearson Education.

This accessible book discusses key concepts linking to developmental psychology and applies them to practice.

Robinson, K. (2010) *The Element: How Finding Your Passion Changes Everything*. London: Penguin Books.

This book was mentioned in the case study called 'state of flow' and will help you understand further how to reconnect with your true self.

THREE
THE SOCIOLOGY OF CHILD DEVELOPMENT

This chapter will help you to

- develop an understanding of sociological perspectives, such as functionalism, interactionism and conflict theory;
- develop an awareness of the new sociology of childhood movement and how social factors influence child development.

Introduction

Sociology has existed as a social science from the late nineteenth century and is considered to be a relatively new discipline where Comte, Durkheim, Weber and Marx are often described as the founding fathers (Meighan, 1981). Sociology is about finding out about human society and understanding how humans interact with the social environment. German sociologist Norbert Elias (1897–1990) argued that an important role of a sociologist is to understand how nature, culture and society relate to one another (Gabriel, 2017).

The discipline helps to explain changes in society, as well as understand how power is distributed between social groups such as adults and children (Barry and Yuill, 2008). Moreover, it is a discipline that sets out to explain the social world which is viewed by sociologists as multi-layered and is associated with radical thought and challenging assumptions. Wharton (2005: 2) states that the things people accept as 'the ways things are, may be most in need of close, systematic scrutiny'. Ingleby and Oliver (2008: 24) describe sociology as 'a discipline that is often associated with politics, especially left-wing politics', but they also highlight that this is a stereotypical view of sociology. In brief, social equality/justice, progressive ideas and liberalism are associated with left-wing politics.

Sociology is also helpful in understanding how young children learn about and enact gender through the process of socialisation. Gallacher and Kehily (2013) highlight that there are numerous sources available in children's lives, such as in the family, the education system, the media, children's peers, to name but a few where children develop gender identity.

Social factors

Sociology is important for understanding how children's development, behaviour and life chances are influenced by social factors (Barry and Yuill, 2008; Ingleby and Oliver, 2008) such as age, gender, socioeconomic background (Pells and Woodhead, 2014). Pells and Woodhead (2014) who worked on the Young Lives Project describe the macro environment as economic growth, adverse events (such as drought), education and social attitudes towards children, which can alter the experience for children growing up. This is important because on a global scale, children are the largest group to be affected by poverty.

Moss and Urban (2020) who write about the latest findings from the Organization for Economic Co-operation and Development's (OECD) international early learning well-being study, argue that there is nothing new about the results. For example, poorer children do worse in all measures for early literacy and numeracy skills, self-regulation, and social and emotional skills. These (they argue) are 'easily measured common outcomes' (2020: 6). Furthermore, what parents do is the most important for their child's growth and development, where children from advantaged backgrounds tend to have more learning opportunities. They further highlight what the report does not tell us, which is the complex system of a country's early childhood education and care programme.

According to Penn (2014), the pace and degree to which a child's growth and development changes depends in part on where a child grows up. Every year since 1980, the United Nations International Children's Emergency Fund (UNICEF) publishes a report on the state of the world's children. The 2019 report featuring data from 202 countries worldwide found that despite improvements over the last two decades:

- one in three children under five is not getting the nutrition they need to grow well;
- two-thirds are at risk of malnutrition;
- 340 million children suffer from the hidden hunger of deficiencies of vitamins and minerals – 'iron deficiency reduces children's ability to learn' (2019: 3);
- 49.9% of children in South Asia are not growing well compared with 11.6% in North America who are not growing well (2019: 18).

In 2015, the Welsh Government reported that girls outperformed boys in all aspects of the early years curriculum called the Foundation Phase. The greatest difference occurred in language, literacy and communication skills (WG, 2015b). In terms of a UK English context, boys are reported to be 'nearly twice as likely as girls to fall behind in early language and communication' (Save the Children, 2016: iv) and this has been a similar picture for the past decade. Save the Children (2016) further reports that boys are behind their female peers and the gender gap is highest among children from poorer backgrounds in every local authority in England. A child's circumstances at birth has a significant influence on how they achieve and succeed in life.

According to Barry and Yuill (2008), sociology provides rich opportunities for critical thinking and questioning, and this is at the heart of the discipline. They further state that sociology is 'one of the most controversial' (2008: 11) disciplines in academia and it is the critical questioning that generates hostility. As with all disciplines, different perspectives are adopted and the following discussion explains some of them.

Functionalism

A functionalist perspective in sociology is focused on *society* rather than on the *individual* and is interested in understanding how systems such as healthcare and education, and subsystems such as families and culture make society function (Barry and Yuill, 2008). Social behaviour is often described in this perspective as a product of society. This perspective assumes that societies have basic needs, such as social order, if they are to survive. Functionalists believe that in order for social order to exist there needs to be a shared understanding of norms and values, and one way of ensuring that these norms and values are commonly understood is by individuals socialising. American sociologist Talcott Parsons (1902–79) reported that childhood socialisation is 'a process whereby they gradually learned about and internalised social conventions in order to become a full member of their culture or society' (Gallacher and Kehily, 2013: 220).

As well as being interested in social order, functionalists are also interested in social disorder and conflict. However, functionalism is criticised because it places too much emphasis on social systems and less emphasis on how individuals make choices and socially interact (micro elements). It is also criticised for seeing society and the individual as separate entities (Ingleby and Oliver, 2008).

A pivotal time in the UK was 1946, whereby the welfare state was introduced as a dominant idea for taking care of the needs of children and families. With the introduction of the National Health Service (NHS), social security and social services, it was recognised that the wider social system could impact on the life chances of children and their families (Ingleby and Oliver, 2008). However, the drawback of the welfare state has reinforced or, some would say, perpetuated the vulnerability of children (Shanahan, 2007).

In terms of child poverty, functionalists would be interested in understanding how it threatens the social system and would ensure that there is a strategy in place to counter the negative impacts of poverty (Ingleby and Oliver, 2008).

Case study: 30 hours free childcare – government policy

Peter has a part-time job at a local garage and is a single dad of three young children – Harry who is 7 years old, Katie who is 3 and Bradley who is 1. He recently became a widow and lives in the family home in a rural village. When he is at work, his mother looks after Katie and Bradley, and he has just heard about a new government policy that offers working parents 30 hours of free childcare for children aged 3–4. He is so pleased, as this means that Katie will have a place at the local nursery,

(Continued)

but the policy states that childcare providers must be approved in order for Katie to receive the free offer. The nursery closest to the family home is not on the government's list of approved childcare providers, but the nursery, which is listed and approved, is thirty-five minutes away by car, which makes it difficult for Peter to get to. Due to Peter's circumstances, he is unable to make use of the childcare offer. Therefore, his mother will continue to look after Katie as the policy states that a parent cannot claim the hours if childcare is provided by a relative.

The case study above highlights how a government policy focuses on society as a whole, in particular the early childhood education system, and does not cater for Peter's individual circumstances and offer flexibility so that his daughter can attend a setting.

Reflective question

What can you learn about children, their families and social policy when applying a functionalist perspective to this case study?

Interactionism

Interactionism is another sociological perspective that focuses on how individuals interact with one another. Social behaviour in this perspective is viewed as a result of inventive and creative individuals whereby interactionists view human experiences as continuously shifting and are not considered fixed entities. They are interested in understanding the negotiated meanings that people attach to their experiences and endeavour to find out how individuals navigate different social systems (Ingleby and Oliver, 2008).

Sociologist William Corsaro is well known for his work on peer cultures and focused on understanding children's interpretations of their culture. He suggests that during socialisation children are not simply internalising the adult culture, they are contributing to it by their interactions and negotiations with adults and other children (Gabriel, 2017). American sociologist Norman Denzin agrees with Corsaro in that the process of socialisation is fluid where children are shaped by socialisation and are also shaping it (Gallacher and Kehily, 2013). Shanahan (2007) states that Corsaro's study was one of the first in sociology to report children's perspectives and raise the importance of child culture.

An interactionist perspective focuses on meeting the individual needs of a child, acknowledging the many ways in which they communicate and views young children as meaning-makers (Ingleby and Oliver, 2008). Smidt (2013) also views children as meaning-makers, as well as symbol weavers and users. Cameron and Moss (2020) suggest that all those involved with early childhood education and care need to ensure that they have a rich image of the child where the multiple ways in which they communicate are authenticated.

Interactionism is criticised because it is thought to be too localised and small scale in nature (micro elements), and therefore might not always apply to global contexts. It is also criticised for seeing the individual in isolation and disregards the important role that the social system can play in child development (Ingleby and Oliver, 2008).

In terms of child poverty, an interactionist perspective would be interested in understanding how poverty is impacting on an individual and recognises that individuals experience poverty in many different ways. Interactionist sociologists are interested in finding out how individuals creatively deal with social challenges such as poverty or migration (Ingleby and Oliver, 2008).

Case study: Meeting individual needs

Natalie, a newly qualified primary school teacher, really enjoys working as a reception teacher with 4- to 5-year-olds. She has some awareness of the socioeconomic status of the children in her school and class as there is a very high percentage of children receiving free school meals, which is often used as an indicator for low socioeconomic areas. Joe, one of the boys in her class, arrives at school on time but always seems very hungry by the mid-morning break. He would eat his banana very quickly which is provided by the school and then on some occasions Natalie found him eating the leftover apple cores from his classmates. She started to get a little concerned about this and started to note this behaviour. Then, during an activity about favourite foods and healthy eating, Joe explained to Natalie that he loved eating in school and would have tasty toast at home. He said, 'I love treat Tuesday and sweet Sunday'.

When Joe was collected from school the following Tuesday, Natalie said to his mum 'He's really looking forward to going home today because it's treat Tuesday'. An hour later Natalie received a phone call from Joe's mum who explained the challenging financial circumstances of feeding her family. Her low income meant that she had to be very resourceful and creative with food and calling it 'Treat Tuesday' and 'Sweet Sunday' was her way of dealing with the lack of luxury foods throughout the week but maintaining some kind of dignity as a mother to her children. Joe's mum explained how she had to rethink how to use basic ingredients, cook a healthy meal and save money. On reflection of the conversation with Joe's mum, Natalie realised that many other parents might be experiencing something similar, so she approached her headteacher with an idea to start a ready, steady, cook club. The aim was to bring families together to cook healthy meals. The headteacher agreed and provided a small budget for the group.

This case study shows how the class teacher really focused on the interactions and individual context of Joe's circumstances and made every effort to put in place a plan to ensure that other families would benefit from learning about being creative with food when on a low budget.

> ### Reflective question
>
> What can you learn about children, their families and poverty when applying an interactionist perspective to this case study?

Conflict theory

Conflict theory is similar in nature to functionalism because it focuses on the social system, but sociologists are interested in the conflicts that exist within a social system, particularly the economic system. The concept of ideology is important in conflict theory and is interpreted as being the 'beliefs and values [of the rich and powerful] which disguise truth and distort the reality of the social system' (Ingleby and Oliver, 2008: 30).

Conflict theorists such as founder Karl Marx (1818–83) and Pierre Bourdieu (1930–2002) were interested in the conflicts between two main groups – the rich/ruling class (*bourgeoisie*) and the poor/working class (*proletarians*). Smidt (2013) explains that both theorists were interested in power and class, and they believed that capital (acquired through work) underpins the class system. Marx argued that capital is someone's salary, and their capital determines where they live and what they have, whereas Bourdieu further argued that capital means more than just the economic; there is cultural (what you know) capital and social (who you know) capital. In terms of the latter, young children in early years settings develop social capital among their peer culture.

Bourdieu also used the term habitus and family habitus to help understand and explain the habits, attitudes and behaviours of people within society. He argued that cultural and social capital explained why some children might find it difficult to thrive and achieve in early years settings, rather than a result of a child not trying or being capable (Smidt, 2013). Gabriel (2017) uses the term primary habitus for family and states this is where children begin to internalise their thinking and act out behaviours from their parents/carers.

As with functionalism, conflict theory is criticised because it focuses too much on the social system and not enough on the micro elements of society (Ingleby and Oliver, 2008). Gabriel (2017) explains that Bourdieu's work is particularly important because it sets out to overcome the micro–macro divide in sociology. This means that children's interactions and relationships are understood within the immediate context, as well as within the broader social structures of society.

Conflict theory is useful in understanding the relationship between a child's socioeconomic background and their growth and development. While we know that a number of factors influence a child's development, Ingleby and Oliver (2008) suggest that economic factors are the most influential. The Millennium Cohort Study (MCS), also known as the child of the new century study, is an important longitudinal study that follows the lives of 19,000 young people across the UK born between 2000 and 2002. The study is led by Professor Fitzsimons, based at University College London (UCL), who is interested in finding out how a child's/young person's experiences and circumstances impact on their skills later on. The latest sweep of data collection took place in 2018. The study reports that despite the UK being a wealthy country, the rates of poverty are much higher than in other Western countries. Schoon et al. (2010) report that there is a large gap between the cognitive ability of five-year-olds from those families who receive financial support and those who do not. They conclude that poverty has the most negative impact on children's cognitive development. Conflict theorists would be interested in understanding the social disorder that poverty creates in society (Ingleby and Oliver, 2008).

In 2011, the Welsh Government secured funding to analyse data from the MCS for children in Wales. It reports that maths and reading scores for 7-year-olds were poorer when there is low parental education and income. They further report that when a child is read to on a daily basis, their cognitive scores at 7 years of age are 5 months ahead (WG, 2011).

Case study: Finding out

The Williams family live in an inner city social housing estate where there are issues of unemployment, drug and alcohol misuse and crime. The family consists of a mother and father called John and Sally and their two children – Craig who is 5 years old and Donna who is 3. Craig is very lively and likes to play in the street with much older children and ride his bicycle, whereas Donna is very quiet and likes to play in the garden with her toys. Sally has recently noticed that Craig is getting very aggressive around Donna and provokes her when she is busy playing with her toys. Donna likes playing with lots of Craig's toys but Sally often hears Craig saying 'girls don't play with them' and 'girls can't do that, they're not strong enough'. John and Sally both work and admit they don't have a lot of routine in their life or spend much time with their children to do reading.

This case study highlights the challenges that some parents face in carrying out routine daily activities such as reading to their children, which can boost cognitive development when they are working many hours to stay out of poverty and financially take care of their family.

Reflective question

What can you learn about children and their families when applying a conflict theory perspective (cultural and social capital) to this case study?

Postmodernism

Postmodernism, a theoretical standpoint, originates in disciplines such as sociology, politics, art, cultural studies and literature, and became more prominent from the 1970s (Albon, 2011).

Albon (2011) suggests that it helps to disrupt commonly held assumptions/truths such as universal understandings of children and childhood, moulding children into social beings and the normal child. She further states that knowledge framed from a postmodernism standpoint is socially constructed and not free from 'culture, time and space' (2011: 40).

Postmodernists are interested in finding out how knowledge about the social world is constructed and in order to do this sociologists apply critical questioning techniques to understand the world (Barry and Yuill, 2008). An important feature of postmodernism is examining discourses, which are described by Ereaut and Whiting (2008) as 'more-or-less coherent, systematically-organised ways of talking or writing [about a topic or concept], each underpinned by a set of beliefs, assumptions and values' (2008: 10). Barry and Yuill (2008: 20) describe a discourse as 'the language used to express thoughts'.

In terms of childhood discourses, Dahlberg et al. (2007) set out five discourses and claim that discourse five – *The child as a co-constructor of knowledge, identity and culture* – characterises a postmodern perspective. This discourse views childhood as one of many important life stages and there is neither a natural nor a universal childhood. Children are viewed as social actors, agents of change, and the voice of the child is promoted. Discourse three, *The scientific child of biological stages*, focuses on the individual child, biological stages and natural ladder like progression where children are measured by separate developmental areas. Context is overlooked in discourse three and is associated with developmental psychology.

The new sociology of childhood movement

By the 1980s, researchers were dissatisfied with the dominance of two disciplines – namely, developmental psychology and functionalism in sociology (conforming to social rules and internalising roles needed for adulthood), and consequently the new sociology/social studies of childhood emerged, which offers an alternative perspective (Gabriel, 2017; Gallacher and Kehily, 2013; Quennerstedt and Quennerstedt, 2014). Penn (2014) describes the new movement as understanding what it is like for children in society which is dominated by adults. Mayall (2000) describes the new movement as taking children seriously and viewing them as people.

Sociologists Alison James and Alan Prout are well known for their contribution to the new sociology of childhood movement. They believe that children's lives are interconnected with other variables such as social class, gender and ethnicity, and therefore childhood is a variable of social analysis. Moreover, they criticise the belief that a universal and global understanding of childhood exists and oppose the way in which developmental stages are used as standard and apply to all children. They avoid assuming that children across the world are the same and place more emphasis on the cultural contexts in which they grow up. James and Prout (1997; cited in Gabriel, 2017) highlight that a universal and global perspective of children is grounded in the *minority world* countries that represent children mainly living in Europe and North America, whereas the *majority world* countries, such as Asia, Africa and Latin America, is where the majority of young children live.

Therefore, adopting a universal and global perspective is not representative of all children. The movement recognises that multiple childhoods exist.

Traditionally, families were considered extremely important in shaping young children's lives. However, Gabriel (2017: 5) states: 'in contemporary society young children are not mere receptors of daily socialisation, but active generators of their own social and cultural capital'. A key feature of the new sociology of childhood movement is acknowledging and recognising that young children are active participants who construct their own lives and relationships with others. The movement focuses on researching children's perspectives as worthy in their own right independent of adults' perspectives (Gallacher and Kehily, 2013). Moreover, the movement is closely connected with children's rights, participation and the concept of agency, which, if facilitated authentically by adults, provides opportunities for children to shape society and become active citizens of the world (Barry and Yuill, 2008; Waller, 2009). However, MacBlain et al. (2017) point out that some of these ideas within the new sociology of childhood movement are unsustainable in postmodern times.

Uprichard (2008) argues that in order to increase a child's agency it is important to adopt a human *being* and human *becoming* perspective. The 'being' perspective is often associated with the discipline of sociology where adults view children as social actors who construct their childhood and are seen as competent and present oriented, whereas the 'becoming' perspective is usually associated with the discipline of psychology where adults view children as adults in the making and is future oriented. Uprichard (2008) concludes that both perspectives complement each other and are interconnected. She further states that at times it will be beneficial to focus on either the present or future context and vice versa. To summarise, sociologists James and Prout (2004; cited in Gallacher and Kehily, 2013: 228) state:

> childhood is a developmental stage of the life course, common to all children and characterised by basic physical and developmental patterns. However, the ways in which this is interpreted, understood and socially institutionalised for children by adults varies considerably across and between cultures and generations...

Case study: Childhood memories

Jody was the lead researcher on a project about understanding childhood memories. The following participants reflected back and shared their memories:

'I remember when I was in nursery [3- to 4-year-olds] and Mrs Hedges shouted at us for mixing the sand with the water... '.

'I was 11 at the time, but I remember being told off by my mum when I painted the back gate with my friend. My dad worked away and my mum was always going on about how the gate

(Continued)

needed painting so I thought I'd help her out. But it turns out we used the wrong paint and got too much paint on the floor... '.

'I remember starting Year 1 [5- to 6-year-olds] and Mr Johnson asking us where we wanted the furniture to go, and what we should put on the walls. As a class of twenty-five, we designed our learning space and made it our own... '.

'I remember crying every Thursday morning before going to school because we had to do writing. I was 4 years old and found it so difficult... '.

'I remember being on the school council in Year 6 [10- to 11-year-olds] and going around the other classes to ask their opinions and views on what needed changing in the school. I loved visiting the nursery and reception classes [3- to 5-year-olds] because they seemed to have so much fun. I know it must have looked funny to the teachers, but I put on an apron and started playing with the water... '.

'My favourite teacher was Miss Norman because she always listened to us and was caring and funny. She let us climb outside, take risks and always trusted us with different jobs... '.

'I remember my mum would always let us prepare and cook the meals. My sister and I would look in the cupboards and freezer to see what we could make. This must have been so time-consuming, but such a happy memorable experience... '.

The case study above includes various childhood memories from different people. They highlight how adults made them feel – for example, some adults made them feel empowered and respected, whereas some reflections show how adults made them feel underrated and devalued their capabilities.

Reflective question

How would you want a child to remember their time with you when they reflect back on their childhood?

Summary of chapter

- Sociology is a discipline that seeks to understand the multi-layers of the social world and explores the many different social factors that influence a child's development and life chances.
- Economic factors are reported to be the most influential in children's growth and development.

- A functionalist and conflict theory perspective in sociology focuses on understanding the various systems and subsystems that make society function and behave.
- An interactionist perspective in sociology examines how individuals navigate the different social systems. Interactionists believe that children are shaped by socialisation but they are also shaping it at the same time.
- The new sociology of childhood movement focuses on understanding what it is like from a child's perspective living in a society dominated by adults and social systems. Concepts such as agency, rights and participation are associated with the new movement.

End-of-chapter questions

1. What is your understanding of sociology and child development?
2. How would you respond to an adult who says that young children are annoying and ask too many questions?
3. Can you make a list of ten things that young children are capable of doing well?

Further reading

Corsaro, W. (2018) *The Sociology of Childhood* (5th edn). London: SAGE.

This book provides you with an in-depth discussion of social theories and helps you understand children's peer cultures.

Mayall, B. (2002) *Towards a Sociology for Childhood: Thinking from Children's Lives*. Buckingham: Open University Press.

This well-organised book draws extensively on sociological studies and will help you understand the importance of validating children's experiences.

Wyness, M. (2019) *Childhood and Society* (3rd edn). London: Red Globe Press.

This accessible book discusses key concepts linking to sociology and provides global empirical examples.

FOUR
THE ECONOMICS OF CHILD DEVELOPMENT

This chapter will help you to

- gain a basic awareness of concepts relating to economics such as neoliberalism and cost–benefit analysis;
- develop an understanding of the relationship between economics and early intervention.

Introduction

As a discipline, economics is bound up with context, political values and beliefs, and is very 'influential in determining national and international policies' (Penn, 2014: 149). While this book explores a range of disciplines, policies about early childhood education and care are generally underpinned by economics and psychology (Penn, 2014). Governments must make decisions about where to spend money – for example, do they invest in wind-power technology or early childhood education and care? If both, this raises questions such as how much money should each investment get? Should more money be invested in one over the other; if so, why and how do governments/politicians decide? It is worth noting that evidence, as well as people's values and political judgements inform policy-making (Miller and Hevey, 2012). Various reviews such as the Field review (2010), Allen review (2011) and the Tickell review (2011) have been commissioned by the United Kingdom (UK) government to improve the evidence base that will inform future policy-making decisions (Miller and Hevey, 2012).

A more recent example where economic analysis has been useful is the decision that Welsh policy-makers had to make about an additional twenty hours of childcare for 3- to 4-year-olds. Paull and Xu (2015) conducted this piece of work and in order to estimate the potential impacts for the Welsh Government, they examined two options: the first was a universal offer for all 3- to 4-year-olds and a second option involved a work requirement for parents. They concluded that within the current climate the working requirement for parents would offer better value for money in ensuring parental employment. Therefore, the decision was made to go with the working requirement option. However, they also report that both options would offer 'similar value for money in reducing poverty' (Paull and Xu, 2015: 2). In this instance, economics as a discipline was helpful but also problematic, as policy-makers had to choose between encouraging parental employment or reducing poverty – achieving both was not an option.

Penn (2014) explains that economists mainly take a positivist view of the social world, which means that facts, figures, generalisations and predictions are very important to them (Creswell, 2014). The discipline helps to make predictions about people's behaviour and puts a value on something. There are different economic analyses/measures of doing this, such as cost–benefit analysis and economic evaluation which can be applied to human activity to help understand the value or impact of something (Penn, 2014). However, applying economic analyses to health and education is problematic – humans are complex beings.

Gross Domestic Product (GDP)

A more traditional economic measure would be Gross Domestic Product (GDP) (O'Donnell et al. 2014), which is used to measure the success of a country (Organization for Economic Co-operation and Development (OECD), 2011). Many agree that GDP is a useful 'objective' measure of economic growth, but it only captures part of a picture. In 2009, economists Joseph Stiglitz, Amartya Sen and Jean-Paul Fitoussi (2009) stated that too much emphasis is placed on GDP which is being used as a standard economic indicator for measuring quality of life. They suggest that more emphasis should be placed on measuring people's 'subjective' well-being; this dimension focuses on people's life satisfaction, positive and negative feelings and how someone feels about the purpose and meaning of life (OECD, 2011). Chapter 17 explores the concept of well-being in more detail.

Penn (2014: 142) explains that economics as a discipline

is theoretical, in the sense that it proceeds from certain assumptions about how people make decisions about money and increase their wealth. But it relies on quantitative data, a particular way of computing the consequences of transactions of goods and services between people.

Classical economics

Many daily acts involve a commercial exchange – for example, buying food, making a telephone call and running a tap – and this exchange in economics is known as 'the market'. In classical economics, supply and demand is often used to describe the market, which means that when there is high demand and a short supply of something, the price/cost will go up and when there is too much supply of something, as in day nurseries, the owners/suppliers will compete with one another (Penn, 2014). For some services, competition can have a negative impact (Penn, 2014) – for example, if day nursery owners are having to make their business more competitive and productive, they might increase work hours for staff and/or in order to have more children attend, they may employ lower qualified staff to keep costs down. Tired staff working longer hours and lower qualified staff could impact on the quality of provision for young children. A recent study by the Nuffield Foundation which explored staff qualifications in the early years in England with children's outcomes found 'a positive but small association between the presence of degree-qualified staff and children's outcomes as measured at age five by the Early Years Foundation Stage Profile' (Bonetti and Blanden, 2020: 6).

Economics is an important discipline for those working with children and their families. It helps practitioners understand the impact of decisions made by policy-makers and the relationship between the economy and the workplace. Therefore, the remainder of this chapter discusses concepts such as neoliberalism and cost–benefit analysis within the context of early childhood education and care.

Neoliberalism

Capitalism can be explained as a country's economic and political system whereby trade is controlled predominantly by private enterprise rather than by the state. Neoliberalism is a type of capitalism (Clouston, 2015) which, according to Smith et al. (2016), is rooted in eighteenth- and nineteenth-century liberal philosophy. Penn (2014) explains that in the 1990s, the dominant paradigm in economics was neoliberalism, defining it as 'a view that the state should interfere as little as possible and should not arbitrate in the way people exercise their self-interest… ' (2014: 145). However, if the state/government interferes less and does not provide financial support, inequality perpetuates. Neoliberals view poor/disadvantaged children and their families as a nuisance in society rather than an injustice (Penn, 2014), and they take this view because poor families are not contributing to the production cycle of generating wealth (Clouston, 2015). Moreover, neoliberals see children more as 'the property of their parents' (Penn, 2014: 146) rather than as the property of the state.

Words often associated with neoliberalism are privatisation, deregulation, free trade, consumerism and globalisation. Similarly, individualism is another word associated with neoliberalism which, in the context of the workplace, means 'greater levels of scrutiny and control in order to ensure that this notion of individual responsibility is fully implemented' (Clouston, 2015: 12). In neoliberalism, more accountability and tighter control is placed upon professionals working with young children in meeting pre-specified standards and school-readiness measures rather than giving practitioners autonomy (Cameron and Moss, 2020). Moreover, the agenda of a neoliberal would be to 'promote a standardised, one-size-fits-all approach' (Cameron and Moss, 2020: 100); arguably, this is easier to control. But, as stated in Chapter 2, developmental norms are representative of certain groups of children.

Activists and advocates

Activists who contest neoliberalism champion 'for local democratic, participatory and authentic assessment that respects and values both children and teachers' (Cameron and Moss, 2020: 185). Basford and Bath (2014) provide an excellent analogy in their work, whereby they suggest that practitioners working in the Foundation Stage in England are having to play the assessment game and are torn between strategic (neoliberal) and authentic (activist) acts. Practitioners are torn between competing paradigms, one of which is developmental psychology focused and centres on the universal/typical child and expected learning behaviours (neoliberal); the other is described as the sociocultural approach (activist). The sociocultural approach to assessment in early years settings focuses on context and working collaboratively with parents/carers and embeds assessment into practice; it is used as a cultural tool to extend children's ideas and capabilities rather than being used in a summative way to find out what has been learnt (Basford and Bath, 2014).

Advocates of neoliberalism focus more on competition, private provision, individualism and, according to Cameron and Moss (2020), is more prevalent in Western countries such as the UK and the United States of America. In Western economies, the main goal is productivity and growth, where the priority is to make money and spend it in order to stimulate the market and generate wealth (Clouston, 2015). Conversely, Marxism privileges co-operation over individualism and is associated with countries such as China and Russia. Marxism has its origins in the work of Karl Marx and Friedrich Engels (Thurtle, 2005).

In neoliberalism, the market is stimulated in various ways, such as offering more power to organisations through deregulation and reducing the welfare state, which collectively impacts negatively on the rights of workers (Clouston, 2015). Therefore, the working person is important in the production cycle of generating wealth, but, as Clouston (2015) explains, 'paid work can be greedy in terms of our personal resources of time and energy and can cause work–life imbalance, resulting in stress and exhaustion' (2015: 13). Human capital theory, which is explored in more detail in Chapter 8, is interested in someone's knowledge, skills and abilities, and how they interact with the production cycle of generating wealth (Smith et al., 2016).

Case study: early years workforce

Emma was in her early twenties and was excited to qualify as a Level 3 early years practitioner and managed to secure a full-time job in a well-established private day nursery, which was part of a national chain. Her hours were Monday to Friday, 8.30am to 6.30pm, equivalent to a 45-hour week. She was pleased with her salary and working conditions, particularly after hearing from friends who were working at other nurseries where the working conditions were not so great. Emma was pleased that her uniform was provided, there was a mini gym on site, refreshments were provided throughout the working day and there were monthly bulletins with plenty of opportunities for continuing professional development. Emma felt looked after as a member staff and nurtured by other staff who were qualified to degree Level 6 and Master's Level 7. Eight years later, Emma had successfully completed an early childhood studies degree, partly funded by her employer, and was still very happy and content with her job, despite the long working week.

While Emma was studying for her degree, another day nursery opened nearby and over the period of a few months she started to see the directors/owners of her day nursery place more demands on staff, and in order to be more competitive they removed the mini gym to accommodate more children. They also reduced professional development opportunities and Emma started to feel that the priorities had changed to being very competitive and a money-making workplace. It became impossible for Emma to get her work done in the allocated hours, so she started to take her work home – for example, daily/weekly observations to analyse. Gradually, over time, Emma's work took over her life and there was no work–life balance. She felt overworked, stressed and exhausted, and often wondered whether she had chosen the right profession.

The case study above highlights two important points. The first one relates to paid work being greedy with someone's time, energy and good will in the context of the production cycle of generating wealth. The second aspect relates to the supply and demand of the market, so when there is more supply of something (in this case, day nurseries), then businesses/companies start to compete with one another. However, this raises the question about what lengths will businesses go to in order to be more competitive – reductions in staff, professional development and quality of provision, etc.

Reflective question

What does your work–life balance look like and how do you achieve one?

Early intervention

One way of providing more opportunities for people to contribute to the production cycle of generating wealth is to invest in programmes targeted at those families in need, such as vulnerable families living in deprived areas (Smith et al., 2016). Investing in early childhood education and care is believed to reduce unemployment and crime, and dependency on state welfare (Heckman and Masterov, 2014; cited in Smith et al., 2016). Moreover, James Heckman, Nobel Prize winning American economist (2005; cited in Penn, 2014), argues that investing in early childhood interventions brings the most returns/profit compared with any other phase in education, and bases his analysis on the three studies (which are discussed later on) that took place in the 1960s, 1970s and 1980s. However, in a research brief for Sure Start programmes targeted at families living in disadvantaged areas in England, the Department for Education (2011) states that it usually takes about fifteen years for the economic benefits to show.

Intervening early can make a difference and Bauer et al. (2014) specifically demonstrate the importance of perinatal care. They highlight the estimated average cost to society (in England) of one case of perinatal mental health problems, which is the time during pregnancy and the first year of a child's life, 'is around £74,000, of which £23,000 relates to the mother and £51,000 relates to impacts on the child' (Bauer et al., 2014: 2). They state that more previous research tends to focus on postnatal depression, but explain that mental health problems can start to develop well in advance of a baby being born. Around 10–20 per cent of females will develop a perinatal mental health condition and therefore should be taken seriously as a public health issue, as left untreated can have a detrimental impact on women and their families.

Alleviating pressures

Early intervention has an important role to play in children's lives and has the potential to alleviate pressure on children's services in the longer term, but it is not a panacea for changing children's life chances (Penn, 2010). In other words, an intervention on its own is not a universal cure; there must be a coming together of a range of services to provide consistent, tailored support for children and their families in order to make a decisive difference.

When children and their families face many challenges that go unnoticed, this impacts on society and the economy in two major ways: first, it can eat away at someone's well-being and second, it hinders people's opportunities to live a successful, healthy life (Early Intervention Foundation, 2018). Therefore, avoiding the issues and challenges that some families face is not an option.

Adverse Childhood Experiences (ACEs)

There is evidence to suggest that ten adverse childhood experiences (ACEs), or multiple risk factors, increase the risk of health problems in later life, and that social inequalities will increase the likelihood of ACEs (Asmussen et al., 2020). ACEs are described by Asmussen et al. (2020) when children experience or witness abuse, have a close family member who misuses drugs, has mental health problems, has been to prison, or when a child is exposed to parental divorce or separation. Addressing children's early experiences is an ethical, moral and political matter and should be prioritised.

In 2018–19, it was reported that 4.2 million children were living in poverty in the UK, 44 per cent of children were living in a lone-parent family and 72 per cent of children were living in a household where at least one person worked (Child Poverty Action Group, 2020). Furthermore, in March 2019, the National Society for the Prevention of Cruelty to Children (NSPCC) reported 59,890 children on the child protection register across the UK (NSPCC, 2020). The child protection register is a list of children who have been identified as being at risk of harm. It should never be underestimated that the context for some children and their families can be very challenging.

Case study: Supporting families in need

Matthew is a 2-year-old boy who lives with his mother (Charlotte), father (Craig) and younger sister, Amelia, aged 9 months. Charlotte and Craig are new to the area and don't know anyone. Craig is a construction worker and usually manages to find work, but it is often away from home. Charlotte has suffered with depression since the birth of Amelia, and has difficulty coping with the children and everyday life, particularly when her husband is away for days or weeks at a time. After a few months, Charlotte decided to register with a local doctor's surgery to book an appointment for her repeat medication of anti-depressants. When she visited the surgery, staff informed her about her entitle-ment to free part-time childcare for Matthew and she was introduced to Julie, one of the health visitors. Julie explained to Charlotte that her address was in an area that offered a programme of support to families with young children under the age of 4 years. Julie gave Charlotte an introduc-tory pack for new parents which included lots of helpful contacts and leaflets relating to parenting, activity and support groups.

When Charlotte returned home and settled the children, she looked through the pack and was drawn to a flyer that was titled 'Does this sound like you? You are not alone!' It was a new parent to the area writing about their first experiences of meeting new people, making new friends, fit-ting in and trying to cope with the stresses of everyday life. On reading the personal experience of a mother in a similar situation, Charlotte started to feel relief and comfort, but at the same time overwhelmed with the prospect of the weeks ahead. Over a period of weeks and months, Charlotte started to develop a positive, trusting relationship with her health visitor who was able to signpost Charlotte to lots of other professionals who could help with depression, parenting, managing a home and budgeting.

The case study above highlights the importance of knowledgeable professionals who can inform families of the services on offer and the importance of professionals building positive relationships early on so that parents feel nurtured, guided and supported. Lastly, it highlights how some parents need support with a wide range of other family matters such as running a home and budgeting.

Reflective question

What local services are you aware of that offer support to children and their families – for example, targeted/universal?

Cost–benefit analysis

There is a general understanding and argument that if the lives of some of the poorest and most vulnerable children are supported early on and invested in, this will save money for governments in the longer term and reduce the costs of specific services and support to a child when they are older (Penn, 2010). Penn (2014) and colleagues examined the claim about the substantial evidence base suggesting that early interventions are beneficial and effective for children. Their work concludes that only three American studies exist that support this claim – the 1960s' Perry High Scope study, the 1970s' Abecedarian study and the 1980s' Chicago Child–Parent Centers study. van Huizen et al. (2019) explain that for every dollar invested, these programmes generate 'a total return to society of 7–12 dollars' (2019: 387).

However, Penn (2014) argues that these studies are overused as a rationale for calculating economic benefits and are used as a model for early childhood development in some countries where the original context of the study is very different. Penn states that the findings are 'endlessly recycled in the economic and childcare literature' (2010: 53). Similarly, Karoly (2016) suggests that predictions of the long-term benefits of various programmes are based on programmes that took place decades ago. Penn (2010) suggests that economists are drawn to the three American studies because they used a specific type of methodology called a randomised controlled trial and a control/experimental design. These types of designs are often seen as providing rigorous, robust and unquestionable evidence.

Challenges

Despite attempts, it is difficult to calculate the long-term benefits of early interventions (Penn, 2014) and this might explain why many early childhood education programmes have been evaluated for their educational effectiveness rather than their economic effectiveness (Karoly, 2016). Cost–benefit analyses are challenging because putting a price/cost on the outcomes that are being measured is not straightforward. Another challenge is calculating the benefits throughout the life course, which involves making connections between outcomes at a young age with outcomes at an older age. The final challenge argued by Karoly (2016) is the ripple effect of various programmes and the impact on parents and siblings which may not be captured at all.

Other challenges of cost–benefit analyses relate to the complexity of some interventions that are diverse in nature. For example, the Flying Start flagship programme for families with children under 4 years old in Wales offers four different entitlements – enhanced health visiting, part-time childcare, parenting support and speech, language and communication support. The four entitlements are delivered in slightly different ways across local authorities, and the generational effects range from short to long term. Therefore, 'estimating the rate of return on investment would require more detailed knowledge of local data and decisions' (Feinstein, 2015: 1).

While evidence is growing for targeted interventions, the evidence is still limited about the cost-effectiveness of expanding universal early childhood education (van Huizen et al., 2019). In 2013, the Department for Education (DfE) commissioned an eight-year study called the Study of Early Education and Development (SEED) and part of the study set out to explore the value for money of childcare and education. The DfE highlight that 'the estimated benefit-to-cost ratios should not be treated as measures of absolute value for money but as indicators of the financial return to spending on different types of early education' (Paull et al., 2020: 8). The study found that part-time and full-time early education had a positive impact on the verbal development of 2-year-olds, but there was limited evidence for 3-year-olds, and there was little evidence to show any impact on children's socio-emotional development for 2- and 3-year-olds. They also found an association between

2-year-olds attending childminding settings on a full-time basis and a higher impact on verbal development. Despite Early Years settings (also known as providers) and age groups, the study reports there are greater returns in verbal development (measured using the British Ability Scales (BAS) than socio-emotional development (measured using the Strengths and Difficulties Questionnaire (SDQ)).

Case study: Giving children a chance

Mrs Peters and Mrs Smith worked in the same school, which had been identified as an area of deprivation and challenge. Mrs Peters was the Year 1 teacher working with 5- to 6-year-olds and had been teaching for almost twenty years, and was popular with most staff and parents. Mrs Smith was the nursery teacher working with 3- to 4-year-olds and had been teaching for eighteen years. She was well liked by everyone and known for organising many community events. Both teachers had very different personalities: Mrs Peters was very outgoing, flamboyant, confident and somewhat false at times, whereas Mrs Smith was very kind, genuine and caring. They both appeared to really love their job and both were experienced.

Conversations started one morning in the staff room about jobs and ambitions, and Mrs Smith explained to Mrs Peters that she only ever wanted to be a teacher or a farmer's wife. Then the conversation started to take a different turn, whereby Mrs Peters began joking about the future and the ambitions of the children in the school. Mrs Smith started to feel uncomfortable with the following conversation, as she deeply cared about the children and their futures.

Mrs Peters: You can't honestly believe that the children here will grow up and get a decent job?

Mrs Smith: Well, yes, I like to think positively and yes, many of the children, if given a chance and the right support, will be able to flourish and get a job.

Mrs Peters: I often think, what is the point in teaching them to read – they'll probably end up in prison, wasting their life away.

Mrs Smith: Do you really believe that?

Mrs Peters: Yeah, I think 'What a waste of my time... '

Mrs Smith: I'm sorry that you feel that way, when it's the children's circumstances that put an obstacle in their way; it's not their fault... Don't you ever try to imagine what it must be like for some children and their families, and the struggles they face?

Mrs Peters: We are a school, not a family support centre!

Mrs Spencer: (Headteacher) Well, you're not going to like my ideas and plans for improving the way we support parents and carers, then!

The case study above highlights the different views that practitioners have of children's school experiences, home life and their future opportunities, which is important as it can have an impact on how practitioners interact and work with children from disadvantaged communities. It also highlights how a school can become a place for parents to turn to if they need additional help and support.

Reflective question

How do you perceive the role of a school – is it at the centre of the community, a support hub, embedded in the community or stand-alone?

Summary of chapter

- Economics is a very influential discipline in policy-making for early childhood education and care, whereby economists are interested in facts, figures, generalisations and predictions.
- Applying economic analyses to health, education and society is complex and often problematic.
- Neoliberalism is an economic concept associated with privatisation, deregulation, consumerism and individualism, and places more control, scrutiny and pressure on professionals to make children 'perform the norms' of development.
- It is estimated to take up to fifteen years to see the long-term economic benefits of an early intervention programme.
- There is some evidence to suggest that early interventions are effective, but cost–benefit analyses are challenging; it is not always straightforward to put a cost on some of the outcomes being measured.

End-of-chapter questions

1. What is your understanding of economics and child development?
2. If you were given a very large sum of money to invest in Early Childhood Education and Care (ECEC), what would you do with the money and why?
3. What is your view on universal early childhood education and care versus targeted interventions/services?

Further reading

Hall, M. and Stephens, L. (2020) *Quality Childcare for All: Making England's Childcare a Universal Basic Service*. London: New Economics Foundation.

This report extends some of the discussions in this chapter, and focuses on the risks of private provision and overworked and underpaid staff. The New Economics Foundation is a British think tank that focuses on transforming the economy so that it works for the people and planet. You can visit the website at: https://neweconomics.org/

Heckman, J. (2011) 'The economics of inequality: The value of early childhood education', *American Educator*, 35 (1): 31–6. Available at: https://files.eric.ed.gov/fulltext/EJ920516.pdf (accessed 17 December 2020).

This paper will provide you with further information about Heckman's ideas around the value of early childhood education.

Lloyd, E. (2012) 'The marketisation of early years education and childcare in England', in L. Miller and D. Hevey, D. (eds), *Policy Issues in the Early Years*. London: SAGE. pp. 107–21.

This chapter will help you to understand the concept of the childcare market and the notion of quality childcare.

FIVE

THE ANTHROPOLOGY OF CHILD DEVELOPMENT

This chapter will help you to

- understand key concepts relating to anthropology, such as cultural relativism, enculturation, acculturation and ethnography;
- develop an awareness of the importance of culture within the context of child development.

Introduction

The discipline of anthropology is broadly about understanding the traditions, habits and views that a group of people, community or society possess, and the roles they play in people's lives; it is these traditions, habits and specific behaviours that often seem mysterious, bewildering or even barbaric to those outside the group/culture (Penn, 2008; Rogoff, 2003; Smidt, 2013). Therefore, to understand another culture and its views and behaviours, an anthropologist would usually study outside of their own culture/in a different part of the world in order to achieve what is commonly associated with anthropology as 'making the strange familiar and the familiar strange' (Penn, 2008: 95). Another way of understanding this statement would be to say that when we engage in a genuine quest to understand another culture, their beliefs and traditions, and so on, we learn something about ourselves and our own culture and start to ask, 'Why do I do what I do?'. Montgomery (2013) adds that anthropology is about studying human beings and their social relationships, as well as 'family structures, religion, political and economic life' (2013: 163).

As with psychology, there are different branches within anthropology, such as psychological, social and linguistic anthropology, but generally anthropology is mainly concerned with studying human culture and other concepts, such as self-identity, with poverty and injustice as cross-cutting themes. Understanding culture is important because it influences how a child interacts with others and their environment, as well as how they grow and develop (De Gioia, 2009; Gonen et al., 2019; Matsumoto, 2000). Some argue that children exist within their own subculture where they have their own ways of thinking and being, views of the world and cultural understandings (Montgomery, 2013) but the important question is whether adults respect, uphold and value a child's subculture. It is important to remember that the concept of culture is contested and the meaning is always shifting (Penn, 2008). Woodhead (2005) highlights that beliefs about healthy, holistic child development vary considerably among societies, cultures and over time.

Culture – the development niche

Culture can influence child development in complex ways. For example, Gonen et al. (2019) examined the relationship between executive functions such as attention and impulse control and other development domains among low-income families in America and Turkey. They found more advanced abilities in problem solving and executive function in the American context, and more advanced abilities in fine motor development in the Turkish context. The development niche, made up of three elements, helps to explain how culture in America and Turkey influenced the children's development. The *first* element is the child's physical and social settings, the *second* element is the culturally regulated customs and practices of early childhood education and care settings, and the *third* element is the beliefs or ethno-theories of parents (Smidt, 2013).

In relation to elements one and three of the development niche, anthropologists advocate that family members are 'the product of cultural history and circumstance' (Woodhead, 2005: 90) and this shapes parenting practices. Therefore, a child's development is best understood within the cultural practices of their community (Rogoff, 2003). A study by Levine et al. (1994; cited in Levine and Munsch, 2016) involved showing American mothers videos of Gusii people in Kenya who were shocked to see first, children not being praised and second, older siblings taking on the role of carer for younger children. Gusii people in Kenya were equally shocked when they viewed videos of American mothers not immediately attending to their babies when they cried and could not understand why they would talk to their babies when they could not understand them. The circumstances are different for mothers of both cultures – for example, the American mothers focus on stimulating cognitive development and using toys to interact, whereas the Gusii mothers in Kenya focus on preventing stress and unnecessary crying in their babies because infant mortality is high in Kenya and mothers want to ensure that their babies remain calm to support healthy development.

Expectations

Expectations of when children should be able to do something varies considerably across cultures and relates to traditions and routine circumstances (Rogoff, 2003). Barbara Rogoff, Professor of Psychology and Fellow of the American Anthropological Association, explains how American middle-class adults usually allow young children to use knives at age 5 years onwards or older, whereas in other cultures infants in New Guinea and central Africa handle knives, small spears and fire by the time they are able to walk. Rogoff (2003) provides a powerful and somewhat controversial image, in one of her chapters, of an 11-month-old child using a machete to cut a large piece of fruit. The image raises the importance of understanding and respecting children's cultural contexts.

Case study: Making the strange familiar and the familiar strange

Luke was an Early Years student studying for a degree in the United Kingdom and was looking forward to his exchange visit to America to work with kindergarten children (5- to 6-year-olds). His last placement was in the UK in Year 1 with 5- to 6-year-olds, so he was keen to compare practices. Luke received a warm welcome to the kindergarten class and gradually got to know the children and teacher. It was around mid-morning on Luke's first day, when a loud announcement was made via a tannoy system in the classroom: 'Good morning, all, and welcome to Monday.' Everyone stopped, stood up, placed their hands on their hearts and pledged allegiance to the flag. Despite this being a serious act of the day, Luke found it strange because first, he was not used to the practice, second, he did not have an American identity and third, he was unaware of the historical tradition, which started in 1892.

In the afternoon of his first day, he experienced his second strange encounter. The children were busy engaged in different activities when the kindergarten teacher asked the children to tidy up the classroom and reminded them that nap time was about to start. The children were familiar with the routine, located their individual sleep mat (like a yoga/exercise mat) and proceeded to relax. The children were encouraged to take a nap, read a book and relax in some way. Luke was taken aback with the ambience of the classroom, which was quiet, calm and peaceful. This was a very different kind of afternoon from the one he had experienced in his previous placement in the UK Year 1 classroom where children would be engaged in various adult-led tasks and child-led play. The classroom was constantly lively and loud with no scheduled nap time.

As part of Luke's degree, he had to submit a reflective essay about his experiences of the exchange visit and he discussed his first two strange encounters and tried to explain what made them strange. He also started to question why the UK Year 1 classroom did not have nap time for young children – how strange?

The case study above highlights the importance of visiting other countries, learning about traditions and customs, which in turn provides rich opportunities to better understand and question our own practice. The case study is also an opportunity to reflect on how others plan for children's learning during a day – what should it look like and why?

Reflective question

What kinds of practices have you observed in early childhood education and care settings, and what is the rationale for them?

Ethnography

The method that anthropologists mainly draw upon to go about their work is ethnography, which consists of gathering thick descriptions of the natural environment via participant observation. Ethnography is a method in research which is about 'living the life of the people you are trying to understand' (Penn, 2008: 95). For example, if you want to know what it is like to live the life of a Gypsy, Roma or Traveller parent, an anthropologist would live with the community for an extended period of time and immerse themselves into the cultures and lifestyles of the Gypsy, Roma or Traveller people.

Polish-born Bronislaw Malinowski is well known for his contribution to anthropology in which he advocated for fieldwork that involved learning the local language of the community and participating in the daily rituals. He kept daily field notes and believed that the people of the community were the experts in their own lives (Montgomery, 2013). However, as with all research methods, there are weaknesses and there are critics of ethnography who suggest that observations can be exaggerated (Penn, 2008). In addition, there might be researcher bias in how they interpret their daily observations (Levine and Munsch, 2016).

Unlike psychologists and sociologists, anthropologists have not extensively investigated childhood and child development. However, in the 1920s and 1930s, Margaret Mead, an American anthropologist, was keen to understand whether parenting was the same everywhere. Her work demonstrated that different communities/groups of people held very different views on parenting (Penn, 2008). She also researched young people in America and Samoa and revealed that 'disorderly behaviour in adolescence was caused by cultural conditioning rather than biological changes' (Montgomery, 2013: 175). Mead argued that there were many cultural reasons as to why young people in Samoa were less stressed than those in America (Montgomery, 2013). In 1927, the work of anthropologist Malinowski was instrumental in leading Piaget to withdraw his claim that teenagers 'universally reach a formal operational stage' (Rogoff, 2003: 7) in cognitive development. Therefore, it is important to remember that different research approaches bring about different findings and conclusions.

Cultural relativism

Researching culture tends to fall across a continuum with behavioural universalism (biological) at one end and cultural relativism at the other. Behavioural universalism is a belief that patterns of child development appear in all children around the world that can be compared, and there is an acceptance that a few minor variations will exist (Penn, 2008). For example, Piaget initially demonstrated that all children across cultures progress through the same four stages of cognitive development and identified age groups for each stage (MacBlain, 2018; Woolfolk et al., 2013) until he was forced to withdraw his claim about teenagers. On the other hand, cultural relativism is a belief that children cannot be compared around the world due to the unique way that societies and communities behave and attach meaning (Penn, 2008). Moreover, anthropologists argue that it is impossible to discuss norms of development (Penn, 2008).

As discussed in Chapter 2, behavioural universalism is characterised by developmental charts or milestones with ages and stages, and is associated with the branch in psychology called Developmental Psychology. Arguably, this means that many children are being compared to milestones that have been generated from the experiences of those in North America or Europe (Waller and Davis, 2014; Penn, 2014). This explains why anthropologists are opposed to discussing norms of development.

Developmental Psychology is a very traditional, Western way of viewing children and is used to represent children all over the world, but it tends to disregard race, class and culture (Walkerdine, 2009). It is argued that the majority of research, theory and information that has been written about young children in terms of developmental charts originates from North America or Europe (Penn, 2014; Waller and Davis, 2014) and therefore misrepresents many children (Rogoff, 2003). Smidt (2013) states that information about child development represents a minority of children rather than the majority. She explains that child development texts and major studies and experiments largely relate to '18 percent of the world's children' (Smidt, 2013: 29). Therefore, cultural research is very important because it examines theories that dominate child development texts and the findings challenge the assumptions about child development that are widely communicated in Western contexts. Moreover, research that focuses on culture helps to reduce the overgeneralisations that are made about children's development (Rogoff, 2003). This is important because the 'majority of children grow up in Asia, Africa, Latin America, and the Pacific under conditions differing drastically from those familiar to Westerners' (Levine and New, 2008: 1).

Ethnocentrism

Developmental outcomes are considered by Rogoff (2003) as being ethnocentric in nature. Ethnocentrism can be seen in Early Years settings by thinking about sleep and feeding routines; both are universal practices and needed for young children to survive and develop, but the way in which they are enacted and lived out are vastly different across ethnic groups and within individual families (De Gioia, 2009). For example, some children eat their food while sitting at a table, while others will be fed walking around, some will eat with cutlery and some will eat without cutlery. With both practices, families decide when children should sleep/eat, how they should sleep/eat, where they should sleep/eat and what they should eat and this varies greatly. Moreover, when children enter an early years setting, the practices and expectations will more than likely vary from the home culture, and this may create a feeling of insecurity for the child and parent.

Being ethnocentric is when someone imposes a value judgement from their own culture on to another culture, also described as 'prejudging without appropriate knowledge' (Rogoff, 2003: 15). So, in the context of sleep and feeding routines, practitioners may judge parental practices in a negative way and try to impose their own cultural value and way of doing something because they see it as better and more correct. Matsumoto (2000) suggests that everyone perceives others through their cultural filters and therefore ethnocentrism is not a good or bad thing.

Case study: Taking action

Many children who attend Woven Primary School are from diverse, ethnic minority backgrounds. Very recently, the school had a large intake of Syrian refugee children starting in the reception year (4- to 5-year-olds). At the start of the new year, it was time for the teacher, Mr Greenaway, to carry out on-entry baseline assessments. He was an experienced teacher who loved working in the early years, but did not always agree with the expectations placed upon him and the reception-aged children. One of these expectations was to carry out a baseline assessment in order to find out what children would score against development norms. Every year, he felt uneasy about the task and asked himself the following questions: Why is the score of some children never representative of who they really are or what they can do? Why don't we assess in the child's first language – maybe this would provide a better representation of their capabilities and strengths?

Mr Greenaway loved to observe the children's talents and abilities, and documented these in a celebratory, creative journal in partnership with the child's parents. He soon started to realise that the baseline assessment score and the celebratory creative journal were presenting two very different pictures of the same child. Therefore, in consultation with the head teacher, he decided to pursue a more effective use of bilingual assistants across the school and started a campaign (with support from other schools with a similar demographic) to revise the developmental norms to better represent children from across the globe.

The case study above highlights two important points. First, the ethical dilemma that practitioners find themselves working within when it comes to assessing young children from refugee backgrounds. Second, it shows how practitioners begin to take action about an aspect of their practice that they feel is a child's right issue.

Reflective question

To what extent are Western norms appropriate for assessing *all* children?

Enculturation and acculturation

Enculturation or 'socialisation' is the process of transmitting culture to the next generation or initiating and inducting new members to it and learning their culture, whereas 'acculturation' is about the process of learning another culture and adapting to it (Montgomery, 2013) or, to put it another way, fitting into the new culture, which is usually the dominant culture (Lavelli et al., 2019). Both processes involve social, emotional, cognitive and moral domains of development (Matsumoto, 2000).

During the process of enculturation, a child begins to identify with a particular group and starts to feel a sense of belonging, which in turn contributes to the process of cultural assimilation where a child adopts the attitudes, traditions, practices and norms of their group (De Gioia, 2009). By the time children are adults, they have learnt and practised numerous cultural rules and codes of behaviour that have become second nature (Matsumoto, 2000). The cultural rules tend to be explicitly shown and implicitly absorbed (Levine and Munsch, 2016). According to Matsumoto (2000), learning a culture is a prolonged process and as humans become more and more enculturated, they add more and more layers to their cultural filters, which they use to perceive the world.

Emotional co-regulation

To further explain enculturation and acculturation, the work of Lavelli et al. (2019) will now be discussed. It is well documented (and often perceived as universal) that in Western contexts emotional co-regulation and socialisation between baby and adult occurs when there is face-to-face visual, communicative exchange (Lavelli et al., 2019). But Lavelli et al. (2019) set out to explore emotional co-regulation between mother and baby in different cultures and found that Italian mothers responded to their baby's cooing and smiling in much the same way because they welcomed and valued liveliness and individuality (i.e., the Western way), whereas rural mothers in Cameroon welcomed a calm baby and therefore did not respond to their emotional expressions in the same way and, after a period of time, the babies displayed sober faces (i.e., the West African way). The developmental goals and demands of life are different between the two cultures and the babies are stimulated in different ways – for example, the Italian parent encourages a lively exchange of emotional expressiveness which involves more visual attention, whereas the parent from Cameroon provides more physical attention and tactile stimulation where the baby becomes more accustomed to the rhythm of body movements, vocalisation, body warmth and social cohesion, and community is promoted – two different examples of enculturation.

The study by Lavelli et al. (2019) also included observations of West African immigrant mothers and their babies born in Italy, and they found patterns of emotional co-regulation between mother and baby that were evident in both the Cameroon (original culture) and Italian (new culture) mothers – an example of acculturation. Levine and Munsch (2016) highlight that cultural values can change due to acculturation. Moreover, Bergnehr (2018), who researches acculturative stress in refugee families, states that more research is needed to understand the changes that children and families go through when resettling into a different country.

Case study: Fitting in

My name is Anika. I am 4 years old and speak some English and now live in Birmingham. My parents recently moved here from India, South Asia. I love being at home and playing with my brothers

(Continued)

and sisters. My parents love cooking and on the weekends we all prepare the food together. I wash the vegetables and my brother chops them. We always have delicious food and we eat with our hands. At the end of our meal on Sunday evening before I started school, everyone started singing the family song and wished me well for starting school on Monday morning.

It was my first day of starting school and my mum said that I would make new friends and have lots of fun, but I really wanted to stay at home because I had friends and lots of fun at home. I arrived at school and it was a bit scary – all new faces, new building, new smells – and new things, so I wasn't so sure. Everyone sounded different. My mum came into the classroom and stayed with me until lunchtime, then we went home together and we did this for the first week. It went okay and I was really looking forward to week two and seeing some of my new friends. But then it was lunchtime and I sat at a very long table with my food on a bright yellow compartment tray. I just stared at it because the tray was so bright and it wasn't in a bowl. Mrs Hughes, the teaching assistant, said 'Come on, Anika, make a start, use your knife and fork'. I didn't really know what she meant, so I started eating my food with my hands, like I always do. The food was okay and I was enjoying it, but I jumped when Mrs Hughes said 'What are you doing, Anika, eating here like this?' She picked up these spiky-looking things and used them to cut my food. I thought I was doing okay with my hands, as this is how I do it at home, so what was the problem? When I got home, I told my mum about Mrs Hughes and the spiky-looking things at lunchtime and she said 'Don't worry, that's how they do it here. You'll need to remember.'

The case study above is written from the perspective of a young child who is starting school from a different culture and shows how one practitioner is unaware of the child's cultural context. The case study highlights the importance of supporting a smooth acculturative transition between home and school and Indian to Western culture in order for a young child to feel comfortable, settled and accepted.

Reflective question

What is the rationale for some of your cultural actions?

Identity

For the purpose of this chapter, identity relates to someone's awareness of their own culture and as children grow older their awareness of their cultural identity develops and matures, whereas a young child is much more aware of their racial identity early on (Matsumoto, 2000). Some cultures focus on 'individualism' and countries like the UK and USA value this more, whereas other cultures focus on 'collectivism', which tends to be observed in countries such as China and Africa. These two distinctions are important because they influence how the self is conceptualised (Levine and Munsch, 2016). As children develop a sense of who they are, they are establishing and working out who they are 'similar to', as well as who they are 'different from'. According to Smidt (2013), identity like culture is not something that is fixed; it is continuously shifting and relational in nature.

According to De Gioia (2009: 11). 'young children develop a secure sense of identity through consistent care practices'. De Gioia (2009) also argues that working in partnership with parents will help create consistency of care. Furthermore, practitioners should view the parents as the primary source of knowledge of care-giving practices and be keen to learn and value the micro culture of a child's family (De Gioia, 2009). Practitioners often assume that parents from minority backgrounds have a lack of interest in being involved with a setting, but there are often language and cultural differences at play which make it difficult for parents to engage, and this is often overlooked by settings (Khalfaoui et al., 2020).

However, there are many competing values and beliefs about caring for and educating young children. Working in partnership is problematic as it assumes that parents/carers will happily share their parenting practices with settings in order for them to be understood and appreciated. Research by De Gioia (2009) revealed that some parents did not see the point in sharing their child-rearing practices/ways of doings things with staff; they wanted their child to be integrated into the wider community and to adopt practices other than those within the child's micro culture (another example of acculturation). Therefore, a balance needs to be found between respecting individual family practices and preferences, and the practices and policies of an Early Years setting. In addition, the parents in the research by De Gioia (2009) recognised that their home practices would not always be easily transferred or replicated in the early years setting.

Case study: Valuing each other's identities

Welcoming new parents to Mountain View Nursery School was something that head teacher Mrs James really enjoyed doing. Children aged between 3 and 4 years old attended the school and were from diverse backgrounds. Mrs James was an experienced head teacher and was keen for everyone (children, families and staff) to learn about each other and become friends. It was an ongoing tradition in the school to hold 'family fun days' throughout the school year.

When parents first started, Mrs James would take time to find out about parenting practices and always explained the family fun days by showing them photographs of the events. Past events involved families and staff bringing their favourite food, wearing traditional dress and reciting a nursery rhyme or telling a story in their home language. There were also plenty of bilingual support assistants to explain the rationale of the events. Notices, letters and flyers were always provided in the home language. Ultimately, the event was to promote and value each other's identities. However, the following conversation between two parents was overheard by a member of staff.

Hibaaq: Have you heard about these family fun days?

Jamilah: Yes, Mrs James explained the other day, but I don't feel comfortable with them to be honest. What about you?

(Continued)

Hibaaq: Yes, it's a great way for us to share with others about our community and culture. We can bring some food, dance and read stories in Somali. Haroon would love it.

Jamilah: Yes, I think ours would love it, but not sure others will. Mrs James was also asking me loads of questions about routines at home – was she like that with you too?

Hibaaq: Yes, nothing to worry about, though. She explained it was important information in helping to settle Aaden and trying to keep his day smooth and stress-free. And don't forget if you're ever unsure about why something is happening, don't be afraid to ask for clarification.

The case study above shows how two parents feel about how a setting promotes and values identity. Hibaaq feels excited and comfortable, and sees the benefits of family fun days and sharing routine care practices from home, whereas Jamilah feels somewhat agitated and uncomfortable about joining in and sharing routine care practices. She also feels ill-informed about the reasons why settings do certain things. There are many reasons why both parents feel different and for Jamilah it might take a little longer to build a trusting, positive relationship.

Reflective question

What other strategies could be effective in promoting and valuing identity with children and families?

Summary of chapter

- Anthropology is about studying human culture and understanding the traditions, habits, values and practices of others. When we learn about another culture, we begin to learn something about our own culture. Therefore, anthropology is about making the strange familiar and the familiar strange.
- Culture influences child development in complex ways and cross-cultural research can help challenge dominant discourses, such as Developmental Psychology, and provide a deeper/ alternative insight into understanding childhood.
- Ethnography is a research method used by anthropologists to study the micro culture of human behaviour and culture, and involves participant observation.
- Enculturation (often called socialisation) is the process whereby children actively learn their own culture, whereas acculturation is the process whereby children and families adapt to another culture.
- Consistent care practices between home and Early Years settings help children develop a secure sense of identity. However, there are many ways that settings can promote and value identity, so for everyone to participate and feel comfortable, a rationale needs to be clearly communicated and shared.

End-of-chapter questions

1. What is your understanding of anthropology and child development?
2. To what extent are differences in children's development related to biology or culture or both?
3. What is your view on parenting practices and practices within early childhood education and care settings, and to what extent do they differ?

Further reading

Brown, M. and White, J. (2014) *Exploring Childhood in a Comparative Context*. London: Routledge.

This book will help you understand and appreciate the practices in other countries, such as the Czech Republic, Finland, Japan and rural South Africa. The book explores key themes such as child development and provides you with an overview of theories that underpin their practice.

Gottlieb, J. and DeLoache, J. (2017) *A World of Babies: Imagined Childcare Guides for Eight Societies*. Cambridge: Cambridge University Press.

This book will provide you with a detailed insight into child-rearing practices from around the world.

Papatheodorou, T. and Moyles, J. (eds) (2012) *Cross-cultural Perspectives on Early Childhood*. London: SAGE.

This book will provide you with a deeper understanding of culture in the context of learning, teaching, pedagogy and professional development in the early years.

SIX
THE PHILOSOPHY OF CHILD DEVELOPMENT

This chapter will help you to

- develop an understanding of some concepts relating to philosophy, such as poststructuralism, discourse, ontology and epistemology;
- begin to appreciate how philosophy can help develop critical thinking and support reflective practice.

Introduction

Various definitions suggest that philosophy can mean any one of the following: 'the study of the meaning of life, knowledge, thought... a theory or set of ideas held by a particular philosopher... or a person's outlook on life' (*Collins Dictionary*, 1992: 368). MacBlain (2018) suggests that understanding philosophy is not always straightforward. However, he further states that as a discipline, it can help explain how we think about something and why we do certain things. Moreover, it is important to remember that philosophers are influenced by the following:

- events that surrounded them growing up;
- their personal narrative and experiences;
- the historical period of that time (also known as the chronosystem).

History as a discipline does not appear as a separate chapter in this book; instead, it is embedded throughout the book and is particularly important for this chapter.

Much like anthropology, the discipline of philosophy can help us understand that there are different ways of living, being, doing and thinking (Hobbs, 2018). It has also been described as a type of enquiry (Hand, 2018) or, as the following explanation suggests, philosophy attempts to explore, explain and justify the structure and content of our thoughts in response to perceived problems and puzzles about reality, knowledge, value and meaning… the hope is that by doing philosophy we learn to think better, to act more wisely, and thereby help to improve the quality of all our lives. (The Philosophy Foundation, 2021: 1)

In terms of child development, Murris suggests that philosophy can help make the shift in thinking about 'children as knowledge producers, rather than knowledge consumers' (2017: 531). Ultimately, philosophy is an important discipline and overlooking it or disregarding it may ignore 'the complex and often messy reality of being human' (Clack, 2012: 507).

Pound (2011) suggests that the disciplines of history and philosophy used to dominate the training of early childhood professionals and were considered central to their training. One of the benefits of this is that philosophical thinking provides people with the skills to question authority figures and those in high-status positions (Hobbs, 2018). However, towards the latter part of the twentieth century, both history and philosophy became less favourable. This is probably due to the developments around scientific thinking and the progressive movement. Writing from a 'critical realist' perspective, which is a philosophy of the social sciences, Alderson suggests that philosophy is often ignored because it can raise 'unnecessary complications in social research' (2016: 200) and she further argues that when philosophy is avoided, it 'can leave unresolved confusions and hidden unquestioned assumptions that distort research' (200).

Greek philosophers, Enlightenment and Modernity

There are many ancient Greek philosophers, such as Plato, Aristotle (his student) and Aristippus of Cyrene, who was a student of Socrates, the founder of Western philosophy. Their ideas can often be linked back to the present day and Pound (2011) states that psychology has its roots in philosophy. For example, Plato was interested in understanding the good life and how best to live life, and arguably posed questions that fitted within an ethics and flourishing framework (Hobbs, 2018). The functionalist perspective in sociology, discussed in Chapter 3, originates from the ideas of Plato who placed more emphasis on society as a whole than individuals and believed that intelligence exists beyond that of individual people in society. The opposite idea of this, which is a key feature of German philosopher Immanuel Kant's work, is the belief that people in society create their social worlds and are consciously constructing intelligence (Ingleby and Oliver, 2008).

Enlightenment period

Kant is well known for being a key thinker of the Enlightenment period or the Age of Reason, which is often described as being the philosophical, historical movement of the seventeenth and eighteenth century in Europe. Swiss philosopher Jean-Jacques Rousseau shared his ideas, such as the freedom to move and learn at a time in history (eighteenth century) when children were viewed as little adults and were expected to work and contribute to manual labour. Like Piaget, he also believed that children developed through stages – for example, Rousseau suggests that birth to 12 years old is a period when children's actions are influenced by emotions; the second stage up to the age of 16 is a period when reason and thought influences actions, and then the final stage occurs, which is the move to adulthood. Rousseau believed that the role of the adult was to channel children's emotions, needs and desires in a positive and meaningful way because children were traditionally perceived as 'wicked' at that time in history (MacBlain, 2018).

Modernity

In the late nineteenth and early twentieth centuries, Modernity emerged. It is often described using words such as individualism, scientific thought, industrialisation and technological advances. According to Pound (2011), it was a time of extraordinary change – for example, compulsory education was introduced for children aged 5 and over, and it was a time when psychologists such as Piaget and Vygotsky were instrumental in making a contribution in understanding children's thinking, learning and development. The twentieth century is often called the Progressive movement. However, modernity is criticised for disregarding diversity and complexity (Albon, 2011).

Complexity theory can be useful because it seeks to understand the 'whole' – for example, holistic development, which includes various child development domains (discussed in Part 2 of the book). Complexity theory also focuses on understanding how the 'domains interact' and is concerned with non-linear systems. It is usually described as interdisciplinary in nature, which means different disciplines intersecting to understand various phenomena (Doolittle, 2014).

Postmodernity

The historical period from the mid- to late twentieth century and thereafter is known as Postmodernism, which has been explained in Chapter 3. Postmodernism is criticised for leaving practitioners with very little suggestion or ways forward in practice, and making them wonder what practice should look like. Albon (2011) states that there are different kinds of theories associated with Postmodernism, such as Poststructuralism, which is briefly discussed after the timeline.

Timeline

1693 Childhood started being viewed as a distinct stage of life. John Locke published his book called 'Some thoughts concerning education'. Locke viewed a child's mind like a blank slate waiting to be filled.

1760 Opening of the first toy store in London, reinforcing childhood as a distinct stage of life.

1833 The Factory Act made it law to protect 9- to 13-year-olds to work no more than 9 hours per day and 13- to 18-year-olds to work no more than 12 hours per day. The law also made it legal for children to have ninety minutes for meal breaks throughout their working day.

1840 Vaccinations were introduced in England for the poor and disadvantaged.

1880 The Education Act made schooling compulsory for 5- to 10-year-olds.

1929 Piaget became Professor of Child Psychology and advocated that children's cognitive processing was different from that of older children and adults.

1989 The United Nations Convention on the Rights of the Child (UNCRC) was introduced. This international treaty consists of 54 different articles linking to provision, protection and participation.

2011 Wales introduced the Rights of Children and Young Person Measure, which means that the voices of children and young people need to be considered when developing policies and passing legislation.

2020 In Wales, the Senedd and Elections Act was passed, which gave 16- and 17-year-olds the right to vote.

The timeline above demonstrates some of the significant points in history and the developments that have taken place over centuries. The timeline provides an opportunity to reflect on how improvements have been made to the lives of children and their families.

Reflective question

When you look at the key dates on the timeline, can you distinguish the shift in historical movements?

Poststructuralism (a theoretical paradigm)

Poststructuralists are interested in finding out 'how particular ideas come to dominate our understandings of and actions in the social world and contribute to inequalities in it' (MacNaughton, 2005: 8). Moreover, a Poststructuralist will challenge the following thought: 'things are the way they are just because that's how it is'. In addition, they believe there are many truths in the world and they argue that 'all knowledge is culturally prejudiced' (MacNaughton, 2005: 23). Therefore, knowledge about child development cannot be applied universally, and this is a similar argument posed by anthropologists in the previous chapter.

Michel Foucault, a French philosopher, is often associated with poststructuralist thinking and the concept of power plays a significant role in understanding the world (Albon, 2011). Power is a concept that Foucault described as something that 'operates through the entire social structure and is embedded in the daily practices of professionals' (Gabriel, 2017: 9). According to MacNaughton (2005) and Pound (2011), Foucault made a very significant contribution to how people think about aspects of society, such as schooling, policing and gay rights, to name but a few. Moreover, Foucault was a radical thinker because he believed that truth does not exist and a significant part of his work involved exploring discourses (MacNaughton, 2005). Nolan et al. remind us that Poststructuralists challenge 'knowledge that is taken for granted' (2013: 16).

Understanding the concept of discourse

Discourses are 'more-or-less coherent, systematically-organised ways of talking or writing, each underpinned by a set of beliefs, assumptions and values' (Ereaut and Whiting, 2008: 10). Martin and Ebrahim draw upon Foucault's work from 1980 for their research on examining teachers' discourses of literacy and state that discourse is 'the space where power and knowledge intersect' (2016: 2). Foucault further highlights that discourse is a concept that helps to explain how power is justified. Martin and Ebrahim (2016) explain that power is present within various discourses, as well as being a discourse in its own right.

The discourse or language that is in use shapes people's perspectives of the world. Some discourses are dominant and Foucault calls these 'regimes of truth' (Gabriel, 2017). For example, a developmental discourse in early childhood can be described as a regime of truth where developmental norms mainly represent white, Western, middle-class expectations. MacNaughton (2005) explains that regimes of truth are what people think are appropriate and correct ways of working with children, and they are a form of regulation; they are believed to be true and rarely explored uncritically (Albon, 2011).

In addition, discourses govern 'the normal and desirable ways to think, act and feel about young children in early childhood institutions' (MacNaughton, 2005: 27). Therefore, it can be challenging and overwhelming to think, act and feel in a different way from the one that has been officially sanctioned (i.e., the regime of truth) at a policy or practitioner level (MacNaughton, 2005). It is important to remember that as one truth becomes sanctioned (or normalised), another gets marginalised and silenced (MacNaughton, 2005).

Interestingly, the work of Foucault is rarely included in texts about child development or early childhood education and by including it, MacNaughton (2005) believes that it will help support 'activist educators' among the early childhood profession to disrupt the regimes of truth (also known as dominant discourses). It is argued that inequalities are produced and reproduced within regimes of truth, so it is important for them to be disrupted.

Dominant discourses in early childhood

Dahlberg et al. (2007) suggest there are five dominant discourses that exist which adults tend to use when constructing/conceptualising early childhood. They claim that discourses one to four (below) characterise Modernist perspectives, while discourse five characterises a Postmodern perspective. The five dominant discourses are briefly described as follows.

- Discourse one: 'The child as knowledge, identity and culture reproducer'. For example, this is where a child is viewed as an empty vessel needing to be filled with knowledge, needing to develop specific skills that benefit society, learn values and be trained to conform to school. Childhood is viewed as a progressive journey, preparing children and getting them ready for adulthood and the workforce.
- Discourse two: 'The child as innocent, in the golden age of life'. For example, this is a view about children requiring shelter and needing protection from a corrupt, commercialised world. Childhood is viewed as an innocent period of life and considered sentimental and precious, with a focus on the beauty of childhood.
- Discourse three: 'The scientific child of biological stages'. For example, this view focuses on the individual child and biological stages, and views development as a natural ladder-like progression where children are measured by separate development areas/domains. However, context tends to be overlooked.
- Discourse four: 'The child as labour market supply factor'. For example, this view challenges the belief that mothers should be the main carer for their child and it can be harmful for children to be cared for by different people. This discourse places emphasis and importance on the labour supply and sees young children and early childhood education and care playing a significant part in this. Some would argue that the focus is on what is best for society and the labour market not necessarily the child.
- Discourse five: 'The child as a co-constructer of knowledge, identity and culture'. For example, within this discourse childhood is viewed as one of many important life stages and a universal childhood does not exist. Children are viewed as social actors and agents of change, and the voice of the child is advocated. This discourse is sometimes known as the Postmodern child.

Case study: Old ways and new beginnings

Mrs Trent had been teaching in early years (3- to 5-year-olds) for almost 38 years and had just begun working with a new early years teacher called Mrs Jenkins who had extensive experience of working in the playwork profession. The school was quite large and had two classes per age group, so both teachers would do curriculum planning together. However, when they had their first planning meeting, their views about the curriculum, purpose of education and children's capabilities were quite different, as the following conversation reveals.

Mrs Trent: It's so exciting that you have started. Here is the planning for autumn term last year, so there won't be much to do – for example, it has all the links to the curriculum. It also includes planning for the different learning areas of the classroom. I must say, all the activities worked really well in the past and the Year 1 teachers are always so pleased with the children's skills when they arrive to them.

Mrs Jenkins: Yes, I can see there is a lot of information and it looks very detailed. It's good to hear that the activities were a success with the children last year, but do you mind if I ask a few questions?

Mrs Trent:	Of course, go ahead.
Mrs Jenkins:	How will we know that the activities will be a success this year if we haven't met the children or had the time to get to know their likes, dislikes and strengths, etc.? Also, I notice from the planning that the role-play areas change every half term, but what if the children I work with really like the shop or the café and we want to keep it the same for the whole term?
Mrs Trent:	From my experience – and I have a lot – the children year on year have always enjoyed the activities and developed the appropriate skills that are needed for Year 1 and other school years. I find that all children are the same and they like the same things, so it has always worked. I feel that the children should have variety in the role-play areas and each half term we can link different curriculum skills to the areas.
Mrs Jenkins:	Mm, I can see where you are coming from, but from my experience – and I have a lot – I find that children have such great ideas, lots of capabilities and strengths, and lots to share that we can learn from. I will spend time getting to know each of them, letting them plan the environment and the role-play areas with me, and then seeing how the curriculum fits with them rather than making them fit the curriculum.
Mrs Trent:	Well, that does sound different; this year will definitely be an interesting one!

The case study above highlights how two teachers use contrasting discourses when discussing curriculum planning. Mrs Trent is articulating aspects of discourse one where children are viewed as knowledge reproducers, whereas Mrs Jenkins is articulating aspects of discourse five, where children are viewed as knowledge co-constructors.

Reflective question

What skills are needed to challenge dominant discourses such as discourse one?

Ontology and Epistemology

Ontology and epistemology are philosophical concepts that impact the way we understand the world, and can be daunting to understand and grasp in the first instance (they were for the authors!). Ontology is associated with existence and the nature of reality/being, whereas epistemology is associated with the ways of knowing about the nature of reality/existence (Mukherji and Albon, 2018). Both concepts raise the following questions: What are the things we know (i.e., what exists)? And how do we come to know about them (i.e., knowledge production)? Nolan et al. (2013) explain each concept by stating that ontology is 'the study of reality' and epistemology is 'the study of knowledge'.

Ontology

In terms of ontology (i.e., what exists), these are the things we can see and touch which are more concrete in nature, but there are also things we know about that we cannot see or touch and are more abstract in nature, such as love and self-esteem. Zina O'Leary, who published the social science jargon buster in 2007, posed the following questions about things we cannot see or touch and asks 'are they real, or just constructs of the mind? And if they are just constructs of the mind, are they any less real? (O'Leary, 2007: 180). Abstract ontological categories would also be things such as space, time and numbers that cannot be put in your pocket, argues O'Leary (2007). Is God real? Are myths and legends real? Who decides what's real or not? These are all controversial, philosophical questions. Debates about ontology have been ongoing since Plato and Aristotle were around, and they will continue to do so. Therefore, it is important to start to understand the concept, as it can help you appreciate the different perspectives of early childhood development – and there are many different perspectives, as this book demonstrates.

Epistemology

In terms of epistemology (i.e., ways of knowing), this is about the ways we go about understanding what exists and there are rules about the production of knowledge. Since the Enlightenment period (the seventeenth and eighteenth centuries), the dominant view/epistemological understanding was empiricism, which means that 'all knowledge is limited to what can be observed through the senses' (O'Leary, 2007: 76) and involves the recording and measurement of behaviours (MacBlain, 2018). To some extent, this view is central to the positivist, scientific method and arguably dominates thinking around young children's development in the twenty-first century. It raises the following question: is child development only perceived as real if it is externally and physically observable?

Other concepts such as 'a priori' and 'a posteriori' will also help you understand how we come to know what we know. *A priori* knowledge relates to knowledge that comes from theoretical deduction and excludes experience, whereas *a posteriori* knowledge is generated from experience alone. In sum, it might be easy to think of concepts such as ontology, epistemology, a priori and a posteriori as tools to understand how knowledge is produced.

Case study: Let's discuss

Mrs Kom was a newly appointed head teacher working in a small school who had recently embarked on a part-time Master's degree in early childhood studies. One of her assessments for her first module was to undertake short interviews with staff to find out about their ontological and epistemological understandings of development. Mrs Kom explained the task to her staff and gained ethical consent from those who were interested in taking part. Part of an interview transcript with Mr Roberts, the nursery teacher, is included below.

Mrs Kom:	Thank you for taking part and talking about your understandings of development. So, in your own words, can you tell me what development means to you in the context of your work?
Mr Roberts:	Yes, but I'll have to think about that for a moment [pause]… so development to me is about something you can see happening. But for some children, it can happen fast and for some it can be really slow. I get really excited when a child meets one of their milestones or targets.
Mrs Kom:	That's a really interesting response, thank you. Can you tell me how you came to know about those things that you just described?
Mr Roberts:	Well, it's easy to see because our assessments are informing us about a child's development; it's written down and recorded so we can use it for evidence.

The case study above shows the ontological and epistemological understandings of development from one nursery teacher. Mr Roberts explains that development is tangible and is something he can see, observe and record (which refers to ontology). In addition, he is able to explain how he knows what he knows – for example, through observation and assessment (which refers to epistemology).

Reflective question

Think of a concept that you can discuss with a friend or colleague, and compare your ontological and epistemological understandings.

Philosophy for Children (P4C)

According to Stojanov (2019), engaging children in philosophical activity and thinking is an effective way of helping them understand and articulate their formation of self. American philosopher Matthew Lipman is the founder of the movement called Philosophy for Children (P4C) and argued that if children's philosophical thinking is strengthened, this will make a positive contribution to a good functioning, democratic society (Murris, 2017). Gareth Matthews, a strong supporter of Lipman, rejected Piaget's claims about developmentalism and argued that children were natural philosophers. Matthews (1980; cited in Murris, 2017) states that 'children's thinking is similar to that of well-known adult philosophers' (537).

P4C involves children and young people engaging in dialogue about various philosophical issues such as fairness, bullying and truth. Children sit in a circle and the adult would start with an introductory activity and then provide a stimulus, which could be a story, video, image or object. The group would be encouraged to discuss the stimulus and identify a range of questions; then, as a group, they agree to take one question forward to discuss (Siddiqui et al., 2017).

Research and evaluation of P4C

The aim of the approach is to develop children's confidence and ability to ask questions, build arguments and participate in logical and rational discussions and debates (Gorard et al., 2015). In 2015, Gorard et al. (2015) conducted a process and impact evaluation of P4C to find out if the approach would lead to higher attainment among 8- to 10-year-olds in the areas of reading, writing and maths. The evaluation team also wanted to find out if the approach had any impact on cognitive ability tests.

There were five key findings to the study by Gorard et al. (2015): first, P4C had a positive impact on children's progress and attainment in reading and maths. Second, researchers found that P4C had the most positive impact on children from disadvantaged backgrounds. Third, there was a positive but small impact on cognitive ability tests. Fourth, teachers who were implementing P4C reported that embedding the approach into the timetable on a regular basis contributed to the success of the approach. Lastly, both teachers and children reported that P4C was having a positive influence on other outcomes such as pupil confidence and self-esteem. In a more recent study, Siddiqui et al. (2017) showed that children who had engaged with P4C had higher self-reported rates in communication skills, teamwork and resilience, and less in empathy compared with those who had not engaged with P4C. They highlight that for P4C to be effective, it needs to be implemented as a whole-school approach. Moreover, notions of fairness, kindness and politeness need to be enacted by all; in other words, practitioners and children need to be fair, kind and polite to each other.

Case study: Making decisions

Children in Year 1 who are aged between 5 and 6 years sit in a circle on a bright sunny Monday morning. The teacher sets the scene by explaining that she met a monster on the weekend while out walking. The teacher only shows a picture of the monster's face, which is neutral (i.e., not friendly or frightening), and explains that he wants to come to school the next day. The children take a vote and are split into those who say yes and those who say no. The children are then encouraged to give reasons for their answers. The teacher then gives the children additional information about the monster – for example, would you still want the monster to come to school if he had a bad smell? Children are then encouraged to take a second vote to see if this changes their mind. If they change their mind, they are then encouraged to give reasons for their answer. The teacher continues to share different facts about the monster – for example, what if the monster was in a wheelchair? Once different facts are shared with the children, they all revisit the original question to see if anyone has changed their mind.

The case study above briefly explains a typical P4C activity for young children. It highlights how children are encouraged to listen to each other, make decisions and explain their choices. The teacher's role is to set the scene, pose questions and facilitate discussion where children are given the opportunity to think rationally about their choices.

Reflective question

What are the benefits and limitations of P4C?

Summary of chapter

- Philosophy is a discipline that helps us understand the many different ways of living, being, doing and thinking.
- Historical movements such as the Enlightenment/Age of Reason, Modernity and Postmodernity play an important role in the production of knowledge.
- A discourse is the coherent and systematic way of talking and writing about a concept, such as child development, children, childhood, and the language in use is underpinned by a set of beliefs and values. Discourses can be conflicting and controversial.
- Ontology and epistemology are two important philosophical concepts that inform our view of what exists (ontology) and how we know about what exists (epistemology).
- Philosophy for Children (P4C) is an approach that encourages children to engage in philosophical debates, ask questions and to form arguments, and there is some evidence to suggest that P4C has a positive impact on areas of learning and development.

End-of-chapter questions

1. What is your understanding of philosophy and child development?
2. How do you know when a child's development is flourishing or if they are living a good life?
3. To what extent is it realistic in the day-to-day job of an early years professional to disrupt the regime of truth?

Further reading

Dahlberg, G. and Moss, P. (2005) *Ethics and Politics in Early Childhood Education*. Oxford: Routledge.

This book is part of Routledge's contesting early childhood series and will provide you with a challenging and stimulating read. It will extend your knowledge and understanding about philosophers such as Foucault and Deleuze. You can access the link to the series here: www.routledge.com/Contesting-Early-Childhood/book-series/SE0623?pd=published,forthcoming&pg=1&pp=12&so=pub&view=list

Mercer, J., Hupp, S. and Jewell, J. (2020) *Thinking Critically About Child Development: Examining Myths and Understandings*. London: SAGE.

This book will help you understand and appreciate the importance of thinking critically in the context of child development. The authors set out 74 child development-related claims to be examined and it provides opportunities to develop the skills of a social scientist.

Moss, P. (2019) *Alternative Narratives in Early Childhood: An Introduction for Students and Practitioners*. Oxford: Routledge.

This is another book from Routledge's contesting early childhood series and will help you understand the meaning of a dominant discourse and introduce you to the theoretical perspective of posthumanism within the context of early childhood.

SEVEN

THE NEUROSCIENCE OF CHILD DEVELOPMENT

This chapter will help you to

- become familiar with the role of neuroscience and the relevant debates in the context of early childhood education and care;
- develop a basic understanding of brain functionality such as myelination, synaptic connections and plasticity;
- become aware of neurodevelopmental conditions and impairments.

Introduction

Neuroscience is about understanding how the brain functions and is an overarching term for neurophysiology, neuropsychiatry and neurobiology (Penn, 2008). Other branches include computational neuroscience (as in predictive text on mobile phones) (Goswami, 2020) and the emerging field of educational neuroscience, which is sometimes called neuroeducation, that aims to understand brain function involved with learning (The Royal Society, 2011). There is also cognitive neuroscience, which is defined as understanding 'what happens in the brain when we have emotions, or thoughts, or when we create art, or music, or when we read and write' (Goswami, 2020: 1). This chapter generally focuses on the latter branch of neuroscience within the context of education.

Goswami (2020) further explains that neuroscience is about studying the science of the brain and the nervous system and, due to its scientific nature, neuroscience is becoming increasingly more appealing to policy-makers (Wood et al., 2017). Over the last five years, many advances have been made in neuroscience, but it is important to remember that while philosophical ideas remain worthy after two thousand years, this is not usually the case for scientific findings whereby seven years is often thought to be the 'shelf life' (Penn, 2008). Therefore, it is important to keep up to date with recent findings, particularly in the field of neuroscience.

The importance and relevance of neuroscience

There is a belief that neuroscience helps educators understand pedagogy – i.e., their methods of teaching and learning in a more scientific way (Tibke, 2019). However, critics such as Jeffrey Bowers (cited in Howard-Jones et al., 2016) argue that 'neuroscience has no role to play in influencing education' (3). Conversely, Boyle suggests that neuroscience 'has opened up new understandings of how sensitivity to young children's needs and responsive interactions may impact on the physiology of brain development' (2019: 454).

Penn (2008) and Archer and Siraj (2015) state that there is no agreement among neuroscientists about whether findings from brain science will be of any use to practitioners working with young children. For example, in 2002, John Bruer questioned the applicability of neuroscience research to professionals working with young children and was very sceptical whether it would be helpful. He also disagrees with the dominant discourse about the first three years of life being critical and argues that all years are equally important. The years 1990–2000 were declared the 'decade of the brain' in the USA (Dekker et al., 2012) and towards the late 1990s, the 'birth to three movement', which aimed to influence parental attitudes to early development and public health policies, was put forward and started to grow globally (Centre for Educational Neuroscience, 2020).

In 2005, Sarah-Jayne Blackmore and Uta Frith were strong advocates of drawing upon neuroscientific research. They argued that research about the brain has the potential to optimise learning for children and could transform the way professionals think, act and work. In 2007, Paul Howard-Jones examined various neuro-myths in an educational context and argued for more interdisciplinary work between educators, neuroscientists and policy-makers to ensure that findings are relevant and significant to education (Archer and Siraj, 2015). In 2014, the Wellcome Trust conducted a survey (where 292 teachers responded) and found that the majority of teachers (85 per cent) 'would collaborate with neuroscientists doing research in education' (Simmonds, 2014: 1). The Royal Society (2011) suggests that long-term dialogue and communication needs to take place between different professionals in order for educational neuroscience to be an effective discipline and to make a difference to the learning experiences of children.

Neuro-myths and Neuro-hits

The training of early childhood education and care professionals has an interesting history, as mentioned in the previous chapter about philosophy, but one of the reasons why neuro-myths have emerged is because they rarely appear on the training programme of those working with young children in education (Howard-Jones, 2014). A neuro-myth is a statement about the brain which is not underpinned by scientific evidence and is a mistaken/incorrect idea that has not been rigorously examined in an educational context; Dekker et al. (2012) suggest they are very loosely based on scientific facts. Howard-Jones describes neuro-myths as 'biased distortions of scientific fact' (2014: 1). Some examples of 'neuro-myths' include 'fish oils improve learning', 'left brain versus right brain thinkers', 'children have different learning styles', 'we only use 10% of our brains' and 'babies need to crawl before they walk to reduce the chance of learning disabilities in later life', but there are many more.

In 2012, Dekker et al., (2012) conducted a survey among teachers in the Netherlands and the United Kingdom (UK) to assess their general knowledge of the brain and neuro-myths. The most prevalent myth believed by the teachers was that 'children learn better when they receive information that suits their learning style', and the next most believed neuro-myth was 'left brain versus right brain thinkers'.

Conversely, 'neuro-hits' are statements about the brain that are underpinned by scientific evidence and are correct in nature. Some examples of neuro-hits include 'diet makes a difference to learning', 'physical exercise enhances learning', 'well rested children do better at school', and 'children do better at school if they were born in the autumn', and many more exist (Centre for Educational Neuroscience, 2020).

Howard-Jones states that communication between neuroscientists, educators and policy-makers has improved, and arguably neuroscientists (and all researchers/scientists) have a responsibility to make data and research findings accessible to those without a background in neuroscience. The aim is to have information that is 'scientifically valid and educationally informative' (2014: 6).

Reflective question

Are the following neuro-myths or neuro-hits?

- The left hemisphere of the brain controls the right side of your body and the right hemisphere controls the left side of your body.
- Brain gym in schools is not supported by a robust evidence base and none of the scientific studies found a significant improvement in academic achievement (Smidt, 2013).
- Babies are capable of producing the sounds of all languages at the babbling phase and sounds that are not associated with the child's home language/not heard by the baby are phased out.
- By the age of 2 years, the infant brain has reached over 80 per cent of its adult's volume (Tibke, 2019).
- Once a baby is born, new synapses can form at an extremely fast rate of one million connections per second (Levine and Munsch, 2016).
- When young children start walking, they will usually take more than 9,000 steps in a day (Levine and Munsch, 2016).
- Newborns need 16–18 hours of sleep a day (Levine and Munsch, 2016).
- The brain of an adult weighs approximately 3lb (Overall, 2007).

Case study: The value of educational neuroscience

Sarah, a neuroscientist, and Hannah, an early years teacher, were excited to be attending the annual educational neuroscience conference in Bristol. They were excited for two reasons: first, they were keen to learn new things and second, they were presenting their research posters. During the refreshment break, conference delegates were encouraged to read and appraise the research posters, and this is where Sarah and Hannah met. Hannah had produced a poster about early years practitioners' understandings of the brain and Sarah's poster was focused around the benefits and challenges of using a non-invasive method of exploring brain function in young children using functional Magnetic Resonance Imaging (fMRI).

Both professionals really enjoyed listening and learning from each other – for example, Sarah learnt that many practitioners working with young children had misunderstandings about the brain and was surprised that some didn't make the link between myelination and repetition in children's activities. Hannah learnt how findings from an fMRI study reinforced the importance of reading to children at a young age and she was keen to keep in touch with Sarah to find out more about language development and brain function.

The case study above demonstrates how beneficial dialogue can be between a neuroscientist and an early years professional. The case study also highlights how professionals appreciate each other's expertise and can learn from each other's work.

Reflective question

If you were to plan a research poster, what would the focus/theme be and why?

Research approaches to neuroscience

Despite different views about whether neuroscience is relevant and important for professionals working in the early years, there is widespread agreement that first, the brain is a complex organ of the human body (Goswami, 2020) and second, that brain behaviour relationships are extremely complex (The Royal Society, 2011). Third, there is also agreement that investigating the brain is not easy because of the inability to gain direct access to it. Traditionally, neuroscientists relied upon animal research, brains of the deceased and studying embryology (Penn, 2008). More contemporary methods which are expensive include electroencephalograms (EEGs) which measure electrical activity in the brain, Positron Emission Tomography (PET), which examines tissue and organ function and can detect disease, Magnetic Resonance Imaging (MRI) which forms three-dimensional images of the anatomy (Penn, 2008), and functional Magnetic Resonance Imaging (fMRI), which tracks blood flow to different parts of the brain when it is engaged in different activities (Tibke, 2019).

According to Archer and Siraj, neuroscience has started to 'shed light on the brain and learning' (2015: 23). They further state in relation to their paper on movement-play in the early years that neuroscientific research conducted on animals has shown that exercise enhances brain function; for young people and adults, there is evidence to show that exercise early on in life can have a positive impact on cognitive function and could improve academic achievements. However, they pose a valid question – to what extent can findings from neuroscience research on animals and with young people and adults relate to younger children under the age of 8? The following sections discuss useful information about brain functionality that could be helpful to those working with young children.

Early brain development: synaptic connections

The brain works on the basis of information flowing through complex circuits which are made up of networks of neurons (Penn, 2008). Brain cells are called neurons and it is widely accepted that babies are born with over 100 billion of them (Goswami, 2020) – like stars in a galaxy, suggests Smidt (2013). Neurons can vary in size and shape, and have lots of different interconnected parts (Kalat, 2014), such as the ones described in Table 7.1.

Table 7.1 Brain cell functions

Name of part	Function/role
Cell body	Contains the nucleus which controls and regulates the cell as well as houses genes
Dendrites	Receives information from other neurons
Axon	Information sender
Myelin sheath	Insulating fatty tissue which surrounds the axon

Even though babies are born with billions of brain cells, they do not have many synaptic connections, which is the small gap between the neurons that pass information to one another. Neurons communicate with one another via chemical and electrical signals, and myelination helps to increase the flow of information and make the communication more efficient between neurons (Smidt, 2013; Tibke, 2019). Myelination is the thickening of the fatty tissue called myelin that surrounds the axon; it acts as a type of insulation (Penn, 2008) and is also described as being like 'the plastic on the outside of electric cables' (Overall, 2007: 19). The rate of myelination depends on a child's experiences (Maconochie, 2019) and it is important to remember that neurons and myelination are both nourished by glial cells (Crowley, 2014).

The very small gap between the neurons where information is passed on is called the synaptic gap; chemical messengers known as neurotransmitters transmit the information between neurons. Synaptic connections are rarely formed when babies are born, but over time and with stimulation and experience, the brain overproduces neurons and synaptic connections. In order for the brain to cope with the overproduction, the process of synaptic pruning (or synapse elimination) takes place, which discards synaptic connections that are no longer being regularly stimulated. During stressful situations, levels of cortisol (the stress hormone) rise and can interfere with the process of myelination and synaptic pruning, particularly for children (Crowley, 2014). As previously mentioned, the brain is a complex organ and consists of various parts (see Table 7.2) that work with one another. The remaining part of this chapter further explains some of these complexities.

Table 7.2   (Some) parts of the brain

Name of part	Function/role
Corpus callosum	These are fibres that connect the right and left hemispheres of the brain
Brain stem	Controls basic physiological functions such as breathing, heart rate and body temperature
Cerebellum	Controls movement and balance
Cerebrum – occipital lobe	Processes vision
Cerebrum – temporal lobe	Processes hearing
Cerebrum – parietal lobe	Processes spatial awareness and sensory input
Cerebrum – frontal lobe	Processes language, movement and self-control
Cerebrum – prefrontal cortex	Controls judgements and planning

Early brain development: plasticity

Plasticity is a useful concept to know about and provides you with an opportunity to understand how experiences shape and change brain structure (Smidt, 2013). The following two models 'experience–expectant' and 'experience-dependent' are now briefly explained to help you further understand the relationship between plasticity and experience. First, 'experience-expectant' plasticity is described as naturally occurring where the brain 'expects' to encounter such things as light, sound, responsive care and language; second, the concept of 'experience-dependent' plasticity is about specific experiences that modify synapses or generate new ones (Crowley, 2014). In other words, neural connections are made based upon what a child sees and does (Smidt, 2013). Moreover, experience-dependent plasticity takes place throughout life and therefore synaptic pruning is a very natural and necessary process (Tibke, 2019). Crowley (2014) states that there is often confusion among parents and teachers about the first three years of life being a race against time in terms of stopping synapses being lost; the reality is that experience-dependent plasticity is lifelong and is not something that just happens to those aged under 3 years (The Royal Society, 2011; Smidt, 2013). 'Sensitive periods' rather than 'critical periods' is now the preferred term to describe certain periods of time in the life span, whereby parts of the brain are more sensitive to particular experiences such as early childhood or adolescence (Smidt, 2013; Tibke, 2019).

Sensory and perceptual development

Learning is something we all encounter and as human beings we learn about the world through our senses; the brain receives sensations from different senses such as hearing, smell, taste, sight, touch, vestibular (balance) and proprioception (awareness of the position and movement of the body). The process of perception occurs when the brain interprets the information and attaches meaning to it. Therefore, experiencing different sensations and sensory experiences are incredibly important for the process of perception to take place (Levine and Munsch, 2016). Babies can see with clarity and precision at 20 feet (6 metres) what an adult sees with the same clarity and precision at around 400 feet (122 metres), so this is why it is important for adults to go close to babies' faces so they can see the detail of the face. Newborns will focus on areas of contrast with dark and light such as the hairline, then, at around the age of 2 months, babies will start to look in the eyes. Hearing is functional in the womb and a baby can recognise their mother's voice in the first three days. Levine and Munsch (2016) explain that for a long period of time, a baby will hear so many different sounds in the mother's womb, such as the mother's heartbeat, sounds of digestion and outdoor sounds which reassured them, but once they are born, some babies for a few weeks find it difficult to sleep without these sounds as they were a part of them for nine months. For example, some mothers might stay at home for the first few weeks so the sounds that a baby encounters are now different and new.

Babies also recognise their mother's smell early on and are soothed by it. In terms of taste, babies prefer sweet foods and are drawn to breast milk because it is sweet. Touch is such another important sense that can be calming and comforting. Up until the 1980s, physicians believed that babies did not feel pain and one reason for this belief was that if the mother had taken anesthesia, this could still be in the baby's system so they would be unlikely to feel or respond to pain. Some research years ago was extremely unethical where physicians would prick babies with pins to see how they would respond (Levine and Munsch, 2016). The goal should be to stimulate all senses (not with pins), which in turn aids the process of perception.

Case study: Sensory experiences

Michael had just started his new role of nursery manager within a children's centre. In a matter of weeks, he completed a resource audit and soon realised that the majority of resources in the nursery were made of plastic. He felt the resources were limiting children's play opportunities as well as their sensory experiences, which he knew would stimulate neural connections and perceptual development. At one of the weekly staff meetings, Michael shared his findings from the resource audit and the team agreed that Roxanne, the final year occupational therapy student, would develop a list of resources and activities that would be suitable to use to develop children's senses. Roxanne presented the following list:

(Continued)

Touch: feely/treasure basket including natural items such as a brush, natural sponge, wet/dry sand, playdough, shaving foam, mud, cooked/uncooked pasta/rice.

Hearing: listening walk, music/musical instruments, listening lotto.

Smell: scents on cotton wool, diffusers, flowers, foods, herb garden.

Taste: different foods introduced daily, foods from different cultures, different textured foods – e.g., crackers versus banana, daily cooking (little chefs).

Vision: sensory walk, food colouring/glitter in water, sensory room with different coloured lights, water tubes.

Vestibular: balancing beams, walking along masking tape or rope, climbing frames.

Proprioception: hammering blocks/DIY, lifting, pushing and pulling carts, singing songs – body parts.

When Roxanne presented the list to the team, practitioners were surprised to see seven senses listed and they wanted to know more about the last one – proprioception. Roxanne explained that proprioception is a sense that is incredibly important for young children to develop as it provides them with opportunities to judge body movements, positions and forces.

The case study above briefly shows how creative practitioners could be in promoting and developing children's sensory experiences. But it also shows how a student training in the allied health professional sector can support the learning of the staff in tasks such as analysis of the environment and occupations (activities).

Reflective question

If you were to write a list of resources, what would it look like for different age groups?

Executive function skills, metacognition and self-regulation

So far, you have been introduced to many concepts relating to brain development, but there are many more. Fitzgerald and Maconochie (2019) explain that executive function skills are associated with the prefrontal cortex part of the brain (the very front of the cerebrum) which controls planning, organising, decision making, resisting impulses/urges and involves working memory. Put another way, executive functioning is the numerous cognitive skills that are utilised in problem-solving situations (Bryce et al., 2014). Closely linked to executive function skills is metacognition. Bryce et al. (2014) explain that when someone studies metacognition, they are exploring what people know about their own cognition, as well as examining how they manage and control their cognition when on task. Bryce et al. found that 'executive functions could be "necessary but not sufficient" antecedents to metacognitive skills' (2014: 181).

Self-regulation is also related to executive function skills and metacognition, but focuses more on social and emotional behaviour. The prefrontal cortex controls and regulates emotions and social behaviour, but matures later than other parts of the brain (Potegal and Davidson, 2003), making it difficult for some children to manage and control their emotions. Emotion coaching is a new approach that started about a decade ago which focuses on helping children regulate their own behaviour as opposed to modifying their behaviour, which is usually considered the long-standing, traditional approach. In emotion coaching, behaviour is conceptualised as a form of communication and aims to help 'children to understand their varying emotions as they experience them, why they occur, and how to handle them' (Rose and McGuire-Sniekus, 2016: 1). Empathy and guidance are at the centre of the approach – for example, empathy involves recognising and labelling a child's emotion in order to promote their self-awareness, and guidance involves engaging with a child in a problem-solving way to help them self-regulate their behaviour and adopt alternatives. However, when a child or person is having an emotional outburst and is very anxious, the levels of cortisol (the stress hormone) rise, which increases blood pressure whereby breathing speeds up and makes the child feel confused and unable to think clearly (Potegal and Davidson, 2003). This is where empathy is needed to calm the child and help them return to a more stable state before being able to reason with them. Ultimately, emotion coaching helps children regulate how they express their feelings and they eventually learn to self-calm and self-regulate (Rose and McGuire-Sniekus, 2016).

Neurodevelopmental conditions and impairments

As previously mentioned, there is widespread agreement that the brain is a complex organ and therefore complications can arise as a result. Certain conditions such as autism and cerebral palsy affect/interrupt the development of the nervous system, which interferes with the typical functionality of brain development and learning (Blackburn et al., 2012). The words 'disorder', 'disability', 'abnormality' and 'development deficits', which are more commonly used in neuroscience and child development textbooks, have been avoided in this section because they simply don't fit with the authors' epistemological and ontological views about children and development; 'condition' and 'impairment' are the preferred choices.

Autism is described by Levine and Munsch (2016) as a condition that impairs social communication and interactions, and is usually characterised by repetitive behaviours, activities or specific interests. Someone with autism might also be under- or over-sensitive to stimulation (Crowley, 2014). Research about brain functionality for those with autism is ongoing, but it is thought that the amygdala within the limbic system of the brain which deals with emotions and memory is larger in size, which makes it more difficult for someone to form relationships and interact. 'Theory of mind', which involves understanding the desires, thoughts, feelings and mental state of others and starts to develop in young children, is a skill that children with autism also find challenging (Crowley, 2014). It is still unknown whether the brain of someone with autism overproduces synapses or whether synapses are pruned away in the typical way with the process of synaptic pruning (Levine and Munsch, 2016).

Cerebral palsy is a condition that affects a child's movement, balance, posture, coordination and sometimes speech. Levine and Munsch (2016) explain that children with cerebral palsy have encountered some sort of brain injury, which often means a reduced blood or oxygen supply that negatively impacts on the brain cell's ability to create myelin (the insulating fatty tissue that surrounds an axon) and as a result the brain cell dies. In the majority of cases, brain injury occurs during foetal development, but can also occur and emerge any time up to the age of 3. Very small percentages of babies can encounter brain injury during the birthing process itself, and infection early on in a child's development can also be a contributing factor. The impairment can vary from being mild in nature to very severe.

Case study: Supporting children

Mrs Khan was excited for her new reception class (4- to 5-year-olds) to start in September. She had met most of the children in the previous July at various transition events, including Robbie who had cerebral palsy. Robbie had moderate mobility difficulties and used a variety of equipment such as a wheelchair, standing frame and walking frame. The equipment played a very important role in improving his posture, helping him walk independently and strengthening his balance and muscle control. This meant additional space had to be made for Robbie's equipment, so Mrs Khan and her team made a number of improvements to the learning environment to ensure that Robbie could make a smooth transition to the class. For example, a few tables and chairs had to be removed and a parking bay for Robbie's equipment was provided with outlines on the floor to make sure the space remained free for his equipment. Mrs Khan also decided to borrow an adult wheelchair so the team could simulate what the learning environment would be like for Robbie and this helped to eliminate any barriers.

The case study above shows how one team adapted the learning environment for a child with cerebral palsy and took a genuine and authentic interest in understanding how Robbie would navigate the classroom environment.

Reflective question

What other neurodevelopmental conditions or impairments are you aware of and how would you support the child's needs?

Summary of chapter

- Neuroscience is about understanding how the brain functions and is very scientific in nature, which makes the discipline appealing to policy-makers.
- There are mixed views about whether evidence from neuroscience is relevant and useful for professionals working with young children in early childhood education and care contexts. Cross-collaboration, also known as interdisciplinary work, is needed between educators, neuroscientists and policy-makers to ensure that findings are relevant and significant to education.
- Many neuro-myths (common misconceptions) exist in the context of children's development, and these are untrue, flawed statements about the brain.
- Synaptic connections, myelination and plasticity are useful concepts that can help early childhood professionals understand how experience shapes the brain's architecture.
- Different neurodevelopmental conditions and impairments affect different parts of brain functionality, and it is important that children are supported appropriately and sensitively.

End-of-chapter questions

1. What is your understanding of neuroscience and child development?
2. Do you see a place for evidence/research from neuroscience in your current or future work with young children?
3. What three questions would you ask a neuroscientist and why?

Further reading

Bruer, J. (1999) *The Myth of the First Three Years: A New Understanding of Early Brain Development and Lifelong Learning*. New York: The Free Press.

This book is very thought-provoking and will provide you with an opportunity to reflect on your position and thoughts about the first three years of life being the most critical. John Bruer explores various brain research studies and discusses how they relate to young children as well as to the life course in general.

Conkbayir, M. (2021) *Early Childhood and Neuroscience: Theory, Research and Implications for Practice* (2nd edn). London: Bloomsbury.

This book will help you to better understand how to use neuroscience research and findings in early childhood education and care contexts. This second edition provides additional chapters about neurodiversity and childhood trauma.

Vandenbroeck, M., De Vos, J., Fias, W., Mariett Olsson, L., Penn, H., Wastell, D. and White, S. (2017) *Constructions of Neuroscience in Early Childhood Education*. Oxford: Routledge.

This book is part of Routledge's contesting early childhood series and will provide you with a more in-depth understanding of the benefits and challenges of a neuroscience discourse within an early childhood context. You can access the link to the book series here: www.routledge.com/Contesting-Early-Childhood/book-series/SE0623?pd=published,forthcoming&pg=1&pp=12&so=pub&view=list

The centre for neuroscience in education, based at the University of Cambridge, has some very useful resources listed on their website – for example, brain facts that allow you to explore the brain in three dimension. You can access the link here: www.cne.psychol.cam.ac.uk/further-resources

EIGHT

THE EDUCATION OF CHILD DEVELOPMENT

This chapter will help you to

- develop an awareness of the history of early childhood education, key longitudinal studies and an interdisciplinary thinking towards child development;
- understand key concepts relating to education such as praxis, curriculum perspectives and human capital theory.

Introduction

There are many views about the role and purpose of education and for Richard Gerver, a former head teacher and author of *Creating Tomorrow's School Today*, 'education begins from the moment of our conception and will shape the people we become, the lives we will lead and the impact we will have on others' (2010: xiii). Gerver (2010) further suggests that there are two perspectives about the role of education: first, those who view 'knowledge acquisition as the aim' of education and second, those who view 'knowledge acquisition as the process'. Moreover, those who view the latter believe that the aim of education is to develop skills to become a successful learner and equip them for dealing with life after school. The educational process model advocated by Gerver in his school consisted of the following elements: 'learning to learn and live, developing skills and competence, applying learning in contexts and developing aspiration and values' (2010: 103). Gerver and his staff developed a nurture suite which replicated a studio flat with a fitted kitchen and welcoming lounge, as well as a living/activity area. The suite was used to help children identify their strengths and weaknesses, to develop self-worth and self-esteem, and to engage in problem-solving scenarios. The outcomes were outstanding whereby the 'children made huge progress, impacting on their ability to develop as learners and as young members of the community' (2010: 110). Gerver's work provides opportunities for people to think about the purpose and role of education.

John Dewey, an American philosopher, psychologist and educationalist, believed that 'schools shape society and must help children to live in a society' (Pound, 2011: 22). There is a belief that education is about meeting and respecting 'children's civil, political and social human rights' (Quennerstedt and Quennerstedt, 2014: 129) and therefore lends itself to interdisciplinary thinking and working practices.

Some view education as an academic discipline, some view it as a field and some view it as an applied subject. This matters because viewing education as a field is often considered to be substandard compared with viewing education as a discipline (Wyse, 2020). According to Krishnan (2009; cited in Wyse, 2020) there are six criteria that can be used to judge whether a body of knowledge can be termed a discipline:

1. academic department at universities/colleges;
2. specific focus for its research;
3. well-established body of specialist knowledge;
4. strong theoretical frameworks;
5. specialist terminology/vocabulary;
6. particular research methods.

Arguably, education is a discipline in its own right.

Case study: Time for debate

Carl and Tim were first-year education students and were asked to debate the purpose and role of education in society. Carl explained that education was about gaining knowledge in important areas such as Mathematics, English, Science and Technology and perhaps Art. However, Tim felt that education was also about preparing children and young people for life after school and should involve teaching life skills, such as budgeting and cooking. Carl felt that it was the parents' role to teach children about such things and not for schools, but Tim argued that not every child will have the same opportunities at home.

The case study highlights that people have different views about the purpose of education and that it is not always easy to come to an agreement. It further highlights how education is entangled with politics and philosophy.

Reflective question

How does a country decide on the purpose and role of education in society?

The historical development of early childhood education

As previously stated, history is not discussed as a stand-alone discipline in this book because it is a cross-cutting theme throughout Part 1 and offers an interesting background context about societal views on children, the family and the state. This chapter begins with an historical overview of how early childhood education evolved.

John Comenius was born in the very late sixteenth century in the Czech Republic and is well known for transforming the Hungarian and Swedish education systems. He believed in young children having an education, was against rote learning, and argued for holistic development and rich sensory experiences. Further, he believed that all children deserved an education regardless of socioeconomic background, gender or ability; while this is not considered revolutionary in the twenty-first century, it was in the early seventeenth century (Pound, 2014). Pound (2011) describes Comenius as the great educational reformer in the seventeenth century. Like Comenius, Robert Owen, born in Wales in the late eighteenth century, also fought for the rights of working-class people and argued against employing children under the age of 10. At the age of 28, he took over New Lanark mill in Scotland and one year later he opened a school to support working parents. Nurturing children's development and access to nature was at the heart of Owen's provision, as well as focusing on practical life skills. He also aimed to bring the rich and poor together to achieve greater social cohesion, but this was extremely radical for his time; he wanted equality of community. It is thought that Owen's work pioneered the way for infant schools for children up to the age of 6 years (Pound, 2011).

German-born Friedrich Froebel opposed the term 'infant school' for young children and in 1837 opened the first 'kindergarten' in Germany, which means 'garden of children' and focused on indoor and outdoor play provision (Pound, 2011). He believed that children's development naturally unfolded and is well known for developing educational materials called 'gifts' (e.g., wooden blocks) which could be used to stimulate thinking and problem solving (MacBlain, 2018). In the mid-nineteenth century, there was a repressive regime in Germany and, as a result, many residents moved to England. In 1851, the first kindergarten opened in London to cater for wealthy German families. Arguably, Froebelian provision did not work as well for working-class children, mainly due to the cost implications because kindergartens required smaller class sizes, highly trained pedagogues (also known as educators) and high-quality play resources, and this would have been considered a luxury at that time (Pound, 2014).

As a result of the Boer War (1899–1902) between Britain and South Africa and the poor health of soldiers, mothers needed to work outside the home, which meant that very young children below the statutory school age of 5 years attended school with their siblings. Classrooms for the very young became available, but they were always overcrowded and the children were penned in their seats to prevent them from being mischievous. Froebelians and others lobbied for improved conditions for young children, but little or no progress was made. When the school age was raised to 11 (in 1893) the numbers of younger children started to drop as the space was needed to accommodate the older children (Pound, 2014).

At the beginning of the twentieth century

Children soon became viewed as the nation's resource and this was due to the fact that soldiers being recruited for the Boer War were in poor health and physical fitness. A shift started to take place in making better provision and services for poorer children, and various legislative acts came into place, such as the Provision of School Meals Act in 1906, which the McMillan sisters (Rachel and Margaret) campaigned for (Pound, 2014). During the end of the First World War (1918) and at the start of the second (1939), progressive ideas about early childhood education were growing at an exponential pace. A key name associated with innovative early childhood education at this time was Margaret McMillan who championed for outdoor provision, space and free play, and advocated for health and well-being as a prerequisite to intellectual development. She was also inspired and influenced by Friedrich Fröbel.

Another progressive thinker was Maria Montessori who opened nurseries in Rome for extremely poor children with working-class mothers; the first Montessori nursery opened in England in 1912. Montessori advocated for a prepared environment, developing a child's concentration and independence, and regarded play and work as the same. Furthermore, Susan Isaacs, who was the first head of the child development department at the now London Institute of Education (IoE), championed for the emotional aspects of development, as well as focusing on the importance of play (Pound, 2014). Like McMillan, Isaacs believed that children needed a generous amount of space to explore and ponder, develop gross and fine motor skills and to be physically active. Isaacs states: 'the nursery school is an extension of the function of the home, not a substitute for it' (1954: 31).

During the Second World War, nursery provision consisted of a mixture of care and education to cater for mothers who were making a significant contribution to the workforce due to men being away at war. However, when the war ended and men returned home, the dynamics of the workforce changed – for example, the birth rate increased and the focus was placed on a child's early attachment to their mother, and much of the nursery provision was reduced to part-time. At the same time, nursery provision took a different pathway in the city of Reggio Emilia in Northern Italy, whereby the decision was taken to maintain and extend nursery provision to what is now internationally known as Reggio Emilia provision (Pound, 2014). This type of provision is explained in more detail later in the chapter.

Soon after the Second World War, health and education services in the UK were reformed and, as time went on, the health services were regarded as successful. However, in the 1950s the education services were considered unsatisfactory because there was low achievement among working-class children and the way in which children were learning started to be questioned (Pound, 2011). It was around the 1960s that literature, mainly from the USA, started to be published about deschooling, whereby some suggested abolishing compulsory schooling and spoke up about their concerns. Brazilian-born Paulo Freire was an activist, particularly around adult education, and tackled the problem of illiteracy in Brazil. He was exiled to Chile in 1964 but was allowed to return to Brazil in 1979 (Pound, 2011). Freire is well known for speaking up on behalf of the oppressed who were subjected to very strict authoritarian ways (Pound, 2011). He believed in transforming society to achieve social justice and strongly advocated for 'praxis', which is about critical reflection that leads to action. In short, praxis means going beyond critical reflection and applying theoretical knowledge and seeing it in practice to take action, and involves deeper/higher level thinking. Lots of interesting developments were taking place in the twentieth century in England and Wales (before power for education was devolved to Wales), such as the introduction of the first statutory early years curriculum in 1996 for 3- to 5-year-olds, called the 'Desirable Outcomes'.

At the beginning of the twenty-first century

In 2008, Wales and England redesigned the curriculum for its youngest children and the Welsh Government introduced a new curriculum for 3- to 7-year-olds called the 'Foundation Phase', and England introduced the 'Early Years Foundation Stage' for 0- to 5-year-olds. To some extent, the pedagogical (learning and teaching) approach in Wales and England is still traditional in nature, whereby knowledge is imparted on children and the practitioner has ownership and responsibility over what, where, how and when the learning will take place. Moreover, this traditional approach mirrors a factory-type model which 'assumes children can be shaped into copies of successful adults' (Andrews, 2012: 157). This is different from the pedagogical approach in the Reggio Emilia practice in Northern Italy, whereby the concept of knowledge is understood as something that 'is the product of a process of construction, involving interpretation and meaning-making' (Moss, 2001: 128) where child and adult are co-learners.

The core belief of the Reggio Emilia practice is that 'children are born with an innate capacity to develop as individuals and to build their own knowledge of the world around them' (MacBlain, 2018: 88). The approach is very flexible with no formal written curriculum, as in Wales and England, and pedagogues are considered to be co-learners where children's interests dominate practice (MacBlain, 2018). A well-known poem called 'One Hundred Languages of Children' is associated with Reggio Emilia, and it highlights an important point about the many different ways that young children express their thinking, feelings and emotions (MacBlain, 2018). In other words, children express themselves in multimodal ways. Therefore, words such as agency, co-construction, rights, creativity and multimodality best describe twenty-first century thinking about pedagogical approaches.

Case study: Choices as a parent

It was a sunny Monday afternoon and Budds Day Nursery were having an open day for new parents. There was lots of chatter and children playing, and Charlotte, the nursery teacher, overheard a conversation between two prospective parents. Sally (one of the parents), explained how she was still undecided on using Budds or Sunbeams nursery situated a few miles away. She said to Donna

(Continued)

(another parent) how Sunbeams had invested in lots of expensive resources and it was very clean, new and impressive. She felt that the wooden resources were a little worn at Budds; it was messy, seemed chaotic and the children had lots of freedom. Donna responded by saying: 'You need to watch your son and see what he does, how he interacts with the environment and what he engages with to know if the setting is right for him. It's about him, not you. It's not about how something looks; it's about how it functions, in my opinion.'

The case study above demonstrates how Sally found it difficult to decide on what nursery to use for her son and Donna tried to offer some advice. Charlotte, the nursery teacher, has an opportunity here to consider why Sally is finding it difficult to make a choice and analyse what is contributing to this. By engaging in higher order thinking and critical reflection, Charlotte can articulate and strengthen why they do what they do at Budds to prospective parents.

Reflective question

In what way can you see praxis benefiting your work?

Child development and Piaget

Penn (2014) argues that learning about child development during practitioner training usually means to learn about Jean Piaget. The Plowden Report in 1976, which set out to review primary education in England, was also heavily influenced by Piaget's work, but since then research about children's development has progressed and moved forward and, to some extent, disputes some of the key conclusions of the report. For example, Goswami (2015: 1) states that 'it is no longer widely believed that there are different developmental stages in learning to think. Similarly, it is not believed that a child cannot be taught until she/he is cognitively "ready"'.

It is also useful to keep in mind that well-known theorists developed their ideas at a particular point in time and were influenced by the cultural–historical context (Levine and Munsch, 2016). Psychologist Marx Wartofsky (1983; cited in Hedegaard, 2009: 71) suggests that 'developmental psychology is constructed because of the need of society'. Developmental psychology is a scientific school of thought that is deeply embedded in the way we work with children and places a strong emphasis on categorising areas of development (also known as domains), which are discussed in Part 2 of the book. It is important to keep in mind that even though domains of development are described separately and are distinct in nature, they interact with one another. The reason for focusing on areas of development is to better understand and manage information relating to 'expected pace, progress and sequences of children's learning and development' (Neaum, 2019: 52). It is also considered useful for helping to understand whether a child has difficulties in a specific area. Perhaps this explains why it is a widely used and accepted school of thought within early childhood education. Developmental sequences and patterns are predictable and each achievement builds on the previous one. Fixed ages linked to stages should be understood in context because the pace of progress will be different for all children (Neaum, 2019). Hedegaard (2009) suggests that in order to understand the variability in children's development, a cultural–historical perspective is essential. This is where the notion of praxis is useful because it affords practitioners opportunities to reflect on children's development from psychology, anthropology and sociology, and contextualise their observations and judgements.

Early years curricula across the UK are underpinned by the key ideas of Jean Piaget and adopt a 'developmental psychology' perspective (Andrews, 2012). For example, the *Development Matters* non-statutory document in use by practitioners working with 0- to 5-year-olds in England presents development as discontinuous in nature (ages and stages). In Wales, practitioners working with 3- to 7-year-olds use the *Foundation Phase* profile handbook which states that the outcomes children reach are broadly aligned with expected ages of development (WG, 2017a). However, it could also be argued that principles of 'humanistic psychology', such as 'uniqueness' and the 'whole child', are also evident in both curricula for England and Wales. For example, the Early Years Foundation Stage in England highlights the 'unique child' as one of its four principles that shape practice and provision for young children. In Wales, the *Foundation Phase* statutory document states that 'children must be allowed to develop at their own unique, individual pace' (WG, 2015a: 4). The curriculum document also states that provision for young children should be holistic in nature. These examples highlight that at least two competing branches of psychology are at play.

Child development and the curriculum

As well as competing schools of thought underpinning child development in a curriculum, there are also different perspectives of the curriculum. Soler and Miller (2003) explain the curriculum as

Progressive and socio-cultural	Instrumental and vocational
Adult as facilitator	Adult as authority figure and controller
No explicit aim/goal in advance	Produces citizens who will benefit society
Child's needs, interests and learning patterns developed	Prepares children for the world of work
Prioritises needs of the child	Prioritises needs of society
Child constructs knowledge	Child absorbs abstract knowledge
Play and culture prioritised	Subject-related learning, school ready prioritised

Figure 8.1 Two different types of curricula

being on a continuum which fluctuates between 'progressive and socio-cultural' (as in the Reggio Emilia practice) and 'instrumental and vocational' (as in Wales and England). Figure 8.1 shows the key features of the two different types of curricula which are described by Soler and Miller (2003).

Human capital theory

One might argue that a curriculum can have features of both perspectives as described above, but human capital theory which relates to someone's knowledge, skills and abilities (Smith et al., 2016) is often the main rationale for investing in Early Childhood Education and Care (ECEC). One of the reasons for it being the main rationale is the 2006 report from the Organization for Economic Co-operation and Development (OECD), which stated that ECEC has a crucial role to play in developing human capital where economic savings can be made. This message can be influential in shaping the thinking of policy at a national level (Campbell-Barr and Nygard, 2014) and is usually positioned towards the 'instrumental and vocational' perspective end of the continuum. However, Campbell-Barr and Nygard (2014) have expressed concerns about this being a narrow view of children and ECEC services. For example, cognitive development and knowledge acquisition is prioritised over social development and tends to focus on the 'becoming' child, which is future oriented and often neglects the 'here and now'.

Case study: Choices as a professional

Rosa, an experienced Reggio Emilia teacher from Italy, had recently moved to the UK because her partner had secured a promotion in the Secret Intelligence Service, London. She was aware of the differences between practices in the UK and Italy and knew that it would take a while to settle in, but she underestimated just how difficult the transition would be for her. Rosa started working in a private day nursery and soon realised that children were perceived differently in the UK (i.e., they were more vulnerable and needy), and the curriculum was too rigid and wasn't working to the child's strengths, capabilities and ways of being. There was not a strong focus on creativity and the setting wasn't part of the community. Rosa decided she had two choices – to leave or embrace the change and draw upon her experiences to shape and extend practitioners' thinking.

The case study above highlights how practices differ from country to country, and how practitioners' training, knowledge and understanding about early childhood can impact on children's experiences. If Rosa decides to stay, she will undoubtedly engage in praxis.

Reflective question

Why did Rosa find it so difficult to work in a UK early years setting?

Longitudinal studies

To strengthen the argument made at the beginning of this chapter about education being a discipline in its own right, key findings from some longitudinal studies are now discussed. The Millennium Cohort Study (MCS), also known as 'child of the new century study', is a longitudinal study that follows the lives of around 19,000 children and young people born in 2000–2002 across the UK. It is an important source of evidence that examines child development and daily life experiences over time. To date, seven data sweeps have taken place, which means that data were collected at different times; the first sweep took place when the child was nine months old and the latest sweep when the young person was 17 years old (University College London, 2021a). The MCS reports that various findings such as ability grouping of children in classrooms (which is very common) might be intensifying the disadvantages that summer-born children face. 'The research found that, by age seven, September-born children were nearly three times as likely to be in the top stream as those born in the following August' (Campbell, 2013: 1). Also, Campbell reports that 97 per cent of young children were grouped by ability by the age of 7, and further states that 'being placed in a particular group can affect children's self-perceptions and behaviour, and possibly how their teachers interact with them' (2013: 1).

More recent findings from the MCS in 2021 suggest that babies born as a result of IVF treatment and weigh under 5.5lb do not tend to have their cognitive development hindered compared to babies born without IVF – i.e., they were naturally conceived. Babies born as a result of IVF treatment tend to be from wealthier backgrounds and therefore the researchers believe that parents are 'able to compensate for the negative consequences of being born small by providing more financial and educational resources for their children' (University College London, 2021b: 1). In cognitive assessments at ages 3, 7, 11 and 14, small babies born from IVF 'performed, on average, similarly or better... as naturally conceived children... ' (2021b: 1).

Another relevant longitudinal study is the Effective Provision of Pre-school Education (EPPE) project which found that high-quality provision was beneficial to children's intellectual, social and behavioural development. Moreover, 'where settings view educational and social development as complementary and equal in importance, children make better all round progress' (Sylva et al., 2004: 1). Data collected from the EPPE study were used in a further study called Researching Effective Pedagogy in the Early Years (REPEY). The REPEY study explored the pedagogical (learning and teaching) strategies that best support children's development and found that sustained shared thinking between adult and child extends children's thinking. Formative assessment during activities and collaboration with parents in establishing a child's learning programme was also effective in supporting children's development. In terms of improving children's social and behavioural development, the most effective settings were proactive in supporting children's social skills via stories and group discussions, and talked through conflict with children and practitioners when they arose (Siraj-Blatchford et al., 2002). Andrews (2012) argues that effective pedagogy is supported by an awareness of and a strong grasp of child development.

A more recent longitudinal study called the Study of Early Education and Development (SEED) in England set out to explore 'how variation in ECEC experience may be associated with cognitive and socio-emotional development' (Melhuish and Gardiner, 2020: 7). Some of the key findings indicate that children who had experienced a larger amount of informal ECEC settings, such as with friends and family, had higher scores in their verbal ability when measured in Year 1 (5- to 6-year-olds), whereas children who had experienced a larger amount of formal ECEC settings, such as playgroups and nursery/reception classes, had poorer outcomes in social and emotional scores when measured in Year 1 (Melhuish and Gardiner, 2020).

The importance of an interdisciplinary focus on child development

Previous chapters that have discussed different disciplines make positive contributions to thinking about child development such as psychology, which is useful for understanding children's behaviour and how they construct and internalise knowledge, as well as the influencing role of the adult and environment. Sociology, for example, makes practitioners aware of social factors and how poverty, age, gender, ethnicity and socioeconomic background can influence development, but also life chances. Conversely, economic analyses can help to predict outcomes for early intervention programmes and help policy-makers shape the direction of services. Anthropology, on the other hand, helps practitioners to understand the habits, values and individual practices of families and appreciate the process of how children learn their own culture and that of others. With similar features to anthropology, philosophy helps practitioners tune into the many different ways of living, being, doing and thinking, and how these interact with development. Lastly, neuroscience helps practitioners understand brain function for ensuring quality learning experiences, as well as appreciating how experience can shape the brain. However, over time some disciplines and discourses become dominant and they can influence children's experiences either positively or negatively. Therefore, praxis is essential in recognising the worth of other disciplines.

Summary of chapter

- Education is a discipline in its own right and one that has competing purposes and roles – knowledge as process or knowledge as product.
- The history of early childhood education has evolved differently across countries such as the UK and Northern Italy, and many progressive ideas that were initiated centuries ago are evident in practice today.
- There are competing perspectives from developmental and humanistic psychology of how children learn and develop in curriculum policy, as well as competing perspectives of the curriculum (progressive versus instrumental) that can make practice challenging.
- Human capital theory is often used to support the rationale for investing in ECEC, but it tends to favour cognitive development and knowledge acquisition.
- Praxis involves critical reflection, but takes it to another level whereby practitioners apply higher order thinking that leads to action.

End-of-chapter questions

1. What is your understanding of education and child development?
2. What is the role of education in promoting children's health and well-being?
3. Talk with a colleague and decide what knowledge, skills, abilities and competencies are important for young children to develop. What do you notice about the discussion?

Further reading

Boyd, D. and Hirst, N. (2016) *Understanding Early Years Education Across the UK: Comparing Practice in England, Northern Ireland, Scotland and Wales*. Oxford: Routledge.

This book will help you understand and appreciate policy and practice in other countries. The book explores the policy context in each country, then provides a discussion about their similarities and differences.

Cameron, C. and Moss, P. (eds) (2011) *Social Pedagogy and Working with Children and Young People: Where Care and Education Meet*. London: Jessica Kingsley.

This book, particularly Chapter 1, provides you with a detailed insight into the concept of social pedagogy which is widespread in continental Europe but less familiar and less well known in the UK.

Noddings, N. (2005) *The Challenge to Care in School: An Alternative Approach to Education* (2nd edn). New York: Teachers College Press.

This book will extend your knowledge and understanding of progressive approaches to working with children and focuses on a caring curriculum for children.

PART TWO

EXPLORING CHILD DEVELOPMENT DOMAINS WITH AN INTERDISCIPLINARY LENS

NINE
PHYSICAL DEVELOPMENT AND GROWTH

This chapter will help you to

- become familiar with the distinction between fine and gross motor skills and how these skills develop.
- discuss the influences of both genetic and environmental factors on physical development and growth.

Introduction

A great many changes take place in terms of physical development over the course of childhood. In its most basic terms, physical development can be defined as 'the progress of children's control over their body' (Neaum, 2013: 50), whereas physical growth covers growth in weight and height.

The human body grows and develops for 20 per cent of the life span, but growth is uneven, with the most rapid growth in the first two years and adolescence. There are two patterns of growth: cephalocaudal development – growth and development proceed from head to toe – and proximodistal development – growth and development proceed from the centre outwards (Crowley, 2017).

In addition to physical growth, the physical development of control over body movements also develops rapidly and is known as motor control. Motor development also follows cephalocaudal and proximodistal patterns with babies holding their heads up first before gaining control of their trunks and arms. Further, motor development can be divided into gross and fine motor skills.

Physical development and growth is dependent upon both genetic (maturation) and environmental factors. Genetic factors include the inheritance of certain physical factors such as height, hair colour and eye colour. Environmental factors, such as nutrition, affect weight, height, puberty and cognition. This chapter explores physical development and growth through the interdisciplinary approaches or disciplines discussed in Part 1. It considers the development of both gross and fine motor skills, and the influences of genetic and environmental factors upon physical development and growth.

Developmental Psychology Approach to Physical Development

As discussed in Part 1 (Chapters 2–8), there are many interdisciplinary approaches to child development. This means that physical development and growth can be viewed through many lenses. From a developmental psychology approach, physical development and growth is considered a domain or an area of development. As discussed in Chapter 2, categorising development into areas or domains enables an understanding of expected sequences of a child's development and learning and is used in education. Therefore, developmental psychology views physical development through established sequences and stages, but also acknowledges that children are all individuals and the rate at which they achieve sequences or stages of physical development and growth will vary.

The developmental psychology view of development occurring in defined stages or sequences is a linear approach and has led to the production of developmental charts or milestones linked to ages and stages. This has facilitated interventions when children are deemed to be not meeting expected developmental milestones, including those of physical development and growth.

Growth charts allow comparisons between children and to determine whether growth is within the normal/typical range (Mercer, 2018). If growth rates are not within the typical range, then this can be the first indication of atypical development and the need for intervention. A child's growth can be described in terms of percentile rank and these are used to establish a normal range of growth. Growth charts also provide information about changes in the speed of growth. In the first four months of life, babies typically double their birth weight. However, this slows down as it takes another eight months to the age of approximately one year old to triple it. Once a child enters educational settings, then physical development is measured in terms of milestones linked to curriculum outcomes.

Early years curricula

Many early years curricula, including the current Welsh Foundation Phase (FP) and the English Early Years Foundation Stage (EYFS), view physical development as an area of learning. Both curricula provide practitioners with policy documents detailing physical milestones of development (WAG, 2009) and early learning goals for physical development (DfE, 2017). The EYFS has a progress check at age 2, where children are assessed using the early learning goals in the prime areas, including physical development, and at the end of the EYFS across all areas of learning. The FP has a baseline assessment for children within the first six weeks of entering the reception class, including an assessment of physical development based upon skills ladders (WG, 2017a). These age-related views of physical development 'are informed by developmental psychology' (Neaum, 2013: 163).

The new curriculum for Wales beginning in September 2022 has six Areas of Learning and Experience (AoLE) and physical development comes under Health and Well-Being (WG, 2020). Here, children will be on a learning continuum from 3–16 years and there are 'What Matters' statements that children need to meet as they progress along this continuum (WG, 2020). This is identical to the Curriculum for Excellence in Scotland in which physical development also sits under the Health and Well-Being AoLE (Scottish Government, 2018).

However, in contrast to previous developmental trajectories being viewed as linear, the Welsh Government (2020) states that 'Progression within the Health and Well-being Area of Learning and Experience is non-linear and follows different pathways within and between progression steps'. Each AoLE has progression steps that link 'to the ages of, 5, 8, 11, 14 and 16 years of age. These progression steps are set out as a series of achievement outcomes, which are broad expectations of learning over two- to three-year periods' (WG, 2020).

As discussed in Chapter 2, there are criticisms of taking a developmental psychology view of child development, including physical development. This view regards the child as meeting a set series of linear stages and steps, but does not take account of individual learning experiences; it views children as one of a kind (James and Prout, 1997). There is also the concern of segregating children into those that meet expectations and those who do not. For some children, passing a physical milestone or step may happen once as they progress along the physical development continuum. However, for others regression in physical development may occur due to injury or illness (Mercer, 2018). The following case study demonstrates why a cautious approach to assessing children against linear milestones is needed.

Case study: Using developmental milestones

Gareth and Susan have three children – two girls and one boy. The eldest girl, Rebecca, walked at 14 months and the middle child, Daniel, walked at 15 months. However, their youngest daughter, Ellie, was 20 months and showed no signs of walking, although she would crawl and had good language skills. Susan took Ellie to an appointment with the health visitor who examined her and could not find any physical reason why Ellie was not walking yet. Susan explained to the health visitor that Ellie had good language skills and enjoyed playing alongside her siblings.

The health visitor arranged to visit Susan and Ellie at home so she could observe Ellie in her home environment. During this visit the health visitor observed the following. She noted that Ellie indeed seemed advanced for her age in her language development as throughout the observations, she asked her older brother and sister to get things for her, which they invariably did. Therefore, Ellie had no need to move to fetch things as she was able to communicate to others, to do it for her. The health visitor reassured Susan that all children develop at different rates and although Ellie was slower at meeting the physical development milestone of walking, she was exceeding the developmental milestone for language for her age. Susan felt reassured and within the next three weeks Ellie started to walk and went on to ably meet her milestones for physical development.

The case study above highlights the importance of viewing milestones as a guide and to appreciate that all children develop at their own rate even within the same family. Without the knowledge of Ellie using her language to get what she wanted, it would be easy to think she was developmentally behind in her physical development, especially when based on linear milestones for physical development. This case study reinforces the need to view a child's development holistically and to view development as a web, with all areas interlinking rather than a linear sequence or a series of steps.

Reflective question

What sources of information do you use to record a child's physical development?

The development of gross and fine motor skills

Like other stages of physical development, motor skills occur in a sequence, but the length of the sequence can alter. As with physical growth, motor development and control follow the cephalocaudal and proximodistal trend. Voluntary movements occur in the upper body before the lower body. An example of this is seen in newborns and is shown when babies will throw out their arms when they have the sensation of being dropped or startled (Mercer, 2018).

The acquisition of motor skills has an impact upon other areas of development and can be split into gross and fine motor skills. Gross motor skills are the actions that help a child get around, such as walking and crawling, and facilitate spatial awareness (Crowley, 2017). Fine motor skills refer to smaller movements such as reaching and grasping. They facilitate cognitive development as the child is able to hold and explore objects, enabling the child to learn about their properties. Once a child is able to walk (usually around 14 or 15 months), locomotor skills advance rapidly and by approximately 4 years old, they can walk like an adult and descend stairs (Crowley, 2017). Children continue to refine their motor skills as they grow, running faster and jumping higher.

Fine motor skill development begins by infants making clumsy attempts to reach for objects known as pre-reaching. This starts to decline at about two months of age, being replaced by direct reaching (Thelan et al., 1993), which is more synchronised and effective. This coincides with advanced eye, head and shoulder control, and facilitates more accuracy in reaching out for objects (Bhat et al., 2005). Initially, infants will use the palmer grip to grasp objects, but gradually they will start to become more precise in their grasping, adapting to the type of object they are attempting to hold. As infants approach their first birthday, they will change to a pincer grasp when they use their thumb and index finger. This facilitates more detailed explorations and allows specific actions to be carried out, such as twisting a knob or dial (Crowley, 2017). By the end of the second year, they become more proficient and can build towers of blocks and begin to scribble.

As fine motor skills develop, children are able to progress from scribbles to more detailed and recognisable drawings. This is dependent upon an increase in ability to hold pens and pencils. Children's developing fine motor skills also support self-help skills such as holding cutlery and doing up zips and buttons on clothing.

Case study: Capturing children's interests to develop fine motor skills

Four-year-old Imran is in the reception class. He enjoys coming to school and has a wide group of friends. Practitioners have been observing the class throughout the first term and have noted some differences in where Imran is in terms of his physical development. Imran has good gross motor skills and loves to be outdoors where he will often be seen kicking or throwing a ball or racing around the yard on one of the bikes.

Imran seems to particularly be interested in anything round, such as balls or the wheels on the bike. However, he does not choose to spend time at any activity that involves fine motor skills such as writing, painting or craft activities. When practitioners sit with him on fine motor skill tasks, he always rushes through them and shows little or no engagement.

One of the practitioners has just been on a training course that has discussed the importance of nurturing children's current interests and building a learning environment around these interests. She has been thinking about Imran's interest in all things *round* and how she can incorporate this into activities that will help develop his fine motor skills. The practitioner suddenly remembers a set of twistable pens her own children had and how much they enjoyed using them. The following day she brings them in and shows them to Imran who is fascinated with them and spends most of the morning twisting the nibs up and down. He then proceeds to draw with them in the writing area. Anyone who enters the classroom is grabbed by Imran who demonstrates the pens and the marks they can make.

The above case study shows the importance of spending time observing children and getting to know them. The practitioner has recognised, through observation and looking at milestones, that Imran needs to develop his fine motor skills. However, she has spent time thinking about how to do this in a way that is relevant to Imran. In doing so, she has adopted a child-centred approach and used resources that captured Imran's interests, but also supported his fine motor skills.

Reflective question

Consider the children you work with. How do you ensure that you are supporting them to meet their motor skill milestones, but are also capturing their interests?

Dynamic Systems Theory

A relatively new theory underlying the development of motor skills is the dynamic systems theory (Crowley, 2017). This places the infant as an active participant in the occurrence of motor skills. Here the infant reorganises existing skills into more complex actions (Shaffer and Kipp, 2010; cited in Crowley, 2017). Research by Goldfield (1989) found that before an infant crawls, they will turn their head towards interesting features in their environment, then reach towards stimuli and finally push their leg opposite to the outstretched arm. This indicates that crawling is preceded by looking towards an object of interest, turning the body towards the object and then kicking to move the body forwards. Thus 'crawling can be seen as the reorganisation and coordination of existing capabilities into a new skill... to achieve a desired goal' (Crowley, 2017: 65).

Sociological Approach to Physical Development

As discussed in Chapter 3, sociology is about finding out about human society and understanding how humans interact with the social environment. It is concerned about how child development is influenced by social factors. If we reconsider the case study about Ellie, then social factors such as communication influenced Ellie's physical development, as she got what she needed through communication, without having to move. Packer (2017: 175) argues that as infants become more capable of 'primary sociability', there is an increased ability to influence others to get what they want.

How active a child is can also be considered in terms of their lived experiences within society and families. As Brady et al. (2015: 176) state, 'children's daily lives play out across the social contexts which structure their lives'. Children who live in a family environment where sport is played regularly are more likely to be physically active compared with a child who lives in a very sedentary family.

Screen time can also be an issue in today's society, where a child who is left for long periods fixated on a TV or computer screen is less physically active. This can have long-term effects on a child's health in terms of obesity. Research by Wethington et al. (2013) concluded that when a child exceeds recommended screen time, they are at heightened risk of becoming obese.

Economic Approach to Physical Development

An economic approach to physical development can be viewed in terms of socioeconomic status. This can be considered as a measure of status in terms of income and education. Children living in poverty may be overweight or obese as their diets may consist of mainly unhealthy foods. However, it is important to note that poverty can also lead to undernutrition, which in turn affects children's physical development (Siegler et al., 2017). From the ages of 1 to 5 years there is a steady pace of growth and 'children require more energy-rich foods than older children and adults' (Crowley, 2017: 62). If families cannot afford such foods, then there will be an impact upon children's physical growth. In addition, parents from poorer backgrounds may not be able to afford after-school recreational activities for their children, which may mean that they miss out on developing some physical skills compared to more affluent peers.

Sleep also plays an important part in physical development as a child's physical activity increases then children need appropriate amounts of sleep. Children from poorer families tend to sleep less well and wake more frequently in the night (Lightfoot et al., 2013). This may be due to cramped unsuitable housing and not having somewhere quiet to sleep properly.

Anthropological Approach to Social Development

Anthropologists are concerned with the studies of human societies, their culture and their development (Montgomery, 2013). In terms of physical development, anthropologists study how different cultures and societies impact upon physical characteristics. An example is in modern industrialised nations where adults today are taller than their great grandparents. This increased growth is primarily due to improvements in nutrition and overall health (Siegler et al., 2017).

Packer (2017) details different infant care within different cultures around the world and its impacts upon physical development. In eastern Paraguay, it is thought that children are behind in motor skills compared with children their same age in the USA. This is because mothers of the Paraguay children are very reluctant to let them explore and as a result spend a long time on their mothers' laps. However, as they get older, they quickly make up for these delays as they spend time climbing trees to chop down branches and quickly overtake their American counterparts in terms of physical development. Crowley (2017) discusses the Kipsigi tribe of Kenya, where motor skills are developed early on. Adults encourage walking early on by holding the infants by their armpits, resulting in them walking approximately a month earlier than Western infants.

Philosophical Approach to Physical Development

Margaret Whitehead writes that 'Philosophical underpinning supports the view that physical activity can enrich life throughout the life course' (2010: 3). She advocates the notion of physical literacy, arguing that people need to maintain physical activity through the life course through motivation, confidence and physical competence. Physically literate children have a positive sense of self and have confidence in their physical abilities (Whitehead, 2010).

Whitehead also talks of a 'movement vocabulary' (2010: 45), used to describe a child's physical growth and movement in the first years of life. These encompass crawling, walking, lifting and clapping. This movement vocabulary is refined as a child grows to include physical development skills such as hand–eye coordination and balance.

The primary school physical literacy framework provides guidance to primary schools on how to embed physical literacy within their pedagogy (Sport England, n.d.). Similarly, in Wales there is the guidance provided through *Physical Literacy: A Journey Through Life* (Sport Wales, n.d.). Both sets of guidance promote physical literacy from the early years onwards, with the key message being to maximise the potential of all pupils.

Case study: Using physical literacy to build confidence

Harley was 7 years old and was in Year 2 of primary school. He had an individual education plan and found it difficult to build relationships with his peers. Harley struggled with his co-ordination and often upset other children as he tended to be quite rough when playing alongside them. He gave up on activities quite quickly and had tantrums (explosive outbursts) if he could not do something.

The classroom practitioners wanted to provide an environment that would support Harley in fulfilling his potential. They attended training on physical literacy and decided to create a bespoke plan for Harley that focused upon a holistic approach to his development. Physical and personal and social skill development were a priority and included Harley accessing extracurricular activities after school. Harley also had weekly mentoring sessions with the practitioners to ask him how he felt his week was going and what support he might need. Throughout this time, Harley's confidence grew and he became much more focused in class and enjoyed working with others to achieve success. Harley is now reaching his physical potential and is a much happier, healthier child. He regularly joins in with group activities and is eager to take part in any physical activities, quite often taking the lead.

The case study above highlights the impact that physical literacy can have upon a child's confidence and self-esteem. Through becoming physically literate, Harley was able to become more confident and positive in his approach to joining in with activities and working with others. He was able to articulate what he enjoyed and what he felt he needed more help with.

Reflective Question

When planning for physical development, how do you consider a child's personal and social skills?

Neuroscience Approach to Physical Development

Child development can also be explored through a neuroscience approach. When considering physical development specifically through a neuroscience lens, a starting point is brain development. The brain can be thought of as being split into three regions – the brain stem, the limbic system and the cerebrum (Crowley, 2017). The cerebrum has two hemispheres, one left and one right. The left hemisphere controls movement on the right side of the body and the right-side controls movement on the left-side of the body. Newborns tend to have a preference for turning to the right when lying on their backs and also tend to use the right sides of their bodies in reflex reactions (Rönnqvist and Hopkins, 1998).

Even before babies are born, their brains are able to support basic sensory and motor functions. This prepares them physically to adapt at the earliest opportunity to their new environment (Lightfoot et al., 2013). After birth, babies demonstrate what are called 'reflex movements', which are movements that are inbuilt to the nervous system. An example of a reflex movement is when newborns are held upright and their feet touch a flat surface, they will make leg movements as if they are walking. This is known as the stepping reflex, but stops at around 3 months of age. Then, at around 1 year, babies use a similar motion as a precursor to walking. However, this is not a reflex movement, but a completely voluntary movement to aid walking (Lightfoot et al., 2013).

Piaget's work also provides an explanation of the transition from reflexive behaviour to coordinated actions and movements. As discussed in previous chapters, he described children going through a series of linear stages in their development, each stage building upon the one before (Piaget, 1973). Piaget developed the concept of assimilation and accommodation where new experiences are assimilated and accommodated into existing thinking or thinking is changed to accommodate the new idea or experience. He believed that initial reflexes present at birth allow infants to connect with their world, but add nothing to development as they undergo very little change or accommodation. However, as infants grow and thinking develops, these reflexes change or disappear as actions and movements become more fine-tuned (Lightfoot et al., 2013).

The influence of genetic and environmental factors on physical development and growth

Genetic Factors

Children's physical size and growth is influenced by heredity or genetic factors, and the rate of growth is directly linked to their parents (Crowley, 2017). Genes affect growth through hormone production, especially growth hormone and thyroxine (Siegler et al., 2017). Growth hormone is responsible for the development of all body tissues except the central nervous system and the genitals. A lack of growth hormone can cause children not to reach their expected height. The pituitary gland releases thyroid-stimulating hormone which stimulates the release of thyroxine. Thyroxine is necessary for brain development and for the growth hormone to have full impact on body size (Crowley, 2017). Infants born with a thyroxine deficiency can, without treatment, suffer with severe mental impairment.

If motor development becomes impaired by problems such as cerebral palsy, then a child may show difficulties not only with physical movements, but also with speech and language. This could make others have the assumption that the child is intellectually impaired, which is not the case (Mercer, 2018). Therefore, when we observe an individual, care is needed not to make judgements based on visible perceptions such as difficulty moving; motor development is only one part of a child's development.

Environmental factors

Environmental factors can play a part in disturbances of growth or atypical growth. A combination of genetic and environmental factors can cause a failure to thrive in infants. Here the infant becomes malnourished and fails to grow or gain weight with no obvious medical reason (Siegler et al., 2017). There are a range of options to treat this from praising a child when they eat to hospital treats and dietary supplements.

There is evidence to suggest that alongside heredity and nutrition, emotional well-being can impact upon physical growth and development. Black et al. (1994) identified that infants can suffer from non-organic failure to thrive, a growth impairment resulting from a lack of parental love. This impairment presents itself at around eighteen months when the infant stops growing but shows no other signs of illness. According to Crowley (2017), positive emotional well-being is important for growth into childhood, as extreme emotional deprivation can inhibit the production of the growth hormone and lead to a condition known as psychosocial dwarfism. However, removing the child from an abusive environment can result in the child catching up growth-wise.

Summary of chapter

- Both genetic and environmental factors impact upon physical development.
- Physical growth and development occur in a sequence.
- Children develop both fine and gross motor skills.
- Socioeconomic status can impact upon physical growth and development.
- Different cultures place different emphasis on aspects of physical development.
- Physical literacy is a concept that can support physical development.
- Early years curricula provide guidance for physical development and include milestones or outcomes that children are expected to achieve.

End-of-chapter questions

1. Which of the approaches to physical development resonates most strongly with your practice?
2. What are the advantages and disadvantages of linking physical development to linear milestones?
3. Why is it important to have knowledge of how both genetic and environmental factors can impact physical development?

Further reading

Healthy Schools (2020) *Healthyschools.org.* Available at: www.healthyschools.org.uk/ (accessed 28 July 2020).

This website explains the initiatives that schools are putting into place to encourage healthy eating and lifestyles.

James, A. and Prout, A. (eds) (2014) *Constructing and Reconstructing Childhood: Contemporary Issues in the Sociological Study of Childhood* (3rd edn). London: Routledge-Falmer.

This book provides an in-depth understanding about viewing child development through a number of lenses.

Malina, R.M., Bouchard, C. and Bar-Or, O. (2004) *Growth, Maturation and Physical Activity* (2nd edn). Champaign, IL: Human Kinetics.

This book provides a comprehensive review of physical development.

TEN
SOCIAL DEVELOPMENT

This chapter will help you to

- understand the basic principles and theories of social development;
- understand how children acquire a sense of self and develop the concept of socialisation with others;
- discuss the impact of maturation, learning and the interactions between genetic and environmental factors on social development.

Introduction

Social development can be defined as the child's ability to relate to others in an appropriate way 'within the social context of their lives' (Neaum, 2013: 61). It can be described as the series of changes that a child moves through, starting with the egocentric stage in early childhood to more adult-like behaviours.

In order to become socially competent, children need to develop adaptive characteristics, such as being cooperative, having good communication skills, a sense of empathy and self-control (Van Ryzen et al., 2015). Crucial to the development of these skills is the growing awareness of a child's social understanding, taking the perspective of others and an understanding of how their behaviour can affect others (Crowley, 2017).

Both families and schools are involved in shaping and influencing children's social development through formative experiences. This chapter outlines factors affecting social development and how it is viewed through the different interdisciplinary approaches. It will consider the theories under-pinning social development, and the development of self and the concept of socialisation.

Developmental Psychology Approach to Social Development

Developmental psychology views social development through established sequences and stages, but also acknowledges that children are individual and the rate at which they achieve sequences or stages will vary. One theory that sits within the developmental psychology approach and views social development as a series of stages is that of Erikson (Neaum, 2013). Erikson proposed eight stages of development from childhood to old age, and each stage is characterised by a specific crisis or developmental issues that need to be resolved (Siegler et al., 2017). If the crisis or set of issues is not resolved successfully, then it will continue into the next stage. The stages are summarised in Figure 10.1.

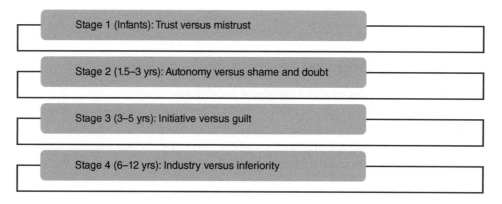

Figure 10.1 The four stages of childhood development proposed by Erikson

The first stage in Erikson's theory (1964) is trust versus mistrust. Here the infant is developing a sense of trust and the basic belief is that people are usually helpful. If this sense of trust does not develop, then the infant will find it difficult to form intimate relationships in later life (Neaum, 2013; Siegler et al., 2017). The second social stage is autonomy versus shame and doubt and is seen in children aged 18 months to 3 years (Packer, 2017). Here the child is battling between being autonomous with increasing social demands.

Between 3 and 5 years old, children enter the stage of initiative versus guilt, and they learn from their parents. Erikson (1994) states that in this stage the child wants to be like their parents. They are setting goals in play, school and work to achieve them. The feeling of guilt is the fear that they will do something wrong, so plans are constricted to those that have already been approved by others (Mercer, 2018).

The next stage, from 6 to 12 years, is industry versus inferiority. This stage is crucial for the development of ego. Children begin to master skills important for their culture, work hard and learn to co-operate with their peers. However, they also feel inferior to others if they cannot master tasks such as schoolwork and helping others (Mercer, 2018; Siegler et al., 2017).

One of the strengths of Erikson's theory is that it covers the whole lifespan, with further stages described from age 12 until death. However, Erikson's theory is rather unclear about how the psychological conflicts that arise in each stage can be resolved as people move through the different stages. Even Erikson (1964) himself stated that his theory is a descriptive outline of human social and emotional development, without adequately explaining how or why this development occurs.

Ecological Systems Theory

Ecological systems theory has influenced research and theoretical considerations of social development. Chapter 2 has outlined Bronfenbrenner's theory (1992) that depicts the child at the centre of concentric circles, being influenced by formative experiences. In terms of social development, the microsystem has the most direct effect upon the child as it involves interactions with people and groups the child has direct contact with. The mesosystem is the interaction between those in the microsystem and could include the relationship between home and school. In developed countries, school experience plays an important part in shaping social development (Mercer, 2018). The outer circles of Bronfenbrenner's theory, called the exosystem, the macrosystem and the chronosystem, affect the child indirectly. When viewed as a whole, Bronfenbrenner's model is able to demonstrate the interrelated influences on children's social development.

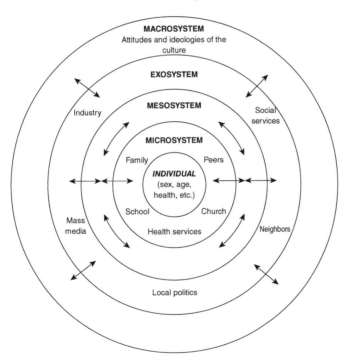

Figure 10.2 Bronfenbrenner's Ecological Systems Theory: Wikipedia (2022) Ecological Systems Theory

Learning Theories

Other influential psychological theories that impact upon social development are those termed 'learning theories'. These theories are concerned with external factors that impact upon social development (Siegler et al., 2017).

One such theory is that of Skinner and operant conditioning, where positive behaviours are repeated and reinforced, and negative behaviours are suppressed (Skinner, 1971). In this way, undesirable behaviours can be changed. An example would be a child who shouts and screams to get their own way and the parent ignores this behaviour; then when the child speaks nicely and behaves in a calm manner, the parent praises the child. In this way the child recognises that they are far more likely to get what they want when they behave in a calm manner and do not shout.

Social-learning theory also considers aspects of social development in terms of learning mechanisms. It argues that social development occurs when children 'observe and imitate the behaviour' of others. In this way, children develop a mastery of the social environment which can 'foster social development' (Mercer, 2018: 173).

Bandura is another theorist who has proposed that learning is intrinsically social in nature, based upon observing and modelling the behaviour of others. In Bandura's theory, there is an emphasis upon children being active agents in their development (Bandura, 1977, 1989). He considered the role of cognition or thought processes and argued that in order to learn from observation there needs to be attention to detail, retention and 'motoric reproduction'. This can be explained as attending to the observed behaviour, remembering the observed behaviour and motoric reproduction of said observed behaviour (Crowley, 2017: 9).

One of Bandura's most famous experiments was that of the Bobo doll. Here, pre-school children who were shown an adult modelling aggressive behaviour towards the doll tended to imitate that aggressive behaviour in their own play with the doll (Bandura et al., 1961). Bandura's later work focused upon the development of self-efficacy or self-belief, and here he contended that this is also learnt by observation (Bandura, 1977).

Case study: Olympic champions on the climbing frame

In a nursery class, there is a large climbing frame outside, with a rope and pulley at one side, fixed to the top of the platform. Jaydon, Amir, Khalid and Ashleigh are quite adventurous in their play and like to set themselves challenges. Today, they industriously tie their scooters one at a time to the rope and pull them up to the platform. They are highly cooperative and each scooter is stored in the corner. Ashleigh, though, excludes other children from this space: 'You can't come up here – Olympic champions only. The next stage of the activity involves the boys riding around the platform as fast as they can in a relatively small space and trying to do skids around the corners.

The practitioners are keen to encourage the boys to play cooperatively, develop their self-belief and to use their imaginations as part of their social development. They observe the play for a few minutes before stepping in to prevent any injuries. The practitioners praise the boys for their cooperative skills, but remind them of the class rules around staying safe and sharing. They ask the boys to move the bikes to the ground level and remind them that everyone in the class can have a turn if they wish.

The practitioners help the boys to make a circuit on the yard and they suggest working in teams so that everyone can have the opportunity to take part if they wish.

The case study above highlights the importance of getting the balance right when supporting social development. The practitioners recognise the need for the boys to be active and to develop their cooperative skills, their self-belief skills and their imagination. However, there needs to be a consideration of safety and inclusivity in this example.

Reflective Question

How do the children in this case study demonstrate Bandura's theory and how do the practitioners demonstrate Skinner's theory?

Sociological Approach to Social Development

In Chapter 3, sociology was defined as finding out about human society and understanding how humans interact with the social environment. Functionalism is a perspective of sociology that considers social behaviour as a product of society. American sociologist Talcott Parsons (1902–79) reports that childhood socialisation is 'a process whereby they gradually learned about and internalised social conventions in order to become a full member of their culture or society' (Gallacher and Kehily, 2013: 220).

Interactionism is another sociological perspective that focuses on how individuals interact with one another. Here a child's social development is dependent upon interacting with adults and their peers. As discussed in Chapter 3, Corsaro focused on understanding children's interpretations of their culture. He suggests that during socialisation children are not simply internalising the adult culture, they are contributing to it by their interactions and negotiations with adults and other children (Gabriel, 2017). This situates the child as an active meaning-maker within their social world.

Kohlberg (1963) developed a theory where socialisation is linked to moral development. This is a stage theory but, as Mercer (2018) states, the links between stage and age are weak; not everyone reaches the later stages, and others reach the later stages at earlier ages. Kohlberg (1963) suggested three levels of moral reasoning, starting with pre-conventional for young children, where they do not recognise community-based moral thinking or behaviour. This is followed by conventional, where children know and recognise community-based behaviour and want to comply. The last level is post-conventional, where reasoning is centred on ideals (Mercer, 2018; Siegler et al., 2017). Figure 10.3 shows the stages within each level.

In the obedience and punishment orientation stage of Kohlberg's theory, wrong behaviour is punished, so children are obedient to avoid punishment. The next stage is the individualism and exchange orientation. Here children recognise that not all rule breaking is punished and that there are 'fair exchanges of behaviour' (Mercer, 2018: 175). At the conventional level, school-aged

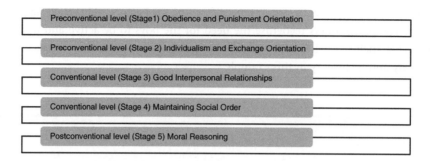

Figure 10.3 The five levels of moral reasoning

children do what is expected of them in terms of society or community. This allows them to develop good relationships with others and is termed the 'good interpersonal stage' (Mercer, 2018). The final stage in this level is known as maintaining social order. Here children understand that obeying rules and conventions benefits society. Few children reach stage five of Kohlberg's theory within the post-conventional level where obeying laws are in the best interests of the group (Siegler et al., 2017).

Kohlberg argued that everyone moved through these stages in the same order, but fluctuate in how far they get. Critics of this theory argue that Kohlberg did not differentiate between truly moral issues and social conventional issues (Nucci and Gingo, 2011). Further, in Kohlberg's theory, children in non-Western cultures do not advance as far as those in Western societies. This is because in several non-Western cultures, group harmony is essential, whereas individual rights and liberties are not (Snarey, 1985).

Economic Approach to Social Development

There is a long history of research on the effect of socioeconomic status on child development. Research has found that socially disadvantaged children are at greater risk of physical, emotional and behavioural problems (Berkman and Kawachi, 2000). As stated in Chapter 3, there are several factors that influence a child's development. However, Ingleby and Oliver (2008) suggest that economic factors are one of the most influential.

Conger and Donnellan (2007) argue that education, income and occupation are separate factors that can impact upon a child's social development. Children from lower socioeconomic backgrounds are likely to have parents who are more authoritarian, and this can result in children who are less competent socially and emotionally (Steinberg, 2001). Both social causation and social selection influence a child's development. A social causation stance argues that social conditions impact upon a child's development, whereas the social selection stance argues that characteristics and depositions of the parents influence social status and a child's development.

Economic pressures such as poverty can affect family functioning through stress and worry, which in turn affects a child's development. Parents and care givers who have higher socioeconomic status can afford to live in more affluent areas and have access to better schools. They are able to afford their children greater opportunities to attend after-school activities where they can develop their social skills in a number of different social contexts.

Anthropological Approach to Social Development

Children inherit and learn to use culture through social processes. One such process is known as social enhancement (Lightfoot et al., 2013). Here children use available cultural resources to enhance the environment. Other social processes through which children inherit culture are 'imitation' or 'observing' and 'explicit instruction' (Lightfoot et al., 2013: 54). Imitation involves children copying the behaviour of others. Explicit instruction uses symbolic communication such as the written and spoken language, but also art and music.

Culture continues to evolve, and this is what Tomasello and Hermann (2010) termed 'cumulative cultural evolution'. Through socialising in groups, knowledge can be shared and new ideas generated and culture can thrive. However, different cultures place different emphasis upon engagement within groups within society. Some cultures place a great deal of emphasis upon family and community achievements. In contrast, other societies place more emphasis on the self (McDevitt and Ormrod, 2010). An example is given by Du et al. (2015) who discuss Chinese culture, which has a strong emphasis upon the value of the group over individual desires.

Philosophical Approach to Social Development
Acquiring a sense of self

A child's knowledge and understanding of themselves is known as a sense of self. A child's sense of self helps them to find themselves in the world, where they are able to feel 'capable, cared for and respected' (McDevitt and Ormrod, 2010: 445). The development of language and perception contributes to an understanding of self-awareness (Crowley, 2017). Harter (2008) summarised the development of self from early to late childhood. Young children between the ages of 3 and 5 years describe themselves in noticeable and specific characteristics, such as the colour of their eyes and whether they have a sibling. At this stage, their self-esteem is positive and they usually state what they can do rather than what they cannot do. Between the ages of 5 and 7 years, children still have a positive outlook, but they will begin to group things together, so they will group things together that they are good at like reading, skipping and singing. They also have a growing awareness of good and bad, but tend to think of themselves as good. This gradual progression in the way children describe themselves coincides with their social development such as comparing themselves with others and understanding multiple emotions (Crowley, 2017).

Factors influencing sense of self

Both adults and peers influence a child's sense of self. Hartup (1989) postulated that children's relationships with adults can be classed as vertical, while those with peers as horizontal and more equal. Experience of both types of relationships is necessary for development, including social development. Vertical relationships provide children with basic social skills, whereas horizontal relationships allow children to develop the skills of cooperation and building relationships with others. Linking back to Piaget's theory as discussed in Part 1 of this book, Piaget saw the worth of interaction with peers of equal status to support cognitive development (Piaget, 1980). In contrast, Vygotsky's theory considered children to need a more knowledgeable other to support their development (Vygotsky, 1978).

Friendships play an important part in social development, such as higher levels of pretend play and conflict resolution (Parker and Gottman, 1998). Hartup and Stevens (1997) found that having friends is linked to a sense of well-being, and that the quality of friendships is important. Children's ideas of friendship change over time and at the ages of 4–7 years, children tend to form friendships with those living nearby and who engage in similar activities (Crowley, 2017).

Case study: Role of the adult on a child's sense of self

Adele is an additional practitioner in a busy reception class in an inner-city school. The surrounding area is classed as deprived and there is a higher than UK average number of children receiving free school meals. The school welcomes children from a range of different cultural backgrounds and is keen to celebrate and promote this diversity. The school has the children's well-being as their priority and have an ethos of ensuring that all children are praised and any negative behaviour is dealt with calmly and consistently.

Adele has worked at the school for a few years, but has only worked with reception-aged children in the last six months. Prior to this, Adele had always worked with older children in the school. She has started to notice that the children are reluctant to come and work with her on any activities. The class teacher has also noticed this and has asked Adele for a meeting. She asks Adele to think about how she interacts with the children and how many times she praises them, and how many times she finds herself nagging or getting cross with them. Adele is asked to keep a diary of how often she praises the children. At first, Adele's diary was blank, but as time went on she started to really focus on the positives with the children and to praise them. As she changed how she worked with the children, Adele noticed that they were much keener to work with her and had started to come up and interact with her spontaneously.

Adele has realised that as an adult, she has such an important role to play in developing children's self-esteem and sense of self. Her relationship with the children is far happier and she is now enjoying her work much more.

The case study above highlights the importance of an adult's role in supporting social development. Adele had not realised the impact of her actions on the children's developing self-esteem. The children, however, were able to show their feelings by being reluctant to work with Adele on any activities. As soon as Adele was able to focus on praising the children, her relationship with them changed.

Reflective Question

Think about your own work with children. Do you offer enough praise to develop their self-esteem and sense of self?

Neuroscience Approach to Social Development

Theory of mind

As they grow and develop, children experience several improvements in their cognitive skills. A growing area of interest is how a child develops cognitively and how this impacts upon their understanding and interaction with others – i.e., their social cognition. Within the field of social cognition, there are a variety of different fields of study, including the ability of a child to 'understand the mental states of others... known as theory of mind' (Crowley, 2017: 185; Wellman et al., 2011).

Theory of mind can be defined as the ability to attribute mental states to others and use them as an explanation for other people's behaviour. This is important for social interaction as it allows an understanding and prediction of the behaviours of others and to adjust behaviour accordingly. This leads to social competence in children and an 'understanding of the physical world around them' (Mercer, 2018: 120).

At about the age of 2 years, children will use words to indicate what they want. Wellman (1990) contends that this is the first indication of a theory of mind and he termed this 'desire psychology'. Between the ages of 3 and 5 years, children begin to understand the concept of false beliefs and that a person may have incorrect knowledge, and that this could lead to doing the incorrect thing (Mercer, 2018). Children begin to realise at around the age of 4 years that a perception is a reflection of truth, but it is not actual reality. This understanding is known as 'representational theory of mind' (Perner, 1991).

Representational theory of mind was shown in an experiment by Wimmer and Perner (1983) where a child is shown two puppets. One puppet puts a piece of chocolate in a box and leaves the room. The other puppet takes the chocolate and puts it into a different box. The first puppet returns, and the children are asked where the first puppet will look for the hidden chocolate. The majority of 3-year-olds fail the task by stating that the first puppet will look for the chocolate where it actually is rather than where the first puppet left it. The 3-year-olds do not appreciate that there can be a discrepancy between what an individual believes and what is actual fact. In comparison, most 4-year-olds correctly understood that the first puppet would look for the chocolate where it had been put before they left the room. This confirms a false belief that conflicts with reality.

Factors in Acquisition of theory of mind

Hughes et al. (2005) studied theory of mind in identical and fraternal twins and showed that both genetic and environmental factors play a part. Social interactions with parents, siblings and peers, and the acquisition of language all play a part. Adults interact with infants and comment on what they see, known as joint attention, and this allows the infant an insight into the mind of others (Crowley, 2017). Language development and social interactions provide the ability to reflect on thoughts and label mental states. Pretend play opportunities with siblings and peers enable the discussion of thoughts, and this in turn may provide experiences that facilitate the development of theory of mind.

Case study: Theory of mind and pretend play

Harry is 5 years old and is in Year 1 of school. He is a solitary child and prefers to play by himself both indoors and outdoors. Harry very rarely engages in conversation with his peers, but he loves playing in the sand and water tray outside. The practitioners are carrying out observations with Harry as part of his child development profile. Today, they are outside observing Harry playing in the sand tray by himself. Harry has made a mound of sand and is pouring sand through the sieve on top of the mound. One of the practitioners tries to engage in conversation with Harry by asking him what he is making. Harry ignores him and carries on pouring the sand from the sieve. The practitioner then starts to make his own mound in the sand and talks to Harry as he does so. He tells Harry that he is making a birthday cake as it is his birthday soon and that his favourite cake is chocolate, but he is not sure anyone will make him a chocolate cake. Harry stops what he is doing and considers this for a moment. He disappears from the sand tray and walks over to the outdoor garden. Here Harry takes a bucket and collects some soil and twigs. He returns to the sand tray and sieves the soil on top of his cake. He then places several twigs upright in his cake. He turns to the practitioner and says, 'Here is a chocolate cake for your birthday.' The practitioner thanks Harry and pretends to blow out the candles and make a wish. Harry tells the practitioner that he would like to make a real chocolate cake and the practitioner tells Harry that is such a good idea and they will make one as a class later in the week. Harry smiles and claps his hands. The practitioners discuss this observation in the weekly team meeting and are pleased they have seemed to find a way to engage with Harry.

The case study above highlights the importance of tuning into a child's thinking. Here the practitioner has used language and pretend play to engage with Harry. Harry has heard what the practitioner has said and has used theory of mind to reflect upon the practitioner's words and how he feels. Harry has then adjusted his behaviour accordingly and has made a 'chocolate' cake to make the practitioner feel better. The practitioner has found a way to connect socially with Harry and will build upon this in planning future activities.

Reflective Question

Can you think of opportunities to use theory of mind in your practice to develop children's social interactions?

Summary of chapter

- There are many approaches and theories to understand social development, as this chapter has shown.
- There is continuous interaction between both genetic and environmental factors in social development.
- The development of a sense of self is important as is the development of self-esteem in social development.
- As children mature, they begin to understand right from wrong and that some people believe different things to them.
- Critics suggest that Kohlberg did not differentiate between truly moral issues and social conventional issue.
- From the age of 4 years, children start to develop theory of mind, understanding that this can help practitioners to support children's social development.
- Socioeconomic status can impact upon a child's social development, both positively and negatively.
- Different cultures place different emphasis on social development.
- Adults can influence a child's social development through language and how they interact with them.
- Erikson's theory is rather unclear about how the psychological conflicts that arise in each stage can be resolved as people move through the different stages.
- Bronfenbrenner considered the influence of the social environment upon a child's development.

End-of-chapter questions

1. What is your understanding of social development?
2. Which theories of social development have you seen used in practice?
3. How can you ensure that you are meeting every child's social developmental needs?

Further reading

Dowling, M. (2014) *Young Children's Personal and Social and Emotional Development* (4th edn). London: SAGE.

This accessible book links research in social and emotional development to educational practice.

Lewis, M. and Brooks-Gunn, J. (1979) *Social Cognition and the Acquisition of Self.* New York: Plenum.

This book, while quite old, gives a good understanding of the acquisition of self and its impact upon a child's understanding through empirical findings.

Mercer, J. (2018) *Child Development: Concepts and Theories.* London: SAGE.

This book will help you gain a more detailed insight into the understanding of social development.

ELEVEN
EMOTIONAL DEVELOPMENT

This chapter will help you to

- understand the basic principles of emotional development and how children's personalities and temperaments develop;
- discuss attachment theory and the causes of variations in patterns of attachment;
- consider Adverse Childhood Experiences (ACEs) and their impact upon children.

Introduction

Emotional development can be defined as the child's 'ability to feel and express an increasing range of emotions appropriately'. It includes the development of emotional responses to other people, oneself and the ability to 'feel and express emotions that contribute to our own and others' well-being' (Neaum, 2013: 61). In the course of development from birth onwards, emotions and the situations that affect them change (Mercer, 2018). However, it is widely accepted that humans are furnished with a set of basic emotions that are universal and have evolved as a means of survival.

Emotions are a rudimentary part of human experience, but how they are regulated can have life-long consequences. Ekman and Freisen (1971) identified six basic emotions: surprise, anger, sadness, disgust, fear and happiness. There is some evidence that these basic emotions are present in infancy, with the main emotional states being those of contentment and distress. This chapter outlines factors affecting emotional development and how it is viewed through the different interdisciplinary approaches.

Developmental Psychology Approach to Emotional Development

Developmentalists attempt to explain why we experience emotions and why we express them through facial expressions or through vocalisation. Here emotions are viewed as 'a combination of physiological and cognitive responses and reactions to thoughts or experiences' (Siegler et al.,

2017: 419). An infant showing happiness through smiling or by laughter will evoke a similar response in a caregiver and this in turn strengthens the bonds between them. By the time infants are 1 month old, they will begin to smile in response to bright objects within their field of vision (Berk, 2008). Between 1 and 2 months old, the infant will engage in the social smile, induced by social interactions, and then at 6 months smiles are evidenced in response to interesting stimuli (Ainsfield, 1982). Laughter appears at around 3 to 4 months, with an increased understanding of the world around them (Crowley, 2017).

Responses to unpleasant things are also present from birth, while anger appears from around 4–6 months. Expression of sadness occurs when an infant is deprived of affectionate responses from a familiar caregiver and fear appears at around 6 to 7 months, with a fear of strangers being evident. This response is known as 'stranger anxiety' and emerges around the time the infant is starting to form attachments with known caregivers (Crowley, 2017: 155).

Attachment

Attachment is the strong and affectionate bond between the infant and the caregiver. The most influential theory of attachment is that of John Bowlby (1969) alongside his collaborator, Mary Ainsworth. Bowlby stated that the ability to form attachments was an evolved behaviour that promoted survival of the infant. Infants are equipped with a set of behaviours that lead them to seek closeness with caregivers who will nurture them and protect them from harm. These behaviours include smiling, crying and moving towards caregivers and Bowlby called these behaviours the 'attachment behavioural system' (Crowley, 2017: 163).

However, for attachment behaviours to be successful, they need to be reciprocated with a corresponding system in mothers to nurture and protect their children. In order to explain how attachment behaviours operate, Bowlby used a control-systems theory, where behaviours related to a particular goal are grouped together. The attachment behaviour system's goal is to maintain closeness to the mother. When this is threatened, the attachment behaviour system is activated until the desired state of closeness has been restored.

Ainsworth et al. (1978) and Bowlby (1969) contended that there were 'four phases over which the attachment relationship develops' (cited in Crowley, 2017: 164).

Bowlby argued that not all attachments are equal and that for healthy attachments to develop, there needed to be a primary attachment with a specific figure, and this should be the mother. If this primary attachment did not develop in the early years of life, then Bowlby contended that there would be long-term detrimental effects on the child's mental health. This is known as monotropism and is the most contested part of Bowlby's theory. The notion of attachment to one adult caregiver has been replaced with a growing awareness that infants can have several familiar attachment figures who are not necessarily biologically related to them (Mercer, 2018).

Ainsworth et al. (1978) devised a laboratory-based observation technique to assess the quality of attachment known as 'the strange situation'. This involved eight episodes where the infant was separated from the mother and exposed to a stranger and then reunited with the mother. The responses

Table 11.1 Development of the attachment relationship

Phase	Known as	Age	Behaviour shown
1	Orientation and signals without discrimination of figure (pre-attachment)	6–8 weeks of life	Smiling, grasping, crying No preference shown at this stage for the primary caregiver over other adults
2	Orientation and signals directed towards one (or more) discriminated figures (attachment in the making)	2–7 months of age	Beginning of differentiation between familiar and unfamiliar figures
3	Maintenance of proximity to a discriminated figure through movement and signals (clear-cut attachment)	7 months onwards	Clear preference for familiar individuals and seeks proximity with these and becomes upset when they leave
4	Goal-corrected partnership	From 3 years of age	More reciprocal relationship with child taking into account the needs of the caregiver. Developments in language and cognition facilitate an understanding of the caregivers leaving but also that they will return

Adapted from Crowley (2017: 164).

of the infants to these episodes led Ainsworth et al. (1978) to identify three categories of attachment relationship, shown in Table 11.2.

Table 11.2 Summary of attachment relationships

Attachment relationship	Behaviour shown
Secure attachment (most common)	May or may not be upset when parent leaves room but are happy when parent returns, actively seeking contact.
Insecure-avoidant attachment	Unresponsive to parent and shows no overt signs of distress when they leave. Infant fails to respond to parent on their return and often actively avoids them.
Insecure-resistant	Infant fails to explore the room and is distressed when the parent leaves. During the reunion the infant is ambivalent to the parent. They seek contact but also show resistant behaviour struggling and being difficult to soothe when picked up by the parent.

Further research by Main and Soloman (1990) has also identified another category of insecure attachment called 'insecure-disorganised'. This is the most insecure form of attachment, where the infant does not seem to know how to manage the reunion, appearing confused over whether to approach or avoid the parent.

Links have been made between secure attachments and positive developmental outcomes. Securely attached children display more pleasant emotions and are more sociable towards other children (Kochanska, 2001; Pastor, 1981). There is an indication that 'the relationship between early attachment security and later development is affected by the stability of these relationships over time' (Crowley, 2017: 169). Children who receive affectionate care in infancy and throughout childhood are more likely to develop better outcomes. Alternatively, children who receive insecure attachment in early childhood are more likely to have negative outcomes.

However, it is important to note that children who are insecurely attached, who then receive sensitive caregiving at 24 months, show improved developmental outcomes. These outcomes are better than for those children who had secure attachment as infants, but then experience a decrease in caregiving at 24 months.

Case study: Creating an emotionally safe environment

It is Garth's first day at school. He cried when his mother left him and was still sobbing when he went into the cloakroom to take off his coat. The cloakroom is shared between the reception class and Year 2 and an older boy in Year 2 bumped into Garth and said, 'Watch where you're going!' Garth followed the rest of his class into the classroom and was told to sit on the carpet. He felt squashed and wriggled over to a corner to sit by the wall. He was trying really hard not to cry and to listen to the teacher. However, he felt overwhelmed and could not concentrate on what she was saying. He looked around and bit his lip while rubbing his nose onto his sleeve. All the other children seemed to laugh and be happy.

The teacher, noticing that Garth was not paying attention, called out his name, 'Garth, what is wrong with you? Why aren't you listening?' The rest of the children looked around at Garth and stared. The teacher carried on and said, 'Why are you crying? Come on, you are in the big class now, not nursery anymore and big boys don't cry! You are going to do some work now, so off you go with Mrs Carter.'

The case study above highlights the importance of practitioners in creating an emotionally safe environment. Here Garth did not feel emotionally safe and secure, and needed reassurance. However, instead he was made to feel silly, and this could lead to him becoming more emotionally insecure in the future.

Reflective Question

What would you do differently here for Garth in terms of developing his secure attachment?

Attachment impairments

There are occasions when a child is raised in an environment that is so pathological that normal attachment is inhibited, and a child can show a condition known as reactive attachment disorder or RAD. Here a child shows highly disturbed and developmentally inappropriate social relatedness (Kerig et al., 2012). Two forms have been identified: an inhibited type where the child constantly fails to initiate and respond to social interactions, and a disinhibited type where the child is indiscriminately friendly and is not selective in their choice of attachment figures (Crowley, 2017).

More recently, there has been the suggestion that three broad categories of RAD can be identified (Kerig et al., 2012). Here the inhibited and disinhibited types of disorder come under a category called disorders of non-attachment and two other types have also been proposed: disordered attachment and disrupted attachments. Disordered attachments are where a child has formed a specific attachment relationship, but it has been disrupted by conflict. The child shows behaviour such as self-endangerment, withdrawal and hypervigilance, which usually occurs when the caregiver has been abusive or unavailable.

Disrupted attachment results from the sudden death or separation from an attachment figure. The child shows normal loss reactions such as protest, grief and detachment. However, Zilberstein (2006) has argued that this classification is best suited for problems with young children and may not apply to older children.

Sociological Approach to Emotional Development

Barbalet (1998: 8–9) argues that sociology seeks to explain social phenomena, and emotions are examples of social phenomena. A range of emotions such as fear, grief, hate and pride can emerge in social situations, social relationships, and interactions. According to Bericat (2016: 495), 'understanding an emotion means understanding the situation and social relation that produces it'. By examining emotions through behaviour and actions, a greater understanding of each emotion can emerge.

Children learn to guide their actions based upon other people's emotional expressions. In the first years of life children tend to monitor the emotions of others, particularly those of their parents and caregivers (McDevitt and Ormrod, 2010). Young children show what is called social referencing where they watch parents' facial expressions to determine how to respond to new or different situations.

As children grow and develop, they learn to read different social situations and manage their emotions accordingly. This emotional regulation allows children to acquire a range of strategies that support them with their feelings and equips them to deal with stressful situations (Saarni et al., 2006).

Chapter 3 described interactionism as a perspective of sociology that focuses on how individuals react with one another. Bericat (2016) argues that individuals try to confirm the image they have of themselves (self-concept) and identities through which they act in social situations (role identity). If a person's self-concept is confirmed by others, then we experience positive emotions; conversely if it is not, we experience negative emotions. Consider the following case study and Ahmed's behaviour.

Case Study: Self-concept and role identity

Ahmed is 7 years old and lives with his parents and brother who is 16 months older than him. Because of their birthdays, Ahmed is only a year behind Jamal in school, Jamal being one of the oldest in his class and Ahmed being one of the youngest. Jamal has always achieved well in school. He started talking early and was reading simple books before he started school. The family value academic excellence very highly, with both parents having professional jobs.

Ahmed has always been in Jamal's shadow. Because he is a stocky child and is almost the same height as Jamal, his friends and family sometimes forget that he is 16 months younger than his brother. Ahmed is always trying to keep up with Jamal and gets upset when he cannot play football as well or do the same bicycle tricks as Jamal.

Ahmed is finding schoolwork a struggle. Both his parents and teachers keep telling him that he is not as bright as his brother. Whatever Ahmed does, he cannot seem to do it as well as his brother and Ahmed is starting to become disruptive in class. He is a very sociable child with lots of friends and has become the class clown, to the detriment of his and others' ability to concentrate and learn. Ahmed will do anything to avoid reading at home or school because he finds it difficult.

The mother of one of Ahmed's friends has discovered that Ahmed loves music and spends most of the time at her house playing their piano. He has a lovely voice and enjoys acting, and he is often seen directing his friends in little plays in the playground.

The case study above highlights the notion of self-concept and role identity. Ahmed has developed the role of 'class clown' to deflect from his difficulties with schoolwork. Here he is getting a positive reaction from friends when he misbehaves, thus reinforcing his self-concept and role identity as the class clown.

Reflective Question

What advice would you give to Ahmed's parents and teachers to improve Ahmed's self-esteem?

Economic Approach to Emotional Development

There is a broad agreement that child development is multifaceted and is shaped by both biology and experience. This means that factors such as socioeconomic status will help to shape children's emotional development. Social competencies such as feelings about identity, self-worth and well-being are dependent upon a person's relative social position, their competence, and the ability to access opportunities for personal and social advancement (Boyden and Dercon, 2012).

Poverty impacts upon emotional development as research has shown that children from lower socioeconomic backgrounds are more at risk to the effects of adversity. Other risks for children linked to poverty include exclusion from after-school activities, which may mean they do not develop the same skills as more affluent peers or form as many friendships, leading to low self-esteem.

Children living in low-income families are 'more prone to anxiety, depression, and behaviour problems' (McDevitt and Ormrod, 2010: 424–5) compared to children from more advantaged backgrounds. Children living in disadvantaged circumstances can feel sad or fearful and angry as they may be worried where their next meal is coming from. McLoyd et al. (2006) state that parents living in poverty may have limited resources and cannot always address their children's needs.

However, not all children who are from poorer backgrounds are emotionally troubled. Some children, although poor, have stable, loving care from their families and develop strong coping mechanisms (McDevitt and Ormrod, 2010). Similarly, children from middle- to high-income backgrounds are not immune to stress. Parents can be driven to push their children too quickly and thus affect their emotional development. This can lead to children worrying that they are not good enough.

Reflective Question

If you work in an area of high deprivation, what strategies do you put in place to negate the impacts of poverty on emotional development?

Maslow's Theory

Abraham Maslow (1943) developed the hierarchy of needs model, illustrated as a triangle (see Figure 11.1). There are five tiers of human needs, and the lower needs must be satisfied before moving further up the triangle. The aim is to reach the top of the triangle and self-actualisation (Thomas and Lewis, 2016). The first set of needs are physiological needs and biological requirements such as food, drink and warmth. Maslow considered that these needs were the most important. The next set of needs (safety needs) are secondary until the physiological needs have been satisfied. Safety needs include security, including emotional security, and here there is a need for order and predictability in life. Once the physiology and safety needs have been met, the next set of needs are love and belonging, followed by esteem needs. Love and belonging are social needs and are driven by the need for interpersonal relationships – children need to feel that they are loved and belong somewhere. Maslow classified esteem into two categories: esteem for oneself and respect from others. The last need is that of self-actualisation and is the fulfilment of one's potential. Maslow (1943) describes this level as the need to accomplish everything one can.

Maslow (1987) continued to refine his hierarchy of needs and in 1987 stated that the order is not as rigid as he originally thought; the order of needs might be flexible based on external influences and individual differences.

Maslow's hierarchy of human need

Self-actualisation needs

Esteem needs

Social needs

Safety needs

Physiological needs

Figure 11.1   Maslow's hierarchy of human need

Anthropological Approach to Emotional Development

Cultural differences in socialisation practices result in differences in emotional responses. In China and Japan, children are thought to be raised to be shy and unemotional, whereas in Western cultures children are encouraged to be more assertive and emotionally expressive (Camras et al., 2006). Individualistic cultures encourage children to express all their emotions and innermost feelings. In contrast in collectivist cultures, emotions that disrupt group harmony are discouraged (McDevitt and Ormrod, 2010). Nepalese children show little anger as their culture views annoyance as an obstacle to inner peace and harmony (Cole and Tan, 2007).

In many cultures, displaying emotions is different for males and females, reflecting beliefs about how males and females should behave. In some cultures, girls can be more attuned than boys to inhibit their emotions (Cole, 1986). This is true for girls from India, where females are expected to be deferential and only express socially acceptable emotions (Joshi and MacLean, 1994).

When considering attachment theory, described earlier in this chapter, there is an argument that 'human relatedness, which is part of the categorization of attachment is culturally specific' (Rothbaum et al., 2000; cited in Packer, 2017: 207). Packer (2017) discusses research carried out in northern Germany where a low percentage of securely attached babies were found. Here researchers rejected the notion that a large percentage of the parents were indifferent to their children; instead, these parents were following the cultural norm of a large interpersonal distance from their children and weaned their babies from bodily contact as soon as they became mobile. The aim with this type of parenting was to satisfy the children's needs, but not to disrupt family routine by spoiling the child with 'too much attention' (Packer, 2017: 207).

Therefore, differences in attachment can be down to what is considered typical parenting in different cultures. Keller contends that attachment theory as it stands does not reflect 'cultural variation in relationship development' (2013: 179). What is considered normal for one culture will not be for another, and it has been argued that there needs to be a reconceptualisation of attachment theory to consider different cultures.

Philosophical Approach to Emotional Development

Philosophers have been concerned with the nature of emotions since Socrates. As discussed in Chapter 10 on social development, a sense of self helps a child to find themselves in the world. Similarly, with emotional development, young children are aware of how their emotional expressions affect those around them. Rochat (2009) states that by the time children are 6 months old, they have experience of interactions with objects and people, and have developed a sense of self as a result.

Emotions are also linked to temperament, which can be defined as the way a child reacts to events and how they regulate impulses (McDevitt and Ormrod, 2010). Differences in temperament can be seen in infancy where some children are more demanding than others. Although temperament has a genetic basis, it is also affected by relationships and experiences.

Research by Rothbart and Bates (2006) indicates three dimensions of temperament: high, low or somewhere in between. Children who score high on extraversion have high levels of optimism and anticipation, and smile and laugh a lot. Children who score high on negative affectivity tend to be shy and fearful, sad and not easily soothed. Children who indicate high levels of effortful control are able to suppress inappropriate responses and enjoy innovative stimuli.

These differences in temperament are partly due to genetic factors, as shown by identical twins raised in different homes having similar temperaments. However, temperament is also determined by environmental factors, where affectionate families promote children's well-being and non-affectionate families can undermine children's well-being. Parents and other adults foster certain ways of responding that can alter a child's disposition (McDevitt and Ormrod, 2010). Practitioners notice how children behave and react, and understand that a child who is extraverted may need support to channel their energies into more constructive pursuits, while a timid child may need support in joining in with activities.

Personality is affected by temperament, as a shy child will react differently to a situation than a more confident child. Both temperament and personality help understand how children respond to emotions, form relationships, and behave in social situations (McDevitt and Ormrod, 2010). Children's personalities may change in response to situations, so a child may be loud and energetic outdoors, but more reserved and quieter indoors.

Researchers have found the following five dimensions of personality:

- Extraversion (extent to which someone is socially outgoing).
- Agreeableness (extent to which someone is warm and sympathetic).
- Conscientiousness (extent to which someone is organised).
- Neuroticism (extent to which someone is anxious and fearful).
- Openness (extent to which someone is curious and imaginative).

(McDevitt and Ormrod, 2010: 431)

Practitioners can plan activities that address different temperaments and personalities. They can pair more reserved children with more confident peers. They can ensure that all children know the expectations and acceptable behaviours and have routines for children to follow. Children adjust more easily when they know what to expect.

Many early years curricula place personal, social and emotional development at the heart of their frameworks. For example, the Foundation Phase in Wales makes it explicit in their guidance that practitioners need to recognise 'the importance of emotional development and well-being' (WG, 2015a: 4). Similarly, the Early Years Foundation Stage in England states that personal, social and emotional development is one of three prime areas that is 'particularly crucial for igniting children's curiosity and enthusiasm for learning, and for building their capacity to learn, form relationships and thrive' (DfE, 2017: 7). Therefore, nurturing and nourishing emotional development is crucial if young children are to thrive.

Case Study: Supporting emotional well-being

Jimmy is 6 years old and in Year 2 of school. He is normally a happy, energetic boy who loves running around and playing with his friends. The classroom practitioner, Miss Harris, never usually has any concerns with Jimmy's behaviour, and he seems to thrive in the busy classroom environment.

However, today a few of the parents have approached the teacher to say that Jimmy has used inappropriate language during yesterday's afternoon break. Miss Harris is really surprised but has assured the parents that she will deal with it today. As Jimmy walks in and sits on the carpet, Miss Harris notices that he has been crying and he is sitting away from his friends. She asks the additional practitioner to take over and she calls Jimmy to one side.

Miss Harris asks Jimmy if he is OK and he bursts into tears, saying that his mother has told him off as she has also been told by another parent that Jimmy was swearing in school yesterday. Miss Harris asks Jimmy if it is true and he says. 'No, Miss. I wasn't swearing. I was telling my friends what my dad calls me, but I don't like it; it makes me sad and upset.'

Miss Harris asks Jimmy to whisper to her what name his dad has been calling him, which Jimmy does, saying, 'But I don't like it. I tried to tell mum this morning, but she was in a rush and just shouted at me for using bad words.'

Miss Harris tells Jimmy not to worry and she will call mum and explain. Later that morning, Miss Harris speaks to Jimmy's mum and explains what has happened. Jimmy's mum agrees that Jimmy's dad has been calling him a certain name, but that it is family banter, and they didn't realise that is was upsetting Jimmy. She agrees to speak with dad, and they will not use that term any more. Miss Harris explains that Jimmy is at an age where he is becoming much more aware of his emotions like feeling embarrassed and self-conscious, so names that may be used in jest can affect him emotionally.

Miss Harris uses a circle time session that afternoon with all the class to discuss this and explains how sometimes words can hurt people and that they must not be afraid to say if they don't like a word. Jimmy comes to school the next day much happier and tells the teacher that his dad has promised not call Jimmy that name any more.

This case study has shown how, as children develop, their emotions develop too. Here Jimmy has started to feel new emotions such as embarrassment, and this has made him sensitive to the way his dad addresses him. He is becoming self-conscious and does not like to be called names, even if it is considered banter by his parents.

Reflective Question

How do you address children's growing emotional needs and well-being? How would you have dealt with Jimmy's situation?

Neuroscience Approach to Emotional Development

As gains in cognition are made throughout childhood, so emotional development is influenced. Children begin to understand the causes of emotional states and how they in turn can affect behaviour. There is a growing understanding that feelings can also arise from internal causes such as sadness. Children also need to learn how to regulate their emotions through both intrinsic and extrinsic processes. Intrinsic processes are internal and are the thought processes that allow reflection on a situation and determine our reaction. Extrinsic factors are external to the individual and are how a parent soothes an upset child, or the friends someone may talk with to discuss a problem. In developmental terms, emotional regulation is the process of moving on from a reliance on extrinsic processes to more reliance on intrinsic processes.

Emotional intelligence (EI) refers to the capacity to understand emotions in yourself and in others (Crowley, 2017). This started with the work of Howard Gardner (1983) and was further developed by Salovey and Mayer (1990). They identified five domains of EI:

1. Knowing one's feelings.
2. Managing and using the appropriate feelings in a given situation.
3. Self-motivation, making decisions linked to goals and behaving appropriately to achieve them.
4. Recognising emotions in others.
5. Building and maintaining positive relationships with others.

Attention has been given to devising interventions to improve EI in children such as emotional coaching and some settings have adopted the Social and Emotional Learning programme or SEAL (see SEAL Resources for Primary Schools – hwb.gov.wales).

Daniel Goleman has also popularised emotional intelligence and has authored several books on the topic (see Further reading).

Adverse childhood experiences

Mental health is an important part of emotional development. It links to well-being both internally through their emotions and externally in the relationships with their families and peers (Siegler et al., 2017). When children are in frightening or threatening environments, they experience stress. This increases the heart rate, secretion of stress hormones and blood flow to the brain. Stress can be beneficial when it causes a child to flee a dangerous situation or to focus hard for a test. If the stress is not constant and there are supportive adults, then the child learns how to deal with periodic stress.

However, if the stress becomes chronic, then it is problematic. Examples such as conflict at home or abuse and neglect can lead to what is known as toxic stress or adverse childhood experiences (ACEs) (Shonkoff et al., 2009). ACEs were introduced in Chapter 4 and when a child experiences toxic stress, their brain regions that regulate fear become overloaded and suffer atrophying of neuron dendrites and shrinkage (Danese and McEwen, 2012). The more ACEs a participant has experienced, the more the risk of high levels of stress, depression, anxiety, smoking and alcoholism are likely to occur. However, there is evidence that exposure to non-stressful environments and to safe, stable, nurturing relationships and other protective factors can reverse some of the harmful effects.

Research is also focused on preventing ACEs in the first place. Initiatives include community-wide parenting programmes and in Wales, the 'Futures Generation Report 2020' aims to tackle ACEs through the establishment of the Wales ACE Support hub (www.futuregenerations.wales/wp-content/uploads/2020/06/Chap-5-ACEs.pdf). Mental health preventions such as cognitive behaviour therapy, play therapy and parent–child interaction therapy can be effective too (Siegler et al., 2017).

Reflective Question

Are you aware of any other initiatives that can prevent ACEs?

Summary of chapter

- There are many approaches and theories to understand emotional development.
- Secure attachment with caregivers is important for healthy relationships.
- As children develop, they become more self-aware and more self-conscious.
- Different cultures place different importance on the display of emotions.
- Socioeconomic status can impact upon a child's emotional development both positively and negatively.
- Children's personalities and temperaments are affected by both genetic and environmental factors.
- Emotional intelligence (EI) refers to the capacity to understand emotions in yourself and in others.
- ACEs can have a lifelong impact upon a child, but there are strategies and interventions that can prevent ACEs occurring.

End-of-chapter questions

1. Do you use SEAL or other initiatives in your setting to support children's emotional development?
2. Have you had any training on supporting or recognising ACEs?
3. How do you develop children's emotional intelligence?

Further reading

Association of Directors of Public Health (n.d.) Creating ACE-informed places: promoting a whole-system approach to tackling adverse childhood experiences in local communities. England: The Health Foundation (www.health.org.uk/project/creating-ace-informed-places-promoting-a-whole-system-approach-to-tackling-adverse).

This policy document reports on early interventions that prevent ACEs across the UK.

Boyden, J. and Dercon, S. (2012) *Child Development and Economic Development: Lessons and Future Challenges.* Available at: www.younglivesmatter.org.uk.

This is an international study on child development and economic development (including well-being).

Garvey, D. (2017) *Nurturing Personal, Social and Emotional Development in Early Childhood: A Practical Guide to Understanding Brain Development and Young Children's Behaviour.* London: Jessica Kingsley.

This accessible book is a practical guide to understanding brain development and young children's behaviour.

Goleman, D. (2011) *The Brain and Emotional Intelligence: New Insights.* Florence: More Than Sound.

This book provides key findings on understanding emotional intelligence and how to apply this skill set.

TWELVE
CREATIVE DEVELOPMENT

This chapter will help you to

- understand the basic principles of creative development and to understand how children's creativity can be nurtured and developed through different approaches;
- explore what is meant by imitation and symbolic representation;
- discuss the work of Gardener and other theories of creative intelligence.

Introduction

The Welsh Foundation Phase curriculum defines the creative development area of learning as 'the development of children's individual ways of representing their ideas, feelings and emotions imaginatively through various forms of self-expression, such as painting, model making, role play, music, poetry, dance, writing and developing empathy with others' (WAG, 2008a: 4). Similarly, the Early Years Foundation Stage in England states that in the Expressive Arts and Design specific area of learning, children should be given opportunities

> to explore and play with a wide range of media and materials, as well as providing opportunities and encouragement for sharing their thoughts, ideas and feelings through a variety of activities in art, music, movement, dance, role-play, and design and technology.
>
> (DfE, 2017: 8)

Through creative development, young children should be able to communicate, express and reflect upon their work. This chapter will consider the theories of creative development and how it is viewed through the different interdisciplinary approaches discussed in Part 1.

Developmental Psychology Approach to Creative Development

Piaget stated that imitation was an important part of representing experiences. Through imitation children experiment with different behaviours and different ways of drawing, painting and role playing (Bruce, 2011a). Piaget's notion of imitation supports the argument for mixing different age groups of children where the younger children can imitate the older children, and the older children thrive on the sense of leadership and responsibility involved. This was one of the original aims of the Foundation Phase where in theory, children from the ages of 3–7 years could mix and learn with each other. However, in practice it is more likely to find children aged 3–4 years and children aged 5–7 years mixing together.

Piaget also discussed the process of representation and stated that this developed rapidly from toddler age until the ages of 6 or 7 years. Being able to represent means a way to bring back something or someone from a previous situation. Bruner (1990) also explored representation and contended that representation works in three ways:

- the enactive mode;
- the iconic mode;
- the symbolic mode.

The enactive mode is representing experiences through doing and learning through the senses, which coordinate to come together as a whole experience. All early years curricula in the UK advocate an experiential hands-on approach to learning. In the iconic mode, children represent a person, an event or an object through an image. Settings can set up an interest table with objects and photographs as reminders of a previous activity or trip. Here a child can interact with the objects, keeping their experiences alive. In the symbolic mode, children can represent something in a code such as language, writing, drawing, painting, model making or through numerical symbols (Bruce, 2011a). Children need practitioners to provide experiences that facilitate all three of Bruner's modes of representation.

Reflective Question

As a practitioner, *how* would you provide creative experiences for children that support Bruner's modes of representation?

For Piaget, representation, as with Bruner, was a network of processes that developed when the child interacted with others. These processes are as follows:

- active learning;
- imitation;
- memory;
- making images;
- making symbols.

(Bruce, 2011a: 116)

The following case study illustrates the representation of an event through the use of imitation and memory.

Case Study: Representing a trip to the dentist

Ella (5 years old) is playing in the home corner. She has a toy dinosaur and a plastic funnel from the sand tray. She is repeatedly placing the funnel over the head of the dinosaur while talking to herself. One of the practitioners is observing Ella and listening to what she is saying. Ella is saying to the dinosaur, 'Come on, now you need to be brave. I am going to make you go asleep, then I can take your bad teeth out. You must be brave 'cos when the bad teeth have gone, it won't hurt anymore.'

Ella proceeds to keep placing the funnel over the dinosaur's head and then pretends to use a pair of tweezers from the home corner to pull the dinosaur's teeth. She then says: 'Wakey, wakey, all over now. You can go home with mummy and have a treat for being big and brave.'

One of the practitioners watches Ella and notes down what she is doing. She decides to bring this to the attention of other staff in the next staff meeting to see how they can use this to plan further activities for Ella based on her interests.

The case study highlights how children can use imitation and representation in their play. Ella has engaged in all of Bruner's modes and Piaget's network of representational processes. She has been active throughout, and she has imitated the dentist and used her memory to recall an experience that was important to her. She has used language and symbols to represent the experience at the dentist and the dentist's tools (funnel and tweezers).

Reflective Question

As a practitioner, observing this and understanding the representation going on here, what would you do next to support and develop Ella's creative imagination?

Symbolic representation

Piaget valued the personal symbols that children used to represent their earlier experiences, as signifiers to stand for the objects, people or events they are re-enacting. Piaget cited observations of his own daughter engaging in imaginative play representing this stage of development and thinking (Piaget and Inhelder, 1969). Symbolic representation is subdivided into the following two sub-stages: *Symbolic function* and *Intuitive thought*. Within the first of these sub-stages (2–4 years), the infant increasingly uses symbols such as images, words and gestures to represent objects. Then in the second sub-stage – intuitive thought – children begin to be able to search for logical explanations and to classify objects, but have difficulty in arranging things in order (seriation) and to understand conservation.

Vygotsky also valued the use of play props for young children to represent things, people and events. In pretend play, children develop their communication and imagination through stories. This was evident in the case study above, as Ella was retelling a story of a trip to the dentist using the dinosaur, funnel and tweezers as play props. Vygotsky saw pretend play as a product of social collaborations and that the role of the adult was crucial in constructing knowledge (Gray and MacBlain, 2012; Vygotsky, 1978).

Vygotsky believed that in pretend play children could reach higher levels of cognitive development. He believed that imaginary play laid down the blueprints for later life allowing children to become reflective and understand negotiation and cooperation. Vygotsky (1978) stated that symbolic or imaginative play served as a zone of proximal development where a child is able to function beyond their actual development. This is reflected in a quote by Albert Einstein (1879–1955) who said: 'Imagination is more important than knowledge. Knowledge is limited. Imagination encircles the world.'

In the theories of Piaget, Bruner and Vygotsky, the adult's role is crucial from carefully observing children to becoming play partners through to providing resources that can foster imaginative and creative play. Children need access to a range of different creative materials and to hear and experience different stories to fire their imaginations. Dance, music and construction, drawing, painting and drama all offer different possibilities for children to represent something important and unique to them.

Reflective Question

How does your practice support Vygotsky's theory in terms of representation?

Sociological Approach to Creative Development

Chapter 3 describes interactionism as a sociological perspective that focuses on how individuals interact with one another. Here, social behaviour is viewed as a result of inventive and creative individuals. Burns et al. (2015: 179) argue that 'key factors in creative activity are socially based and developed; hence, sociology can contribute significantly to understanding and explaining human creativity'. Interactionism reinforces the importance of meeting individual needs and how social meanings are negotiated by individuals (Ingleby and Oliver, 2008). An interactionist approach to early years is more likely to acknowledge children's individual creativity. Role play where children can use their imaginations and re-enact stories and develop new stories is an important part of their social world. Children can feel free to express themselves as different characters and act out scenarios on their own or with their peers. In early childhood, children use language, fantasy, and play in their social interactions (McDevitt and Ormrod, 2010). However, young children need supportive settings and adults to encourage and enable imaginative role play. Children should not be forced to conform to using creative materials in certain ways. They need to be able to express themselves as individuals and use lots of materials to do this.

Case Study: Individual creativity and social meanings

The termly theme in the reception class is 'Fairytales' and the role-play area is a castle with lots of dressing-up clothes to represent princes, princesses, dragons, and kings and queens. Many of the boys regularly choose to dress up as princesses and enjoy wearing the pretend sparkly outfits, tiaras and shiny slippers. They can often be seen role playing different fairy stories where they are rescued by other children. The practitioners have taken lots of photos of the children dressed up and displayed them around the classroom.

It is parents' evening and one of the dads has spent time looking at the photographs of his son dressed up as Cinderella. When he comes to talk to the teacher, he says he is not happy that his son is dressed up in 'girly clothes'. The teacher allows him to express his concerns and then she explains the following skills his son has developed, She explains that his son has learnt how to do up buttons on the costume, thus developing his hand–eye coordination skills. His language and imaginative skills have also developed, and he has spent a long time writing his own version of the story, and being dressed up in character has really developed his imagination. If the parent had looked past the photo, he would have seen an example of his son's story writing also on display.

The teacher explains to the parent that his son spends just as much time dressing up as a dragon or a prince, and that many of the boys in the class also choose to wear the princess outfits. In fact, the teacher says that they actively encourage all the children to have a free choice in whatever they want to dress up in, as the outfit is a very small part of what the children get out of the role play. Here the dad has attached social meaning only to the outfit and not to the individual creativity his son has developed.

In this case study, the parent has just looked at the appearance of his son and attached his own social meaning to it. It is only when the teacher has explained all of the skills that his son has developed as a result of dressing up and using his imagination, does the importance of allowing children to express their individual creativity become apparent.

Reflective Question

How do you promote individual creativity in your setting?

Economic Approach to Creative Development

Creative thinking is a skill that can help solve problems. In the twenty-first century creative thinking is needed to solve social, environmental and economic problems, so we need to develop children's creative thinking skills from a young age (Englebright Fox and Schirrmacher, 2015). There is an increased emphasis on creativity as a means to improve student attainment and future success in a knowledge-based economy. However, socioeconomic status can impact upon creative development. A study by Lichtenwalner and Maxwell in 1969 found several factors that can affect creative development based upon socioeconomic status. Parents of lower socioeconomic status had larger families, resulting in parents having less time to spend with their children to develop their creativity. Parents of lower socioeconomic status did not seem to approve of creative behaviours or expressions and actively discouraged them. Lastly, the home of children of lower socioeconomic status did not have the same resources or materials to develop creativity as more affluent families. Although this study is more than fifty years old, there are some factors that still hold true today. Children from poorer backgrounds do not have the same opportunities to visit art galleries to develop their knowledge of artists, colour, and textures. They may not have access to out-of-school activities such as taking part in art or craft clubs. Their parents may not be able to afford to pay for music lessons or dance lessons or drama clubs. Further, children from poorer backgrounds may not have access to music or art or craft materials to use at home. This reinforces the importance of settings and practitioners to ensure that all children have equal access to creative activities.

Some schools offer after-school clubs which are free and open to all children. Here, children can access school resources to carry out creative development activities and join in with dance and drama clubs. However, this very much depends upon the school budget and the goodwill of the staff to run these clubs. As argued in Chapter 4, 'economics is an important discipline for those working with children and their families'. Schools can also offer free music lessons and provide instruments, but again this is due to budgets and whether local authorities are prepared to fund peripatetic practitioners to teach music.

Reflective Question

How do you ensure that all children have equal access to creative activities regardless of economic status?

Anthropological Approach to Creative Development

As discussed in Chapter 5, anthropology is broadly about understanding the traditions, habits and views that a group of people, community or society possess, and the roles they play in people's lives. Children's creative development is closely linked to cultural development, 'as the ideas and work of local and famous artists', musicians and dancers, both modern and from the past, can have a significant impact upon children's ideas (WAG, 2008a: 5).

Creativity can be evidenced across all areas of learning. So, for example, learning about different festivals such as 'Chinese spring festival' can support children in their cultural awareness, but can also link to physical development where children can take part in a 'dragon dance' developing their gross motor skills. Similarly, while learning about Diwali, the children can paint Mehndi patterns on their hands, supporting their creativity but also their fine motor skills. Children can re-create different artefacts based upon different cultures, and listen and appreciate music from around the world.

Education policy makes it clear that the role of the adult is important in providing a stimulating and multi-sensory learning environment both indoors and outdoors (WAG, 2008a). Adults need to facilitate conversations about art and artists and pieces of music and dance, asking the children to express their opinions and giving them opportunities to develop their own creative pieces. Children need to listen to stories and poetry from around the world and have opportunities to develop their own writing, thus linking creativity to literacy.

At around the age of 3 years, children usually start to create imaginary play scenarios, and the characters and roles they tend to portray are conventional and linked to their own cultures (Packer, 2017). In Western societies, children have easy access to television programmes and films which they tend to reflect within their creative and imaginary play. Quite often young children will re-create the latest TV craze in their role play and through their drawings and model making, known as popular culture.

Here in the UK, practitioners need to ensure that children's creative and imaginary play is encouraged and broadened to consider other cultures in order to develop their understanding of the world around them. The learning environment needs to have a wide range of resources, including stories, music, displays and craft activities that reflect other cultures. However, care needs to be taken that this is not just tokenistic, but a genuine approach to developing children's knowledge and understanding of other cultures. McDevitt and Ormrod (2010) argue that practitioners need to engage in culturally responsive teaching where teachers use their knowledge of children's cultural backgrounds to develop the curriculum, including creative development.

Case Study: Cops, robbers and guard dogs

Year 1 children are studying the topic 'People who help us'. As part of this, the practitioner, Ben, set up the role-play area as a shop. The intention was that the children would use their mathematical knowledge in buying and selling. The children decided what to sell in the shop, priced the goods and made signs to indicate the opening hours. They made name badges and took it in turns to be the shopkeeper and the customers. At first the children seemed to enjoy this and were enthusiastic about the activity. However, after a few days Ben noticed that the children were no longer role-playing

(Continued)

shop, but were now playing cops, robbers and guard dogs. The children were enthusiastically taking it in turns to be the police officers chasing the robbers around the classroom and some children were scrambling around on all fours and barking like dogs. When Ben asked the children why they were now playing at cops and robbers and not shopkeepers, the children excitedly told him about a new TV show they had watched. This TV show was all about the police catching the 'bad guys' and the children were re-creating the show. Ben believed that the children should have opportunities to develop their imaginations and creative play without adult intervention, but the classroom was not big enough to support the children running around.

Therefore, Ben decided to change one of the outdoor play sheds into a police station and he asked the children to help design the building. The children were then able to choose either to play in the indoor role-play shop area or outdoors in the role-play police station. Ben also invited a police officer to speak with the children about their job as he realised that he needed to nurture and value their current play interests.

This case study has shown how children will sometimes use their creative play based on what they are currently influenced by. Children in the UK are familiar with a culture of watching TV outside of school, so it is of little surprise that they are influenced by this in their imaginative and creative play. Children from other cultures will use other sources to develop their imaginative play, but, as practitioners, it is important to be aware of how cultural norms can impact upon all areas of development, including creative development.

Reflective Question

As a practitioner, consider the children you work with. How do you take into consideration children's different cultural influences when planning imaginative or creative activities?

Philosophical Approach to Creative Development

Although practitioners in the UK follow different curricula, the policies have been influenced by international approaches to early years education. Two such approaches that have particular creative underpinnings are the Reggio Emilia philosophy from Italy and Steiner Waldorf from Germany.

Reggio Emilia

Reggio Emilia is a small city in northern Italy and the Reggio Emilia approach originated after the Second World War in 1945. Loris Malaguzzi led a group of practitioners to set up a community of learners with a philosophical view of children as curious, confident and independent learners (Bruce, 2011a). There is an emphasis on nurturing children's creativity, imagination and problem solving. Malaguzzi believed that all children had rights rather than needs, and could think and act for themselves; the approach is based upon Vygotskian theory. Children learn through interaction, with modelling and support from others.

As discussed in Chapter 8, Malaguzzi wrote the poem called 'Hundred Languages of the Child' in recognition of the multitude of ways in which children can express their ideas, thoughts, feelings or frustrations (Edwards et al., 2012). Children are encouraged to express themselves through painting, drama and sculpting, and the child is viewed as being an active constructor of knowledge. They are encouraged to become thinkers through in-depth projects, and these are cooperative ventures between practitioners, thus fostering quality relationships between teacher and learner (Goouch, 2008).

In Reggio Emilia, children stay for three years from the ages of 3–6 years; alongside teachers, there is a resident artist who works with the children. Creativity is at the core of the Reggio Emilia philosophy and the curriculum revolves around the day-to-day experiences of the children. This can be seen in the Welsh Foundation Phase curriculum where practitioners are encouraged to start with a child's interests and build upon them (WG, 2015a).

Steiner Waldorf

The Steiner Waldorf approach was founded by Rudolf Steiner (1861–1925) and the first school opened in Stuttgart, Germany, in 1919. Steiner integrated science and philosophical thinking into his schools and believed that learning occurred in three cycles of seven-year stages. There is a distinctive need for learning in an ascending spiral of knowledge, with an emphasis on unstructured play. In Steiner settings, formal teaching does not commence until children are 7 years of age. When Wales was developing the Foundation Phase for learners age 3–7 years old, a stage not age approach was advocated. Here, there was an emphasis on not forcing children into reading and writing or number formation until they were ready, mirroring in part the Steiner Waldorf approach (Thomas and Lewis, 2016).

In the first cycle from birth to 7 years, children respond to the world through movement. The spirituality of the child is held in the highest regard and the learning environment is carefully planned (Bruce, 2011a). Learning is through imitation and doing, with imaginary play as the most important, encouraging physical, intellectual, and emotional growth. The curriculum focus is on physical exploration, constructive and creative play, oral language – never written language – through story and song. Steiner, as with Malaguzzi, believed in emphasising what the child can do and building upon this (Bruce, 2011a). Again, this resonates with the ethos of the Foundation Phase (Wales) and the Early Years Foundation Stage (England) (WG, 2015a; DfE, 2017).

Reflective Question

As a practitioner, what approaches to creative development have influenced you?

Neuroscience Approach to Creative Development

Carpendale et al. (2018: 33) argue that 'neural pathways are shaped through experience'. Thus children develop thinking and cognition in many different ways and this led Howard Gardner to develop his theory of multiple intelligences (Siegler et al., 2017). In Gardner's view, children and adults have at least eight different multiple intelligences (McDevitt and Ormrod, 2010). These are as follows:

Table 12.1 Gardner's multiple intelligences

Type of intelligence	Definition	Example
Linguistic intelligence	Effective use of language	Persuasive arguments; identifying subtle nuances in word meanings; poetry writing
Logical-mathematical Intelligence	Logical reasoning	Solving mathematical problems quickly; formulating and testing hypotheses
Spatial intelligence	Capacity to perceive the visual world accurately	Mental imagery; drawing a visual likeness of an object; able to make fine discriminations among similar objects
Musical intelligence	Ability to create, comprehend and appreciate music	Playing an instrument; composing musical work; an awareness of the underlying structure of music
Bodily-kinaesthetic Intelligence	Able to use one's body in a skilful way; able to handle objects skilfully	Dancing; performing; athletics
Interpersonal intelligence	Ability to notice subtle aspects of other people's behaviours	Able to perceive people's moods, intentions and motivations; able to act on this knowledge
Intrapersonal intelligence	Awareness of one's own feelings, motives and desires	Identifying the motives guiding one's own behaviour; using self-knowledge to relate more effectively with others
Naturalistic intelligence	Able to understand and recognise patterns in nature	Classification of natural forms; applying knowledge of nature in farming, landscaping or conservation

Adapted from McDevitt and Ormrod, (2010); Siegler et al., (2017).

Therefore, creative development would encompass bodily-kinaesthetic intelligence, musical intelligence and spatial intelligence. Gardner presents evidence to support the existence of these different intelligences as he describes people who can be skilled in one area, such as playing an instrument, but can have average abilities in other areas. Gardner also presented evidence from people who have suffered brain damage where they lose abilities in one intelligence (McDevitt and Ormrod, 2010). For example, some people with brain damage can function well in most areas, but have no understanding of other people (Damasio, 1999), suggesting that interpersonal intelligence is distinct from other intelligence types. Gardner argues that all kinds of data, and not just test scores, must be considered to get an understanding of people's abilities, and children have a variety of strengths upon which to build (Siegler et al., 2017). Robert Sternberg has also argued that intelligence tests are too narrow, and the type of intelligence needed to succeed in school is too narrow. Sternberg proposes three different types of ability: analytical, practical and creative (McDevitt and Ormrod, 2010; Siegler et al., 2017). Analytic intelligence involves evaluating problems; practical intelligence involves applying knowledge and skills, and creative intelligence involves imagination and invention.

Although there is less supporting evidence for both these theories, they allow for different ways of thinking about and measuring intelligence. Many educators have embraced these optimistic views of different intelligences and that children have a variety of strengths upon which to build including creative intelligence (Siegler et al., 2017).

Reflective Question

Do you plan for and support different intelligences with the children in your care?

Summary of chapter

- There are many approaches and theories to understanding creative development.
- Piaget stated that children use imitation and symbolic representation in their creative play.
- Bruner discussed three ways of representation: enactive, iconic and symbolic.
- Vygotsky advocated the importance of pretend play and imagination as part of creativity.
- Children will engage in creative play in ways that are individual to them.
- Children's creative development will be influenced by their own culture and that of others.
- International curricula including Steiner Waldorf and Reggio Emilia that focus on creativity have underpinned some parts of current UK curricula.
- Gardner and Sternberg have proposed theories that include different forms of intelligence including creative intelligence.

End-of-chapter questions

1. How many different ways do you develop children's creativity in your setting?
2. Do you think children have multiple intelligences and, if so, do you develop all of them equally?
3. How do you ensure that children's cultural creativity is developed?

Further reading

Bruce, T. (2011) *Cultivating Creativity in Babies, Toddlers and Young Children* (2nd edn). London: Hodder & Stoughton.

Tina Bruce provides examples of how to foster creativity with young learners. It explores the journey children take in developing their creativity, and helps students and practitioners to nurture creativity.

Gardner, H. (2011) *The Unschooled Mind: How Children Think and How Schools Should Teach*. New York: Basic Books.

This text explores Gardner's theory of multiple intelligences in more detail. It draws upon science and psychology to make the case for restructuring our schools and the ways that children learn.

Robinson, K. (2016) *Creative Schools: The Grassroots Revolution that's Transforming Education*. New York: Penguin Random House.

This book discusses a revolutionary reappraisal of how to educate children and young people. It is a comprehensive and compelling statement of why creativity matters for everyone.

Sir Ken Robinson, TED talk: 'Do schools kill creativity?' Available at: www.ted.com/talks/sir_ken_robinson_do_schools_kill_creativity?language=en

This powerful talk discusses why creativity should be viewed as equal to literacy, numeracy and science in education.

THIRTEEN
SPIRITUAL DEVELOPMENT

This chapter will help you to

- understand what is meant by spiritual development and how it is developed through different approaches;
- understand how spiritual development is part of a holistic understanding of the needs and rights of children, families and communities;
- explore the theories and theorists underpinning spiritual development.

Introduction

In England, the National Curriculum framework document for learners aged 5 years and above, states that every school must offer a curriculum that 'promotes the spiritual, moral, cultural, mental and physical development of pupils' (DfE, September 2014a: 5). While the statutory requirement for Religious Education (RE) does not extend to children under compulsory school age, it can form a valuable part of the educational experience of children in the Early Years Foundation Stage. As Lunn (2015: 27) argues, spiritual development is a 'crucial part of early childhood, and integral to the holistic well-being of the child'.

Currently, in Wales, spiritual development is considered under the 'National exemplar framework for Religious Education for 3 to 19-year-olds in Wales' (WAG, 2008b). The guidance requires 'the promotion of the spiritual, moral, cultural, mental and physical development of pupils, including those in nursery settings' (WAG, 2008b: 2). The framework explains that children's spiritual development should focus on what it means to be human; an exploration of shared values; alongside the development of curiosity, reflection, and intuition and beliefs (WAG, 2008b).

In Scotland, spirituality forms part of the framework for Religious and Moral Education in the Curriculum for Excellence for learners age 3–18 years. Here, the framework promotes strong emotional, social and spiritual well-being alongside increasing intellectual capacity (Education Scotland, 2014). In the Foundation Stage curriculum in Northern Ireland, Religious Education is a compulsory part of the curriculum. It states that children need 'to develop an understanding of spirituality' (CCEA, 2014: 6).

This chapter will consider what is meant by spiritual development and how it is viewed through the different interdisciplinary approaches discussed in Part 1.

Developmental Psychology Approach to Spiritual Development

Benson et al. (2003: 205) argue that

> sustained, rigorous attention to spiritual development during childhood and adolescence in the social and developmental sciences has the potential to significantly enrich and strengthen the understanding of the core processes and dimensions of human development.

They also contend that spiritual development is difficult to define and difficult to capture in a single definition. Despite this, pioneer psychologists such as 'William James, G. Stanley Hall, J. H. Leuba, and Edwin Starbuck considered religiousness and spirituality to be integral to the field of psychology' (Benson et al., 2003: 206). In terms of development, spirituality can be considered as a change, a transformation, growth or maturation. Initially, spiritual development was considered through a psychological stage theory approach.

Fowler's Faith Development Theory

In 1981, Fowler produced a theory of six stages that people go through as their faith and spirituality develops; the first two stages occur in early childhood. Fowler's theory was based on Piaget's and Kohlberg's stage theories (see Chapters 2 and 10). Stage 0 is termed 'primal undifferentiated faith' (ages birth–2 years) and is very much like Erik Erikson's first stage of 'trust versus mistrust'. The infant acquires experiences from the outer environment that instil in her a feeling of trust and assurance, and a sense of consistency and care from parents. These personalised experiences, according to Fowler, essentially translate into feelings of trust and assurance in the universe, and harmony with the divine.

Conversely, experiences of parental or environmental neglect and/or abuse at this stage of development can result in the formation of feelings of mistrust and fear with respect to the universe and the divine, sowing the seeds for later doubt and existential angst. This stage also compares with Jean Piaget's sensori-motor stage of cognitive development, where thinking takes place in and through the body. Stage 1 is termed the 'intuitive-projective' (ages 3–7 years) and is the stage where fantasy and reality become mixed up, and ideas about God come from parents and society. This stage aligns with Piaget's stage of pre-operational thinking (lacking consistent logical–mental structures) (Armstrong, 2020). The following case study illustrates stage 1 of Fowler's theory.

Case Study: Understanding death

Alys is 4 years old and is in the nursery class of the local primary school. Alys has settled in well and enjoys taking a full part in classroom activities. It is the spring term and the theme is nursery rhymes. Each week, the teacher introduces a new rhyme and plans a number of different activities based on that rhyme. It is Monday morning and Alys had been off school the previous week as her uncle had died. The teacher begins the day by introducing the rhyme for the week and it is 'Twinkle, Twinkle, Little Star'. Some of the children already know the rhyme and they start to sing along, joining in with the actions.

Suddenly, Alys starts to cry loudly. The teacher stops and asks her what is wrong. However, Alys cannot get her words out as she is sobbing too much. One of the other practitioners comes and takes Alys to a quiet corner of the classroom to calm her down.

The teacher resumes singing with the children and then sends them off to choose which activities they want to play with. Alys has stopped crying and she is sitting at the craft table, colouring in a star. The practitioner who comforted Alys comes over to chat with the teacher and explains that Alys's parents have explained the death of her uncle and that now he is a twinkling star in the sky with God; singing 'Twinkle, Twinkle, Little Star' reminded Alys of her uncle's death and upset her. The practitioner has asked Alys to decorate a star for her uncle which they will hang up in the class. Then, when they sing the rhyme, Alys can look at her very own special star. The teacher thanks the practitioner for her handling of the situation and says she will chat with Alys's parents at the end of the day and explain what has happened. They also agree that they will keep a close eye on Alys and tell her that if she feels sad about her uncle, she can come and talk to them at any time.

This case study illustrates what Fowler described in stage one of his theory where ideas about God come from parents, and fantasy and reality become mixed up.

Reflective Question

Have you ever had to deal with a child's perceptions of death and, if so, how would you have dealt with the situation above?

Sociological Approach to Spiritual Development

In 1999, Flanagan contended that spirituality had entered the very soul of sociology. However, in 2007, Holme wrote that sociology had lagged behind areas such as education in considering sociology and spirituality. Moving forwards to 2019, sociologists Bartkowski et al. (2019) undertook research into what the impact of religion, including spirituality, had on child development. They examined the performance of children, who came from religious backgrounds, on psychological adjustment, interpersonal skills, and performance on standardised tests. The results showed that psychological adjustment and social competence were positively correlated with various religious factors. However, the children's performance on reading, maths and science tests were negatively associated with several forms of parental religion.

Bartkowski explained these results as religion prioritising moral codes and social competence among learners with less emphasis on academic performance. This supports the functionalist perspective of sociology as outlined in Chapter 3, where social behaviour is often described in this perspective as a product of society. However, they also pointed out that a limitation of the study was that it did not inquire about denominational affiliation, so some religions may have a better balance between social competence and academic achievement.

Previous research by Bartkowski et al. in 2008 discovered that shared religion among couples and communication between parent and child were linked to positive development characteristics, while religious conflict among spouses was connected to negative outcomes. This would also support a sociological approach to spirituality where the beliefs of the society the child is raised in will impact upon their development. However, Bartkowski et al. (2008) contend that while religion is important, it is only part of child development, and other resources such as academic school clubs and activities are as important.

In the national exemplar framework for religious education for 3- to 19-year-olds in Wales, it clearly states that spirituality needs to focus upon 'the development of intellectual curiosity, open-mindedness, emotion, reflection, intuition and beliefs, including a relationship with God' (WAG, 2008b: 12). This would seem to support Bartkowski et al.'s (2008) research, with the need for academic activity (intellectual curiosity) being as important as spiritual activity.

Case Study: Conforming to different spiritual, ethical and moral frameworks

Six-year-old Isaac attends a Church of England primary school. During assemblies he is told various Bible stories and how God created the world and everything in it. However, both of Isaac's parents are agnostics and this places him in a dilemma. Why did his parents not believe that God created the world and what would the school think if they knew this? Isaac decides not to tell anyone in school that his parents rejected the idea of God creating the world.

He learns about different world issues such as poverty, peace and ill treatment during extended family gatherings, thus developing his ethical and moral framework and an understanding of right and wrong. Therefore, Isaac develops his spiritual understanding through organised religion at school, and at home he develops his ethical and moral understanding through his family gatherings.

The case study above demonstrates how Isaac adapts his spiritual understanding depending on who he is interacting with. This is an example of interactionism as a sociological perspective (see Chapter 3). Interactionists view human experiences as continuously shifting and are not considered fixed entities. Isaac is able to reflect upon spiritual experiences in school, and moral and ethical issues with his family outside of school, thus developing his intellectual curiosity.

Reflective Question

Do you take time to explore what influences children's developing spirituality?

Economic Approach to Spiritual Development

Chapter 4 opens with the following definition from Penn by what is meant by economics. As a discipline, economics is bound up with context, political values and beliefs and is very 'influential in determining national and international policies' (Penn, 2014: 149). Reading this, you may be wondering how this links to spiritual development, but it does at a policy level and through the importance that government and educational authorities place upon spiritual development.

According to research carried out by Lunn (2015), spiritual development needs to be a recognised and valuable part of the EYFS. However, Lunn contends that spiritual development is not recognised in the EYFS and no guidance is given to practitioners. She goes on to argue that spiritual development should be recognised and supported as developing resilience, mental well-being and autonomy in our youngest learners. This is supported by the OECD (2011) which argued for more emphasis to be placed upon well-being and how people feel about the purpose and meaning of life (see Chapter 4).

Adams et al. (2016) also evidenced the paucity of studies on spirituality and how it is enacted in practice. They go on to argue that spirituality is the least understood aspect of development, and there is a need for more research to inform policy and practice.

A more holistic approach

The holistic aspect of spirituality that represents both individuality as well as the significance of humanity and the world has been illuminated by Nye and Hay (2006). Incorporating this holistic approach to spirituality into the early years of the curriculum allows children to respect themselves, others and the broader world. Spirituality not only prepares students for adult life, it also encourages children to respect each other and the wider community, fostering sustainability, again linking into economic growth.

Future economic development and growth will require citizens to be ethically aware and knowledgeable about sustainability. Ofsted (2004) also states that spiritual development helps in the creation of positive relationships within settings, but also within the wider community.

This creation of positive relationships can impact significantly upon economic development on the world stage. Goodliff (2013) argues that children's spirituality should be recognised and understood in education because it supports children in their thinking and to make meaning of their lives. Thus, if we want our twenty-first century learners to be forward thinking, innovative, resilient and problem solvers, adding to our economic growth, then spiritual development has a recognisable part to play in this.

A move away from targets and curriculum goals

Spirituality allows children to consider the wider world and to develop critical thinking skills (Lunn, 2015), a skill required for future economic development. Practitioners and pupils are seen as active co-constructors in their spiritual learning. This approach to learning underpins the Foundation Phase in Wales where policy guidance clearly views the practitioner as accompanying children along their learning journey and being active co-constructors in knowledge development (WG, 2015a).

However, there is a drive in the UK to set targets for children to meet in the early years, and this increases the pressure on practitioners to provide evidence that can be measured and places an economic value upon children and their learning (Adams et al., 2008). This does not fit with spiritual development, which is not linear and cannot be measured in terms of targets.

Eaude (2009) examined the negative effects a materialistic culture has on children, impacting their identity and sense of self. To counterbalance society's culture of consumerism, children need to engage with their spiritual selves. Eaude (2009) believes that children should be motivated by adults to pursue long-term happiness and well-being over short-term immediate gratification. For educational purposes, this is also crucial: short-term performance cannot be prioritised at the cost of lifelong well-being.

Reflective Question

As a practitioner, how do you develop positive relationships, positive well-being and help children to make meanings of their lives?

Anthropological Approach to Spiritual Development

In Chapter 5, Montgomery stated that anthropology is about studying human beings and their social relationships as well as 'family structures, religion, political and economic life' (2013: 163). When considering the different curricula in the UK, policy documentation and guidance for RE, spirituality and cultural awareness, the following statements apply. The Welsh Assembly Government (2008b: 11) contends that there is 'the need for human beings to have a sense of cultural identity, belonging and purpose, which in Wales has been evident by the way in which religion and culture have been interwoven'.

New draft guidance for the EYFS being implemented in September 2021 states that, under the Early Learning Goal (ELG), 'People, Culture and Communities' on page 14 children need to, 'Know some similarities and differences between different religious and cultural communities in this country, drawing on their experiences and what has been read in class.' (DfE, 2012). In Scotland, 'Religious and Moral Education provides a key context for exploring values and beliefs' (Education Scotland, 2014). Lastly, in Northern Ireland children will 'appreciate the role of belief and tradition in identity and culture' (CCEA, 2014: 21). Therefore, there are clear expectations in curriculum guidance for the need to recognise how different cultures shape RE and in turn spiritual development.

Interweaving spirituality and cultural awareness

In practice, young children can learn about their own religious culture and the culture of other religions through role play, stories, music and dance. Through play, children can share their opinions and feelings, reflect upon what is important to themselves, but also what is important to others. Children can learn about different religious festivals from around the world and experience different foods associated with such festivals, explore artefacts, and different stories and folk tales. They can listen to moral dilemmas and consider how they would respond. Children need to be given opportunities 'to explore how religion has influenced and guided people's lives, past and present, including the emphasis of religion on spirituality and religious experience, in Wales and the wider world' (WAG, 2008b: 17b).

The EYFS states that 'enabling environments' (DfE, 2012) provide young children with the opportunity to engage with their own spirituality (Lunn, 2015). Here children can engage in imaginative play, creative activities and meaning making that allows them to reflect and move beyond their own lived experiences (Nye and Hay, 2006). Kimes-Myers (1997, cited in Lunn, 2015: 30) argue that

> spiritual development encourages empathy for others and a deeper understanding of oneself, helping children gain a deeper appreciation of the impact their behaviour and actions have upon not only themselves and other people but upon the world itself.

In the New Zealand early years curriculum Te Whāriki, both spirituality and culture are interwoven in early years education. Spirituality is at the centre of the holistic curriculum, which promotes empowerment of the child through recognition of the diversity of cultural identity (Bone, 2008). In the UK, children do not live in isolation; they are affected by their family values and cultural expectations (see Bronfenbrenner's ecological model in Chapters 2 and 10). Spiritual development allows children to reflect upon these and question their beliefs and values. Therefore, practitioners and settings need to consider a holistic approach to developing children's spirituality that embraces children's own cultural awareness alongside opportunities to reflect and question.

Reflective Question

As a practitioner, how do you empower children to reflect upon their own cultural identity in terms of their spiritual development?

Case Study: A whole-school approach to spiritual development and cultural awareness

Greenwood Primary School decided to adopt a different approach to spiritual development and cultural diversity. The school decided to have a week where each class from nursery through to Year 6 focused on a different religion from around the world. This had worked well with previous subjects such as science week or healthy eating week. Each class focused on a different religion and explored culture, festivals, and stories and artefacts linked to that religion. Then, throughout the week, children in each class immersed themselves in learning all about their chosen religion. They listened to stories, invited in guest speakers to talk to the children about how different religions and cultures developed and influenced spiritual awareness.

At the end of the week, each class presented an overview about what they had learnt about different religions, different cultures and spiritual development to the whole school. This was done through songs, dance, stories and displays. In this way, every child in the school was able to gain an understanding of how different religions and cultures were interwoven to shape both religious and spiritual awareness.

This case study is one example of how children can learn about different religions and how different cultures impact upon spiritual development and awareness. The whole-school approach to exploring different religions over one week did not replace the daily assemblies, but instead allowed the children to immerse themselves in different cultures and nurtured spiritual development.

Reflective Question

Can you think of any other ways you could immerse children in learning about different religions and cultures?

Philosophical Approach to Spiritual Development

Chapter 12 introduced the Steiner Waldorf curriculum and discussed its creative underpinnings. However, as mentioned in Chapter 12, the Steiner Waldorf approach also holds the spirituality of the child in the highest regard. Freedom to learn is at the core of the Steiner Waldorf philosophy and there is the belief that each child embarks upon their own spiritual journey (Lunn, 2015).

Oberski (2011) postulates that spiritual well-being is assumed by the Human Rights Act, which includes the right to 'freedom of thought, conscience and religion' (Article 18). This, he argues, links to Steiner Waldorf education as Steiner's philosophy of freedom leads to spirituality through intuitive thinking. In the first phase of Steiner Waldorf education, which is from birth to 7 years, the spirituality of the child is held in the highest regard, and the whole environment for the child should be carefully planned, positive and harmonious (The Education Hub, 2020).

Steiner viewed the child as an entity with an inner soul and an eternal spiritual nature. There is an emphasis on working with the seasons, nature, festivals and 'embracing diversity and the outdoors' (Bruce, 2011a: 23). Steiner emphasised observing children and building upon the strength of what the child could do. This resonates strongly with the early years curricula in the UK that support starting with the child and building upon their strengths. However, Steiner education has been criticised for not introducing reading until the age of 7.

Two other pioneers of early years education are Friedrich Froebel and Maria Montessori. Both these educators agreed with Steiner's philosophy that childhood is an important phase in its own right, and considered the development of the whole child and recognised the importance of spiritual well-being.

Froebel

'Froebel (1782–1852) is remembered chiefly as the "inventor" of the kindergarten ("children's garden")' (Best, 2016: 1). He was therefore a prominent figure in the provision of education in the early years. The concept of unity in learning and the interconnectedness of learning between adults and children underpin a Froebelian approach to education. To this end, Froebel moved away from a set curriculum and instead became more interested in the process of play. He viewed play as the intermediary between the natural and spiritual, and the emotional and intellectual. Froebel considered play as the highest level of learning and the most spiritual activity of the child, giving meaning to the relationship with the self, others and the universe (Bruce, 2011a; Miller and Pound, 2011). Froebel was an advocate of using the outdoors and nature to develop children's learning. White (2008: 16) describes outdoor play in particular as encouraging an 'emotional connection to the world', assisting children in understanding their spiritual unity with nature.

Montessori

Montessori opened her school called the 'Casa dei Bambini' for children aged 3–6 years in Rome in 1907 (Miller and Pound, 2011). Montessori, like Steiner, believed the environment needed to be prepared, but in contrast to Steiner and Froebel, adults are not encouraged to 'enter the child's world' (Bruce, 2011a: 18). She also, like Steiner and Froebel, did not see the role of the adult as preparing the child for adulthood. Montessori believed that the child was a 'unique individual with a "spiritual embryo" creating its own spiritual characteristics' (Miller and Pound, 2011: 75). For Montessori, the spiritual development of each child was a 'collective mission' for the creation of a better world (Miller, 2002: 19).

There are similarities between Montessori's approach to learning and the EYFS and the FP as follows:

- all children feel secure and valued
- build upon what the child already knows
- observe children and plan based on observations
- the learning environment must be planned and organised.

(Isaacs, 2007: 45)

All three educational pioneers – Steiner, Froebel and Montessori – considered the spiritual well-being of the child as an essential part of their educational philosophy. Further, all three stressed the inner life of the child as one of the most important aspects of child development.

Reflective Question

Reflecting upon your own practice, do you use any of the three approaches detailed to develop a child's spirituality?

Neuroscience Approach to Spiritual Development

Spiritual development can be difficult to define and, as argued earlier, difficult to measure. Zohar and Marshall (2001: 276) found similar issues when they examined the concept of spiritual intelligence, conceding that 'spiritual intelligence cannot be quantified'. Gardner (2000: 30) also cautioned against spiritual intelligence, arguing that the concept of spiritual intelligence is problematic because of a 'lack of convincing evidence about brain structures and processes dedicated to this form of computation'.

Nevertheless, Johnson and Boyatzis (2006) purport that spiritual development is an integral part of normal human cognitive-developmental processes. The cognitive foundations for spiritual development are usually established in the first years of life. Young children are able to understand that people have feelings and thoughts compared to inanimate objects which do not. Religious concepts (including spiritual development) operate under the same conceptual principles and tendencies as everyday cognition. Children's acquisition of religious concepts depend upon how these concepts are assimilated within developing cognitive frameworks (Johnson and Boyatzis, 2006).

Spiritual development and the brain

Richard Griffiths asserts that there are three distinct processing modes within the human brain. These modes are called serial, parallel and synchronous. Serial processing is associated with intellectual intelligence (IQ) and functions in the left brain. Parallel processing is associated with emotional intelligence (EQ) and functions in the right brain. Lastly, synchronous processing is associated with spiritual intelligence (SQ) and functions in the whole brain (Griffiths, n.d.).

The qualities of spiritual intelligence are found in wisdom, compassion, integrity, feelings of joy, love, creativity and peace. Spiritual intelligence and development require children to engage in reflective dialogue and questioning, discussing their thoughts and concerns regarding themselves but also others. Hart (2003) indicated that the phases of spiritual development are more fluid than were once understood, as children have the ability to understand abstract problems, but may struggle to express themselves. He further argued that children were able to recognise complex issues such as injustice, suffering and compassion, thus indicating forms of spiritual intelligence.

In terms of spiritual development (and intelligence) within the curriculum, children are required to develop their thinking skills and engage in critical and creative problem solving (WAG, 2008b). They are required to explore religious education in the twenty-first century through 'a range of philosophical, theological, ethical, and spiritual questions in a reflective, analytical, balanced way that stimulates questioning and debate' (WAG, 2008b: 3). Therefore, it could be argued that as spiritual development requires children to think, analyse, reflect, and question, it does engage the whole brain as detailed above.

Reflective Question

How do you ensure that children are exploring their spiritual intelligence within your setting?

Summary of chapter

- Spiritual development is considered part of religious education in UK curricula.
- Spiritual development is hard to define.
- Fowler identified six stages in his faith development theory.
- Research in 2019 indicated that children from more religious backgrounds performed better in social and moral competences.
- Supporting spiritual development leads to better well-being and economic growth.
- Spiritual development and cultural awareness are interwoven.
- Steiner, Montessori and Froebel all considered spiritual development an important part of their pedagogy.
- There are debates around the concept of a specific spiritual intelligence.

End-of-chapter questions

1. Do you approach spiritual development holistically and, if yes, how?
2. Considering all the approaches to spiritual development detailed in this chapter, which do you think you use the most?
3. How do you evidence spiritual development?

Further reading

Lunn, A. (2015) 'A critical analysis of the role of spirituality within the early years curriculum', *Transformation*, 1 (1). Available at: https://educationstudies.org.uk/journal/tf/volume-1-1-2015/a-critical-analysis-of-the-role-of-spirituality-within-the-early-years-curriculum/

This research paper debates the need for spirituality in the EYFS. This is timely as the draft of the new EYFS framework is out for consultation and it does not mention spirituality within the document.

Moore, K., Gomez-Garibello, C., Bosacki, S. and Talwar, V. (2016) 'Children's spiritual lives: The development of a children's spirituality measure', *Religions*, 7(95): 1–11.

This research paper depicts the initial stages of a children's spirituality measure and considers the limitations of such a measure and future research requirements.

Welsh Assembly Government (2008) 'National exemplar framework for Religious Education for 3 to 19-year-olds in Wales'. Cardiff: WAG.

This policy framework provides an understanding of what is happening in Wales in terms of spiritual development.

FOURTEEN
COGNITIVE DEVELOPMENT

This chapter will help you to

- understand what is meant by cognitive development and how it is viewed through different approaches;
- understand how cognitive development contributes to children's thinking and memory;
- explore cognitive development theories including those of Piaget and Vygotsky.

Introduction

Neaum (2013) defines cognitive development as being concerned with the construction of thought processes and how we understand and use what we learn. Mercer (2018: 103) provides a broader definition of cognition as being 'a range of mental and intellectual states and processes', while Crowley (2017) refers to cognition as the development of skills, including those of memory, thinking and reasoning. Mercer (2018: 111) also states that theory plays an important role in the study of cognitive development 'because cognitive processes are less easily measured or observed than physical ones'.

This chapter will explore these definitions and consider what is meant by cognitive development and how it is viewed through different theories and the interdisciplinary approaches discussed in Part 1.

Developmental Psychology Approach to Cognitive Development

Like other aspects of development, cognition changes with maturation and experience, and developmental trajectories predict a child's cognitive abilities over a number of years. Cognitive developmental tasks, such as learning to talk or read, are associated with age and cognitive developmental charts or milestones are available.

As discussed in Chapter 2, a developmental psychology approach to child development is useful because it is easily understood and provides measurable ways of assessing children

(Neaum, 2019). Here, young children's development is viewed as linear with norms of expected behaviour which naturally lead to adulthood. However, as evidenced in Chapter 2, there are concerns as to whether developmental psychology, by default, normalises child development and privileges certain groups of children in society. Chapter 2 also introduced the theories of Piaget and Vygotsky, and this chapter will further explore the works of both these theorists in relation to cognitive development, starting with Piaget.

Piaget's theory of cognitive development

Piaget's theory of cognitive development is still regarded as the starting point for the development of the child's mind. He developed his theory of cognition through observing his own children and believed that young children were active knowledge constructors. Through exploring their environments and interacting with it, they constructed 'mental structures that allow them to process their worlds' (Crowley, 2017: 78).

Piaget referred to these mental structures as schemas, and these changed through the processes of assimilation and accommodation (1953, 1959, 1970). Piaget believed that children learn through repeated actions and behaviours on objects and materials within their environment. Through these repeated actions, working theories are built up and developed. New experiences are fitted into the existing schema (assimilation) so that equilibrium is maintained or, if the experience is new or different, then the child alters (adapts) their schema to accommodate this new experience. In this way, new thinking and knowledge is constructed and cognitive gains made (Thomas, 2018).

An example is when a child sees a horse and learns that is what it is called (*assimilation*). A little later, s/he sees a zebra for the first time and at first thinks it is a striped horse. Then s/he learns that this isn't the case, but that it is a new animal (*disequilibrium*). S/he needs to *accommodate* the information to take in this new information. When s/he eventually learns that the name of the new animal is a zebra, s/he has accommodated this new information and understanding is restored; s/he has then reached a stage of 'equilibration'. However, although Piaget described the processes of assimilation, accommodation and equilibrium, he did not explain how they operate (Siegler et al., 2017).

Chris Athey (1990, 2007) took Piaget's work on schemas forward in her research at the Froebel Institute and she highlighted that schemas function at four different levels.

Table 14.1 Schema levels

Level 1	Sensorimotor stage	Shown through repeated actions and behaviours
Level 2	Symbolic and language development stage	One thing stands for another and use language to support thinking
Level 3	Functional dependency	Efforts and action
Level 4	Development of thought	Use of logic, reasoning and prior knowledge

Children do not function at one schema level or stage, but move in and out of them in accordance with their developing intellectual capabilities at any given time (Bruce, 2011a). Athey (1990, 2007) further identified the following action-based schemas in her research.

Table 14.2 Action-based schemas

Dynamic vertical (trajectory schema)
Dynamic back and forth (horizontal trajectory schema)
Circular direction and rotation (rotational schema)
Going over, under or on top of
Going round a boundary
Enveloping and containing
Going through a boundary

Athey (2007) confirmed that children gain new ideas and understanding through assimilating experiences (content) into existing thoughts (forms/schemas).

Case Study: Schemas in action

Rashid is 5 years old and is in the reception class. He is quite quiet and shy, preferring his own company. The practitioners have noticed that he enjoys singing to himself and in particular likes nursery rhymes such as 'Humpty Dumpty'. In fact, they have observed Rashid singing 'Humpty Dumpty' over and over in the reading area where he uses a toy caterpillar falling off the bookcase to represent 'Humpty Dumpty' falling down. On a different day Rashid is observed outdoors and spends all his time dropping his jumper into one of the large plastic cubes singing the rhyme '10 green bottles, falling off the wall'. From these observations the practitioners assume that Rashid enjoys singing, so they are surprised when they go over to the main hall for singing time and Rashid refuses to join in and sits on the floor playing with his shoes.

One of the practitioners attends a training course on schemas run by the local authority. On this course she is introduced to the concept of schemas and how they can be seen in action. She reflects upon Rashid's behaviour and thinks he is displaying a trajectory schema. On her return to school, she discussed her thoughts with the other practitioners and comes up with a plan of action for the next singing session. In this session, the practitioners change what they were planning to sing and introduce action-based nursery rhymes such as 'Jack and Jill' and 'Humpty Dumpty'. Rashid becomes very animated and when they ask for children to come out the front and sing the rhymes, he puts his hand straight up. Rashid spends most of the session out the front singing aloud and role playing the rhymes by mimicking the falling down action. Back in the classroom, the practitioners consider other ways they can plan activities that support Rashid's trajectory schema, such as number rhymes that involve jumping actions such as '5 Little Speckled Frogs... '.

This case study illustrates how an informed knowledge of schemas can support children in their ongoing development. Here the practitioners have understood that Rashid has a trajectory schema and have used this to inform future planning, which supports his schema but also his cognitive development.

Reflective Question

Do you use schema as another lens to understand children's actions and, if not, is it something you will now consider?

Piaget's stages of development

Piaget also identified four stages of development: the sensorimotor period; the preoperational stage; the concrete operations stage, and the formal operations stage. A summary of these stages and their links to cognitive development can be found in Table 14.3.

Table 14.3 Piaget's stages of development

Stage	Age	Description
Sensorimotor – includes 6 sub-stages	0–2 years	Cognition is linked to sensory stimulation and movement and understanding object permanence.
Preoperational	2–7 years	Cognition linked to problem solving through thought and active learning. Use of symbols and language development. Lack of understanding of conservation and reversibility. Ability to only focus on one aspect or feature of a problem (centration). Thinking is ego-centric and the belief that inanimate objects have lifelike qualities – i.e., animism.
Concrete operational	7–11 years	Cognition linked to mental processes. Able to solve conservation problems and understand classification and seriation.
Formal operations	11+	End point of cognitive development. Cognition linked to more complex and abstract problem solving. Able to devise hypothetical situations.

As can be seen from the table, Piaget viewed cognitive development in a series of universal stages that follow each other in a sequence. The stages that Piaget suggested are only roughly linked to the chronological ages listed. Some children will show evidence of a particular stage earlier than others or sometimes a bit later, depending on experience and cultural contexts. Children can also be in transition from one stage to another, so may display evidence of two adjacent stages (McDevitt and Ormrod, 2010).

Today, most contemporary developmental theorists now believe that cognitive development occurs in gradual trends rather than discrete stages (Flavell, 1994; Kuhn and Franklin, 2006). Nevertheless, Piaget's view of children as active explorers is still accepted today and forms the ethos of most early years curricula, both nationally and internationally. Further, Piaget's concept of schemas can be seen in early years education as a means of facilitating learning and providing a window into a child's thinking.

Sociological Approach to Cognitive Development

Sociocultural theorists argue that cognitive development takes place through direct interactions between children and other people. This resonates with the sociological perspective of interactionism, as detailed in Chapter 3, which focuses on how individuals interact with one another. Rogoff (2003) discusses the concept of guided participation, where an older, more knowledgeable person arranges activities in such a way that allows younger, less knowledgeable persons to engage in the activities at a higher level than they could manage on their own. The founder of the sociocultural approach to cognitive development was Lev Vygotsky.

Vygotsky's theory of cognitive development

Vygotsky's theory is very often contrasted with that of Piaget, with Piaget emphasising that children understand the world on their own and Vygotsky emphasising the importance of social interaction with others. Piaget emphasised abrupt 'changes in children's thinking and Vygotsky emphasised gradual continuous changes' (Siegler et al., 2017: 173). He recognised that biological factors such as brain maturation played a role in cognitive development. However, Vygotsky's primary focus was on the role of nurture, and how children's social interactions and cultural environments foster cognitive growth (McDevitt and Ormrod, 2010).

Vygotsky viewed language and thought to be integrally related, with thought being internalised speech originating from statements made to children by adults. This again differs from Piaget who viewed language and thought as independent of each other (Siegler et al., 2017). He (Vygotsky) saw the end point of development as the ability to think and reason for oneself, but to get there is a social process. Vygotsky contended that development moves from a stage where children do things with others to a stage where they are independent, and he termed this move from the social plane to the psychological plane 'internalisation' (Crowley, 2017).

Vygotsky identified two kinds of mental processes, which he termed 'functions'. Lower mental functions are basic ways of learning and responding, and higher mental functions are focused cognitive processes that enhance learning and memory. Vygotsky viewed lower mental functions as 'biologically built in', but society and culture are 'critical for the development of higher mental function' (McDevitt and Ormrod, 2010: 211). Vygotsky also developed the concept of the zone of proximal development (ZPD) by suggesting that children had two stages of development: their present level and the next step that required help from a more knowledgeable other (MKO) (Neaum, 2013). Vygotsky did not specify how adults and children could work together in the ZPD, but other researchers have. Wood et al. (1976) developed the idea of social scaffolding where adults continually adjust the support given to children, with the eventual aim for the child to become independent.

A weakness in Vygotsky's theory is that it does not say much about the role of basic cognitive skills in development. His descriptions of development were often lacking in detail (Gauvain, 2001), making it more difficult for researchers to test his theory.

Reflective Question

How do you use the concept of the ZPD and MKO in your practice?

Economic Approach to Cognitive Development

Chapter 4 introduced the concept of human capital theory as being interested in someone's knowledge, skills and abilities, and how they interact with the production cycle of generating wealth (Smith et al., 2016). There is a link between this and what is termed 'cognitive economics'. Cognitive economics is defined as the economics of what is in people's minds and is characterised by its use of a 'distinctive kind of data. This includes data on expectations, hypothetical choices, cognitive ability and expressed attitudes' (Kimball, 2015: 168).

Boyden and Dercon (2012) argue that human capital theory has focused much contemporary thinking and practice. Further, research on human capital has established clear links between 'child development and wider economic and societal development' (Boyden and Dercon, 2012: 23). As a result, studies in this tradition have long focused on exploring the impact of investments in education, health and nutrition on child outcomes (as measured by incomes) and national trends (as measured by economic growth).

Socioeconomic status and cognition

Several studies have reported that children's educational attainment and performance on tests of cognitive ability vary with socioeconomic status (SES), with children from disadvantaged homes and environments having lower achievement than children from advantaged homes and environments (Christensen et al., 2014). Early childhood achievement gaps linked to socioeconomic status emerge before children enter school, and these gaps have been shown to exist and even widen over time (Jefferis et al., 2002; Yeung and Pfeiffer, 2009). These disparities have negative consequences for children's jobs and earnings opportunities, as well as being linked to poor adult health and shorter life expectancy (Christensen et al., 2014).

Researchers have examined the role of family factors, such as the level of cognitive stimulation, parenting style, and parental stress and depression, in explaining the well-documented association between SES and child cognitive development. This resonates with adverse childhood experiences, discussed in Chapter 11, and their impact upon a child's development, including their cognitive development. Low-income families may be unable to have the same amount of cognitively stimulating resources or games, such as books and puzzles, as more advantaged families due to financial and time constraints. Additionally, parents with a higher level of education can be more mindful of the advantages of engaging in cognitively stimulating behaviours early and often (Christensen et al., 2014).

The Welsh Government has attempted to address the impact of SES on children's cognitive development through the Flying Start initiative. It is the targeted Early Years programme for families with children under 4 years of age who live in some of the most disadvantaged areas of Wales. Flying Start aims to make a decisive difference to the life chances of children by mitigating the impact of poverty, which is linked to poor life outcomes in early childhood, and ensuring that young children are reaching their potential (WG, 2017b). Secure attachment, positive parenting and the home environment are key factors in promoting educational success. There is evidence that what happens during the first 1,000 days of a child's life has a significant impact on their outcomes as they grow up. This period covers the time through pregnancy, birth and up until a child's second birthday (WG, 2017b).

Through early intervention programmes like Flying Start, the Welsh Government has stated that it wants a nation of lifelong learners and this is the ethos of the Curriculum for Wales for learners aged 3–16 years, beginning in 2022 (WG, 2020). Although the running costs of Flying Start are high, the Welsh Government believes that in economic terms, this is a price worth paying for the long-term gain of a nation of high-achieving ambitious learners who will bring skills to the workforce and lead to higher economic wealth.

The UK nations have also introduced breakfast clubs in some schools to ensure that all children have a hot meal before they start the school day. This is because research has shown that children's concentration skills and cognitive skills are improved if they start the day with a healthy breakfast (MacGregor, 1999). The cost of breakfast clubs can be met out of the local authority education budget or in some settings charge a nominal amount.

Case Study: Supporting the family to alleviate socioeconomic factors

Eleri and her family live in one of the more deprived areas of South Wales. Eleri is 4 years old and attends the local school, but her attendance is sporadic. When she does attend school, mum is always late and seems very stressed, and there is a younger sibling who mum pushes in a pram when she drops Eleri off. The classroom practitioner has noticed that Eleri never completes any

(Continued)

home school tasks or returns her reading book, and she often seems tired, hungry and lacking in concentration. The practitioner has tried to speak with mum, but she always wants to hurry away and just promises she will send in Eleri's reading book although she never does. During break times, the practitioner notices that Eleri often asks to go back indoors to go to the toilet, so she follows her one day. Inside she finds Eleri going through the other children's lunch boxes and eating their food. Following this incident, the practitioner decides to hold a meeting with the health visitor who is attached to the school to express her concerns and to get advice on the best ways to support Eleri and her mum. Following this meeting, the health visitor arranges to visit Eleri's mum to assess the situation at home. It turns out that Eleri's dad has left the home and mum has been left with little money to feed herself and the two children. The health visitor arranges for Eleri's mum to get Flying Start support for herself and younger child, and directs mum to organisations that can support with finance. After a few weeks, the practitioner notices a real change in Eleri; she is attending the school breakfast club and she has far more energy and her attendance has improved. Eleri is able to concentrate far more, and she shows a real flair for mathematics, jigsaw puzzles and counting games. Mum also seems far less stressed and ensures that Eleri completes any home school tasks and sends in her reading book each week.

This case study is one example of how targeted support can alleviate some of the socioeconomic factors that can adversely affect young children. Once support has been put in place, there is less pressure at home and Eleri is able to thrive in school. Of course, all this is only possible because mum has accepted the support offered and sometimes that is not the case.

Reflective Question

Do you know what interventions or support organisations are available in your area to tackle low SES?

Anthropological Approach to Cognitive Development

Some of the changes that occur in brain development in early childhood are influenced by cultural context. Different cultural activities promote what Lightfoot et al. (2013: 277) term 'experience dependent brain-growth'. A child's brain can develop cells in the region responsible for processing spatial information if the culture emphasises hunting, which requires spatial connections. Conversely, if a child's culture emphasises verbal expression, the language centres of the brain will undergo additional development. One particular cultural activity is termed 'cultural scripts'.

Cultural scripts

Nelson (2009) states that as children participate in organised cultural events, they acquire generalised event representations or scripts. These are referred to as 'cultural scripts' and exist both externally as observable patterns of behaviour through words and daily life practices, and internally as a representation of these tools.

Cultural scripts are a guide to action; they are mental representations that individuals use to understand what will happen next in a familiar situation. Children need a large reserve of scripted knowledge to draw upon in unfamiliar situations, and until they have this, every new activity requires a close attention to detail. Cultural scripts facilitate people within a recognised social group to coordinate actions as the scripts are shared (Lightfoot et al., 2013). Therefore, they become a source of common ways of understanding and meaning making.

As children grow and develop and experience new things, they will acquire a variety of new scripts to add to already familiar scripts. Children are more likely to behave in a logical way in familiar contexts where they know the expected sequence of actions and can correctly interpret the situational requirements. Conversely, in unfamiliar situations they may apply inappropriate scripts and resort to illogical thinking (Lightfoot et al., 2013).

Reflective Question

Have you ever heard of cultural scripts, and how do you think knowledge of them could inform your practice going forwards?

Cultural diversity and metacognition

Metacognition is thinking about one's thinking and learning, and children's metacognitive beliefs are partially a result of the cultural environments they grow up in (McDevitt and Ormrod, 2010). In mainstream Western cultures, knowledge acquisition and learning is for personal benefit in order to understand the world. In contrast, in China, learning has a moral and social dimension to enable individuals to contribute to the betterment of society (McDevitt and Ormrod, 2010).

Children's readiness to objectively assess the knowledge and values that adults hand down to them has also been recognised to have cultural differences. Some cultures place an emphasis on group harmony and discourage children from critiquing and discussing controversial topics (Kuhn and Park, 2005). Many teachers in East Asia favour rote learning and memorisation. In contrast, in Western cultures there is an emphasis on making sense of teaching materials rather than memorisation. However, there are occasions where Western cultures will revert to memorisation and rote learning, such as learning spellings or multiplication tables (Wang and Ross, 2007).

Philosophical Approach to Cognitive Development

Edward de Bono, a Maltese physician and philosopher, is recognised as one of the leaders in critical thinking and problem solving – skills required for the twenty-first century economy (Kivunja, 2015). He wrote the book *Six Thinking Hats* and is a proponent of the teaching of thinking as a subject in schools. Using the metaphor of wearing various coloured hats, De Bono has devised a model that, when properly implemented, greatly enhances strategic thinking and provides opportunities for solving any problems that might arise. De Bono's conviction that 'simple methods used efficiently are more useful than complex methods that are difficult to understand and use' (1992a: 6) is reflected in the model. He claims that 'when we attempt practical thought, there are three fundamental difficulties' (De Bono, 1992b: 8) as follows:

1. **Emotions** We often have a tendency not to think at all, but to rely on instant gut feeling, emotion and prejudice as a basis for action.
2. **Helplessness** We may react with feelings of inadequacy: 'I don't know how to think about this. I don't know what to do next.'
3. **Confusion** We try to keep everything in mind at once, with a mess as a result.

Wearing a different coloured hat allows the wearer to approach a problem from a different angle, allowing them to think objectively about it and come up with possible solutions (Kivunja, 2015). De Bono argues that the six hats method allows the use of emotions at the right time and that helplessness can be overcome by the different hats providing a framework for thinking actions and next steps (1992a). Confusion is avoided by the six hats methods, allowing for one direction of thought at a time. Table 14.1 depicts what each hat represents.

Table 14.4 The conceptual thinking associated with each hat

Hat	Thinking
Red hat	Feelings, emotions, hunches and intuition
White hat	Gathering data to understand the issue or problem
Green hat	Creative critical thinking or problem solving
Yellow hat	Values and benefits of why the solution to the problem might work
Blue hat	Metacognition and organisational thinking
Black hat	Cautious critical thinking and checking out alternative approaches to problem solving

De Bono's thinking hats can be applied in schools across all subject areas and in addressing whole-school issues. Not all the hats need to be used every time, and for younger children it is more sensible to use fewer hats. The hats can be a pen-and-paper exercise, or the actual hats can be worn while thinking about the given problem. The following case study demonstrates how the hats can be used with children aged 6–7 years in addressing issues that occur during lunchtime in the school yard.

Case Study: Using thinking hats to address lunchtime issues on the school yard

The lunchtime supervisors at Fairfield Primary School have been complaining about the behaviour of some of the Year 2 children (6- to 7-year-olds) playing football on the yard. There have been issues with the footballs going on the school roof and being kicked out onto the road running alongside the school. There have also been incidents of fighting and squabbling among the children over who gets to take part in the football games. Younger children have also been hit by the footballs, resulting in several bruised arms and legs. Some children have also complained that only footballs are available to play with. Therefore, the school council (including several Year 2 children) has been asked to think of a solution to this problem.

The problem is addressed using De Bono's thinking hats, and the following solutions are put forward:

Monday: Football

Tuesday: Yard games

Wednesday: Football

Thursday: Netball

Friday: Rugby and other games

This solution is taken back to the children involved and to the lunchtime supervisors. It is agreed that this will be trialled for the next month and feedback discussed in the next school council meeting.

This case study demonstrates using De Bono's hats to address a whole-school problem. Here, the children have gone through each hat in turn to address the problem and to find a potential solution. The hats can be used as a reflection tool, too, once feedback has been received to see if the solution has worked or if the problem needs rethinking.

Reflective Question

Where could you use De Bono's thinking hats in your practice to develop critical thinking skills?

Neuroscience Approach to Cognitive Development

Chapter 7 defined cognitive neuroscience as understanding 'what happens in the brain when we have emotions, or thoughts, or when we create art, or music, or when we read and write' (Goswami,

2020: 1). Although the importance of focusing upon neuroscience and brain development cannot be ignored, a young child's brain is still relatively immature. Various parts of the brain are still developing and connecting at different times and rates, and this may account for the unevenness of cognitive development. There are a number of different theories relating to cognition, memory and brain development, which will be explored further.

Information-processing theories

Piaget and Vygotsky sought to provide a single broad-based theory of cognitive development, but information-processing theories focus on more specific aspects of cognition, such as attention, problem solving and memory (Crowley, 2017). Here a comparison is made between a computer and the human mind, where we receive information from the outside world which is stored, organised, and manipulated and used to provide a useful output such as a solution to a given problem. This theory proposes that information flows through three stores: sensory register, short-term (working) memory and long-term memory (Crowley, 2017).

Table 14.5 How information flows through the three stores

Sensory register	Stores details such as visual images and sounds for brief periods	Can enter short-term or working memory, but only lasts a few seconds
Short-term or working memory	Mental workspace, retains information for brief periods while we operate on it	Example is mental arithmetic where we need to keep numbers in mind while doing multiplication. Information lasts for a period of seconds
Long-term memory	Permanent knowledge base	No capacity limits, highly organised, forms an associative network where related units of information are stored together

Information-processing theorists have suggested that the primary process by which information moves from the sensory register into working memory is attention. More complex processes are then needed to remember information for longer periods by making connections between new information, and concepts and ideas that exist in long-term memory (McDevitt and Ormrod, 2010). The information-processing mechanism does not alter with cognitive development, but the mechanisms that operate on the information do.

Memory development follows a consistent pattern (Flavell et al., 2002). Initially, children appear not to have a strategy, then they go through a phase called 'production deficiency' – There is the capacity to use a strategy, but they do not use it spontaneously, although they can be instructed to use it. This is followed by utilisation deficiency where children spontaneously use a strategy to no positive effect. Some children also show evidence of a strategy inefficiency where a strategy is applied, but in an inefficient and inconsistent manner. Lastly, children acquire a mature strategy where it is used spontaneously and applied to a variety of tasks yielding positive results (Crowley, 2017).

Although research into brain development and cognitive development is ongoing, what has been learnt can support practitioners and others working with children to provide activities and resources to nurture, shape and develop children's cognition.

Reflective Question

What strategies do you use with children in your setting to help develop their memory skills?

Summary of chapter

- Both Piaget and Vygotsky proposed theories of cognitive development.
- Piaget emphasised that children acquire knowledge on their own through a series of universal developmental stages.
- Vygotsky emphasised the role of social interaction in acquiring knowledge and introduced the ZPD.
- Information-processing theory consists of a system with a sensory store, a short-term memory store and a long-term memory store.
- There is a recognition that SES impacts upon cognitive development, and that early intervention can reverse some of the effects of low SES.
- Cultural scripts are a guide to action; they are mental representations that individuals use to understand what will happen next in a familiar situation.
- Edward De Bono introduced the concept of the six thinking hats to develop critical thinking.

End-of-chapter questions

1. Reflecting upon the theories of Piaget and Vygotsky, which do you use most in your practice and why?
2. Are there any new approaches detailed in this chapter that you will now adopt in practice?
3. What research can you do now to develop your own understanding of cognitive development?

Further reading

De Bono, E. (2009) *Six Thinking Hats*. London: Penguin Books.

Although this book dates from 2009, it gives a comprehensive overview of how to use the thinking hats in practice and is a worldwide bestseller.

Gathercole, S.E. and Alloway, T. (2008) *Working Memory and Learning: A Practical Guide for Teachers*. London: SAGE.

An account of how research into short-term memory can be applied to learning. It offers practitioners ways to support children with poor working memory in the classroom.

Louis, S., Beswick, C., Mcgraw, L., Hayes, L. and Featherstone, S. (ed.) (2011) *Again! Again!* London: A&C Black.

This book gives a really clear introduction to schemas and provides definitions, examples and resources of action-based schemas observed in young children.

FIFTEEN
LANGUAGE DEVELOPMENT

This chapter will help you to

- understand what is meant by language development and how it is viewed through different approaches;
- understand the biological and environmental aspects of language development;
- explore language development theories including those of Chomsky and Skinner.

Introduction

Language is the way we communicate, and studies of language development are an essential part of child development (Neaum, 2013; Mercer, 2018). The 'Development Matters' guidance (DfE, 2020: 6) asserts that 'planning to help every child to develop their language is vital'. Language use requires comprehension (understanding what is being said) and production (actually speaking or writing or using sign language) (Siegler et al., 2017). At birth, babies show a preference for speech over other kinds of sounds and within a few days of being born can recognise their native language from foreign languages (Lightfoot et al., 2013). In fact, a typically developing child will learn several words a day during pre-school and by the time they are 6 years old, their vocabulary will have expanded to between 8,000 and 14,000 words (Biemiller and Slonim, 2001).

This chapter will explore how this growth in language development occurs and how it is viewed through different theories and the interdisciplinary approaches discussed in Part 1.

Developmental Psychology Approach to Language Development

There are several theories on language development that have contributed to understanding how children develop the ability to talk (James, 2005). The behaviourist perspective of language development is linked to Skinner (1957) and is based upon the learning theory of reinforcement and operant conditioning. Here, parents and care-givers praise and reward young children's use of speech sounds, thus encouraging the children to continue (McDevitt and Ormrod, 2010). The transition from babbling sounds to word production occurs through 'shaping'. Adults 'selectively reinforce children for vocalising real words and then for vocalising "correct sentences"' (Crowley, 2017: 203).

Bandura (1989) also proposed a social learning theory of language development that stressed the role of observation and imitation in children's language development. Listening to others and imitating their behaviour is how children learn vocabulary and phrases.

Case Study: Imitation and observation in language development

Erin is studying childcare and is undertaking a placement in a busy Year 1 class in a local primary school. She attends this placement on a Thursday and Friday each week as part of her course. The practitioners have been really pleased with Erin so far as she is enthusiastic and engaged with the children. She gets down to their level, asks them lots of questions, listens to them and makes direct eye contact and models correct language.

However, one Friday Erin arrives late, and she looks unkempt and washed out. One of the practitioners asks if she is OK and Erin replies 'yes'. She is asked to work with a group of children in the outdoor space re-enacting the story 'We are going on a Bear Hunt'. Usually, Erin loves being outdoors with the children, so the practitioners hope this will perk her up.

At morning break, one of the classroom practitioners is on duty when she notices a group of children who have been working with Erin seeming to be quite agitated. She wanders over to listen to what they are saying. One of the children is pretending to be on the phone and she is arguing with someone quite loudly. The child is using inappropriate language and the rest of the children around her are giggling and nudging each other. The practitioner asks the children to follow her indoors. Inside, she asks the children what they were doing, and they tell her they were copying what Erin had been doing and saying outside when they were working with her.

The practitioner asks to speak to Erin and for her to explain what she has just been told by the children. Erin becomes upset and apologises, explaining she had been on the phone to her boyfriend, and they were fighting, which is why she had used inappropriate language. She explained she did not realise that the children could hear her. The practitioner explains that this is a serious incident as she will have to let the children's parents know what has happened in case they repeat the language they have heard at home. She also explains that they will need to call Erin's tutor as there is a strict no-phone policy during school hours, which Erin knew about.

This case study illustrates how young children will imitate the language they have heard, regardless of whether it is appropriate or not. Everyone working with young children has a duty to ensure they are a good role model and that they reinforce the correct and appropriate use of language.

Reflective Question

How would you have handled this situation and how would you ensure that the children understand it is not acceptable to use inappropriate language?

Crowley (2017: 203) argues that there is some support for reinforcement and imitation in language development as at a 'basic level children acquire the language they are exposed to'. However, Crowley (2017) goes on to contend that learning theory cannot provide a complete account of language development and that there have been several criticisms of this theory. Reinforcement of language cannot support the speed at which language is acquired and when a child is reinforced for a correct utterance, they do not receive direct feedback on what was correct about their speech. Further, it has been observed that parents do not correct grammatical errors and this criticism of learning theory is termed the 'poverty of the stimulus argument' (Crowley, 2017: 203).

Chomsky (1959, 1965) also refutes this theory of language development. He states that the language children hear is often fragmented, hesitant and provides a poor model for learning. Further, the speech of young children includes many utterances that are grammatically incorrect and which they would not have heard from an adult. He proposed the nativist theory of language development.

Nativist approach to language development

The nativist theory of language development proposes that language is innate and biological. Chomsky stated that children have a built-in language device called the 'language acquisition device' (LAD) (McDevitt and Ormrod, 2010: 315). This LAD enables children to learn complex aspects of language in a short time. However, Chomsky has revised his initial theory to replace the LAD with an innate capability called 'universal grammar' (Crowley, 2017: 204). There are a number of characteristics that are common to all languages, and children are not taught grammar; rather, this innately defined universal grammar allows children to infer the rules of their language. This is done by a procedure known as parameter setting (Crowley, 2017). Many psychologists share Chomsky's idea that babies are born not knowing any specific language but inherit some predispositions that help them in attaining linguistic knowledge and skills. At a very early age, infants can detect differences within similar speech sounds.

Margaret Donaldson disputes the idea of a LAD. She contends that language development happens because the child has other cognitive skills, including being able to make sense of human situations (Donaldson, 1978). In this theory, the child is seen as an active participant in the world and not passive recipients of experience (behaviourist theory of language development) and they do not have an innate ability to learn language (nativist theory). This was categorised by Bruner who stated: 'children... needed to have a working knowledge of the world before they acquired language' (1983: 34).

Regardless of which language is being learnt, children seem to progress through milestones at similar ages. Certainly, nearly all early years curricula have language milestones, outcomes or goals that children are measured against. Table 15.1 summarises the stages or milestones typical children go through in developing language. It also considers the importance of the adult's role.

Table 15.1 Language development from birth to 8 years

Age	Stage of language development	Role of the adult
0–6 months	Eye contact and babbling. Imitation and repetition of sounds.	Good eye contact. Repetition of phrases and praise and recognition of attempts to communicate.
6–18 months	First words, pointing and responses to familiar objects. By 15 months use of up to 15 words.	Getting down to child's level. Eye contact is important. Children need to feel understood and listened to. Introduction of rhymes and books and songs. Adults to provide lots of commentaries for children to follow.
18 months–3 years	Children's vocabulary increases rapidly. At the age of 3, children put sentences together and start to ask questions. They can follow and enjoy stories and remember rhymes. By 3 years of age, they are using up to 900 words.	Allow children enough time to think and answer questions. Be patient as children often repeat questions and like to ask for the same story and song repeatedly. Reinforce the correct use of grammar.
3–8 years	At the age of 5 years most children have a vocabulary of 3,000 words. They are able to use complex sentences and ask detailed questions. They can understand simple jokes. By the time they are 8, they can use language in many different ways such as socialising, expressing needs, recounting and predicting events.	Extend children's vocabulary and support them to use language as a form of thinking. Ask open questions, give children time to respond and show you are listening. Continue to make good eye contact. If they use swear words, explain this is not acceptable. Continue with stories and rhymes.

Adapted from: Tassoni, 2007: 38.

As always, these milestones are a guide, and all children are unique and will meet these language milestones at different rates. 'Development Matters' makes the point that 'development is like a spider's web with many strands, not a straight line' (DfE, 2020: 6).

Nativist theorists also state there is a critical period for language development, when the brain is particularly ready to process language. Language development after this period becomes very difficult (Crowley, 2017). Today, many researchers prefer the idea of sensitive periods for language development.

Information-processing approach to language development

Cognitive theorists such as Piaget put forward an alternative version of the nativist theory. He argued against a specialist inborn language-acquisition device, and instead proposed the role of 'innate cognitive and information-processing abilities' (Crowley, 2017: 206). Piaget (1967) argued that cognitive development drives language development. Language does not appear until after the sensorimotor period/stage (see Chapter 14), and language learning does not start before cognitive abilities like object permanence have occurred. Piaget's view of the learner as being active supports many of the phonic programmes on offer to develop children's recognition of letter sounds. Many of these programmes combine the learning of letter sounds with action rhymes and songs, making learning phonics action-orientated.

Effective communication and use of language is about appropriate eye contact, gestures and tone of voice used (McDevitt and Ford, 1987). Children automise many aspects of language such as pronunciation and the retrieval of common words.

Reflective Question

Which theory of language development resonates most strongly with you, and what have you seen and used in practice?

Sociological Approach to Language Development

Sociocultural theorists argue that language development takes place through direct interactions between children and other people. This resonates with the sociological perspective of interactionism, as detailed in Chapter 3, which focuses on how individuals interact with one another. Information-processing theories, as discussed earlier, consider the cognitive processes involved in language use and acquisition. In contrast, sociocultural theories focus on how social interactions support language development. Here, children are socialised to use language termed 'language socialisation' (McDevitt and Ormrod, 2010: 317). This involves explicit instructions about language (such as saying 'please' and 'thank you') and more indirect, appropriate linguistic behaviours (modelling of turn taking and other social cultural conventions). Social interactions provide opportunities for children to internalise their language, linking to Vygotsky's theory of cognitive development.

Vygotsky and language development

Vygotsky stated that initially children use words when interacting with others and then, through the process of internalisation, incorporate these words into everyday thought processes (McDevitt and Ormrod, 2010). Thought and language are initially separate systems from the beginning of life, merging at around 3 years of age, producing verbal thought (inner speech). Vygotsky's theory was that children learn from being part of a social context and he made the link between the roles of *more knowing* people in helping children to construct knowledge and develop thinking, with dialogue supporting the understanding of the children's learning continuum. What appears first on the social plane is internalised and becomes part of a child's thinking; language supports cognitive development and social interactions benefit children's thinking due to the input of language (Vygotsky, 1978).

Young children will often talk to themselves, and Vygotsky termed this private speech and felt it was 'a powerful tool for regulating behaviour' (Crowley, 2017: 88). Language facilitates children in reflecting upon different situations, allowing them to select ways forward and choose which action to take. More challenging tasks show an increase in private speech and its use showed better task performance (Fernyhough and Fradley, 2005). As children get older, this private speech becomes more internalised and disappears.

Functionalism and language development

Chapter 3 also discussed functionalism. Functionalism argues that social behaviour is often described as a product of society. In terms of language development, functionalism asks why children want to learn language. Some have argued that we have developed language skills because language serves a range of functions, such as allowing us to develop the social behaviours that are expected within society. For children, language helps them to acquire knowledge and develop interpersonal relationships, influencing their behaviours and the behaviour of others.

Functionalists believe that language is closely aligned with development in other domains, such as cognitive development, and social and emotional development. Within cognitive development, symbols allow children to mentally represent and recall events. This allows them to exchange information and ideas with others. In social and emotional development, conversations and conflicts with others enable children to learn socially acceptable ways of behaving and how to function successfully within society (McDevitt and Ormrod, 2010).

Reflective Question

Have you taken the time to listen to children's private speech when they are engaged in tasks and, if so, have you considered using it to inform how you support children's development?

Economic Approach to Language Development

Many chapters in Part 2 of this book have viewed an economic approach to development through a socioeconomic lens, and language development is no exception. The 'Best Start for Life' (Early Years Healthy Development Review, 2021) is explicit in that the first 1,001 days (birth to 2 years) are critical for all aspects of development, including communication skills. Chronic stress through economic hardship such as poverty can and does negatively impact a child's development. The OECD (2002) found that low literacy levels led to social disadvantage over time.

Before the Coronavirus pandemic and the need for lockdowns, initiatives such as 'Flying Start' in Wales and 'Sure Start Centres' in England provided support for disadvantaged families in all aspects of child development, including supporting children's language development. However, since lockdown these initiatives have not been able to fully function, and reduced social contact and social isolation is a concern for children's development, including their language development (Early Years Healthy Development Review, 2021). Socioeconomic status can have a significant impact upon children's language development.

Socioeconomic status and language development

A seminal study by Hart and Risley (1995), cited in McDevitt and Ormrod (2010), recorded the speech that 42 parents used with their children over two and a half years from before the children could talk until the age of 3. Parents varied in socioeconomic status from upper middle-class to working-class to those on state benefits. Results showed that the average child with parents on benefits received half the linguistic experiences as those with working-class parents, and less than one-third of the average child in an upper middle-class family.

This research focused attention on disparities with income and language input, and resulted in various policy initiatives to raise parental awareness of how often they talked to their children. Children from higher socioeconomic backgrounds have a larger vocabulary when compared with children from lower socioeconomic backgrounds. Research with young children from low-income families by Hirsh-Pasek et al. (2015) found that the richness of communication, such as engagement, routines, rituals, and fluency, was able to predict children's language attainment a year later. Here the quality of parent–child interactions were a better indicator of language development than the amount of speech heard. This is important, as children from poorer backgrounds may be living in noisy, overcrowded accommodation, so quality interactions here are even more important.

However, the negative effects of lower socioeconomic status on language development can be negated by interventions such as greater access to books, where parents will expose their children to new words. This is evidenced in the 'Development Matters' guidance which states:

> Reading frequently to children, and engaging them actively in stories, non-fiction, rhymes and poems, […] *provides* them with extensive opportunities to use and embed new words in a range of contexts. (DfE, 2020: 13)

Research has also found that in education settings, if pre-school children who already have low language skills are placed with children who also have low language skills, then language growth is less compared to children who are placed with peers who have high language skills (Justice et al., 2011). However, negative peer effects can be offset by positive practitioner effects. Dickinson and Porche (2011) contended that pre-school teachers who used a rich and varied vocabulary with their children showed better reading comprehension in comparison with teachers who used a more limited vocabulary.

Reflective Question

If you audited all the different ways you develop language with your children, are there gaps in what you do and, if so, how can these be addressed?

Anthropological Approach to Language Development

Pragmatic aspects of language development include both verbal and non-verbal communication strategies. Pragmatic knowledge includes sociolinguistic behaviours that are the polite and socially acceptable verbal interactions in a particular culture (McDevitt and Ormrod, 2010). Children begin to acquire pragmatic skills such as saying 'please' and 'thank you' before reaching school age. They also learn what are not acceptable gestures and language, such as being rude to adults and peers. However, cultural differences in sociolinguistic behaviours can lead to misunderstandings in cross-cultural interactions.

In some Asian cultures children are taught to show neutral facial expressions, and an adult from a different culture may consider this to mean that the child is bored or not paying attention. Some cultures consider talking a lot (as seen in Western cultures) as an indicator of immaturity or 'low intelligence' (McDevitt and Ormrod, 2010: 336). In Southeast Asian communities, children learn only to engage in conversation with adults when they have been invited to do so. These children rarely ask questions, unlike in Western cultures where children are encouraged to ask questions. Eye contact in European cultures is an indication that you are trying to communicate or that you are listening, but in other cultures (African American, Chinese and Hispanic) direct eye contact is seen as being disrespectful. In these cultures, children are taught to look down in the company of adults (Trawick-Smith, 2014).

Knowing about cultural differences can impact upon how practitioners communicate with the children in their care. Practitioners often ask a question and wait a relatively short time for a child to answer. If no answer is quickly forthcoming the practitioner may answer the question themselves or ask another child to answer. In some cultures, it is usual to leave lengthy pauses before responding to a question, so allowing time to respond will increase the participation of different children (Grant and Gomez, 2001).

Children learn many cultural conventions through imitating the behaviour of others (think back to Bandura and role modelling earlier in this chapter). They may copy the language used at home by adults and the feedback received may encourage certain behaviours, but this can result in a culture shock if the language and behaviour used outside of school is very different. This can in turn impact upon children's development and achievement (McDevitt and Ormrod, 2010). Practitioners need to be aware about different sociolinguistic patterns and keep these in mind when devising lessons and activities. They can also provide guidance and role modelling of missing skills such as not interrupting conversations or dominating a conversation.

Case Study: Addressing cultural differences

Xin Yu has recently arrived in the reception class. She is a very quiet and timid child who has found it very difficult to engage in any conversation with her peers or the practitioners in the classroom. Xin Yu does not answer any questions and usually looks down when asked anything.

The practitioners have carried out an initial baseline profile with Xin Yu and she has not scored very highly in any categories, including language development. They have tried to speak with mum, but she has limited English, and she also makes little eye contact with the staff. The staff want to engage with Xin Yu and they try to think of ways to get her to communicate with them and her peers. One of the practitioners researches Chinese culture and discovers that looking down when speaking to someone unfamiliar is a sign of respect and that silence after being asked a question, indicates appropriate thought and consideration. She thinks of an activity that she can do with Xin Yu that will get her to communicate more but in her own time. The practitioner comes up with the idea of communication pebbles. Here pebbles are painted with images and children can pick one or more pebbles as a stimulus to talk about.

The practitioner spends some time with Xin Yu and shows her the pebbles where she has drawn a number of images ranging from animals to colours and simple objects. She waits until Xin Yu is ready to pick one of the pebbles and then she asks her to tell her why she has chosen that one. The practitioner is careful to give Xin Yu as much time as she wants to answer her. Later that week, the practitioner asks Xin Yu to choose a pebble to take home, which she does to share with her family. Over the next few days, the practitioner sits and chats with Xin Yu about the pebbles and then Xin Yu brings in a pebble from home which she has painted red and gold. She is keen to tell the practitioner and other children that red and gold are considered lucky colours in her culture.

As Xin Yu grows in confidence, she starts to take the initiative more in communicating with her peers and the practitioners. Here the pebbles have acted as a stimulus in supporting Xin Yu's growing confidence in communicating with the practitioner but also with the other children.

This case study shows the importance of taking time to learn about different cultural expectations and how they impact upon how children present themselves in settings. By doing some research, the practitioner has realised that not answering questions straight away and looking down does not mean that Xin Yu did not know the answer but is taking time to think about the answer. By introducing the communication pebbles as a way of starting a conversation, the practitioner has allowed Xin Yu to take her time, not to feel rushed and to think about which pebble she wants and why. This has built up her confidence and being at ease with her peers in the classroom. Of course, communication pebbles can be used in any setting and with all children from all cultures.

Reflective Question

What different communication strategies have you used with children in your setting and how have they supported different cultural expectations?

Philosophical Approach to Language Development

One of the oldest philosophical questions asks whether one can have thinking without language, and in the domain of theory of mind, this question achieves new significance (de Villiers, 2000). Chapter 10 discussed theory of mind in terms of social development, but this chapter also recognised that language development and social interactions provides the ability to reflect on thoughts and label mental states. In Western mainstream culture, there is a psychology/philosophy of mind that argues that behaviour is guided by desires and beliefs, and at around the age of 2, children's speech will include particular words concerning desires and intentions (de Villiers, 2000; Crowley, 2017). The child in acquiring the appropriate talk about the mind is learning a type of discourse and discussion that helps her fit into society.

Philosophy for children (P4C) and circle time

Philosophy for children (P4C) is also an approach to learning and teaching that enhances children's thinking and communication skills. P4C encourages participants to engage in open debate rather than simply exchanging thoughts and viewpoints as if they were bits of data; instead, they ask questions, sift through claims, and consider alternatives. A stimulus is shared with a group of children in P4C, such as a story, video clip or picture. The practitioner encourages the children to come up with big, engaging philosophical questions about the stimulus (Sapere, n.d.). Children choose which question they want to discuss, and they are given time to reflect and ponder this question before discussing it.

Similarly, younger children can take part in circle time activities where an object is passed around a circle and children can choose to talk when they are holding the object. Circle time can be used to discuss a range of topics and empowers children through giving them time to listen and think about what they want to say. As White (2009: 31) states: 'circle time is about positive communication and interaction'.

Reflective Question

What is your philosophy of language development?

Neuroscience Approach to Language Development

'Language is a species-specific behaviour – only humans acquire language' and 'it is species-universal, language learning is achieved by typically developing infants across the globe' (Siegler et al., 2017: 242). Scientists have long understood that the left side of the brain has a dominant role in language ability (Lightfoot et al., 2013; Siegler et al., 2017). Neuroimaging studies have shown that spurts in a toddler's vocabulary happens 'only after substantial myelination of language-related brain regions' (Pujol et al., 2006, cited in Lightfoot et al., 2013: 240).

Research has found that injuries to the left hemisphere of the brain are more likely to cause aphasia (inability to understand or produce speech). Research with children who have suffered a brain injury before, during or after birth which has cut off the blood supply to the left hemisphere of the brain, have still been able to acquire language albeit at a lower level than their peers. This is due to brain plasticity in infants where the right hemisphere takes over as the language centre from the damaged left hemisphere. This indicates that the brain's mechanism for supporting language is not fixed at birth, but undergoes specific changes as a child's language abilities progress (Brauer et al., 2011).

Research has also indicated that it is far easier to learn a second language in early childhood than as an adult. Newport (1990, cited in Siegler et al., 2017: 245) stated that children are better at learning another language because their perceptual and memory limitations cause young children to 'extract and store smaller chunks of the language than adults do'. The essential building blocks of language are quite small, so young children's limited cognitive abilities can 'facilitate the task of analyzing and learning language' (Siegler et al., 2017: 245). Adults who do learn a second language after puberty use different neural mechanisms to process that language compared to adults who learned a second language as infants (Siegler et al., 2017).

Autistic spectrum disorders and language development

Children who are on the autistic spectrum disorder can struggle with communication. Some children exhibit echolalia where they repeat back what has been said to them without understanding the meaning. Speech can be stilted and formal, and they can have difficulties with non-literal language such as irony and sarcasm (Kerig et al., 2012).

However, recent studies of language development with children with autism have concluded that the pattern of language development is very variable. Some children will display some features such as echolalia, while others do not, and some children on the autistic spectrum develop language in a comparable way to children who are typically developing (Crowley, 2017). Crowley (2017) concludes that a widely accepted view today of the communication difficulties experienced by some on the autistic spectrum is due to the absence of the ability to understand other people's mental states, known as theory of mind (discussed earlier in this chapter).

Case Study: Communicating with children on the autistic spectrum

The practitioners at Fairfield Infant School are keen to support a little boy who has just started in the nursery and has been diagnosed as being on the autistic spectrum. Sam is 3 years old and has very little speech and does not interact with other children or practitioners. He has been appointed a

(Continued)

one-to-one teaching assistant (David) to support him in the classroom, and David is keen to explore alternative ways to develop communication skills with Sam.

Sam attends a local nurture unit two days a week with David where a specialist speech and language therapist works with Sam and David to learn Makaton (a language programme that uses symbols, signs and speech to enable people to communicate). David is keen for other practitioners and children in the nursery setting to learn Makaton, too, so he arranges some after-school sessions where he teaches the other practitioners some basic Makaton to use with Sam. He also teaches the children some Makaton so they can also communicate with Sam. The children and practitioners learn some basic commands and everyday words to use. Soon this becomes part of everyday practice in the setting.

As the Christmas nativity play approaches, the practitioners decide to learn how to sign 'Away in a Manger' with the children and Sam. On the day of the nativity play, the children sing the traditional Christmas carol 'Away in a Manger', but also sign along to the words with Sam and David. In this way Sam, while not able to be part of the nativity with words, was able to be part of it through communicating via sign language.

The above case study indicates the different ways of communication that facilitate children in becoming part of a setting. David has embraced learning a different way to communicate with Sam and has encouraged other practitioners and children in the setting to join in. In this way Sam can communicate with his peers and with David, and feel a sense of belonging and not feel isolated from others.

Reflective Question

What strategies have you used with children who have communication difficulties?

Summary of chapter

- There are a number of different theories of language development.
- Language is a cultural tool and different cultures embrace different rules of language development.
- Language development is both biological and environmental.
- The left hemisphere is the brain's centre for language development.
- There is a developmental sequence in language development.
- There is evidence to suggest that children from poorer backgrounds can have poorer language development.
- Learning disabilities can vary in their impact upon language development.
- Learning a second language is easier for younger children.

End-of-chapter questions

1. Which theory of language development aligns most closely with your practice?
2. Out of all the different interdisciplinary approaches to language development in this chapter, which one do you feel you need to learn more about?
3. What strategies do you use to negate the effects of social disadvantage and its impact upon language development?

Further reading

Education Endowment Foundation. 'Nuffield Early Language Intervention scaled up as an important response to the impact of the pandemic on school starters'. Available at: https://educationendowmentfoundation.org.uk/news/62000-reception-age-pupils-in-england-to-take-part-in-early-language-programme/

Information on an intervention to negate the impact of COVID-19 on young children's language development.

Elizabeth Jarmen: 'Communication friendly spaces'. Available at: https://elizabethjarman.com/

Visit this website for an overview of Elizabeth Jarmen's work on how to declutter the learning environment to encourage language development.

Fletcher, P. (2016) *Language Development and Language Impairment: A Problem-Based Introduction.* Chichester: John Wiley.

This book explores and examines a child's language development, both typically and atypically.

PART THREE

UNDERSTANDING CONTEMPORARY ASPECTS OF EARLY CHILDHOOD PRACTICE

SIXTEEN

UNDERSTANDING PLAY THROUGH THE DISCIPLINES AND DOMAINS

This chapter will help you to

- appreciate the role of the adult in enabling children's play;
- develop an interdisciplinary understanding of play;
- develop an understanding of how play facilitates child development.

Introduction

Part 3 of this book applies the theoretical content about the seven disciplines from Part 1 and the child development domains from Part 2 within the context of various contemporary aspects, such as play and playfulness, well-being, global curricula, inclusion and shared spaces (i.e., the learning environment) in order to understand the implications for practice.

As a contemporary aspect of practice, play is interpreted in many different ways and there are usually subtle differences in the ways that practitioners interpret play. Moreover, play is often described as being ambiguous in nature and difficult to define. Andrews (2012) suggests that play is used as a noun, a verb and an adjective, and this is why there is sometimes confusion or differences in understandings. Fisher (2013) states that a single definition of play does not exist. According to some, making identical Christmas cards and counting tea cups and saucers in the role-play area constitutes play (Canning, 2011). How you define play will depend on your values and beliefs about childhood and its purpose. Play is not solely a medium for socialisation; it is a process whereby children learn about themselves and discover the world around them (Canning, 2011). 'Play involves a complex interaction of opportunity, motivation, disposition and skill' (Andrews, 2012: 11) and Fisher (2013) highlights that play is something that children naturally do.

Being playful or the notion of playfulness is usually described as a behaviour and an attitude, and is not always owned by a child and can be adult-led (Andrews, 2012; McInnes et al., 2011). Children could be playfully engaging but not necessarily playing in its purest form. McInnes et al. (2011) suggest that playfulness (verb or adjective) can be beneficial for learning rather than the play itself (noun). Children's perceptions of play are very helpful in understanding playfulness, and there is evidence to show how children can differentiate between play and not play activities (McInnes et al., 2011).

Playful pedagogies

Andrews (2012: 155) contends that as play is often considered the opposite to work, then it is 'at odds with the idea of pedagogy'. Pedagogy, defined usually as teaching and classroom management, can lead to concerns over play becoming a mechanism for learning. Rinaldi (2013) suggests that they are not the same, but are closely related. She stresses the importance of a 'play-based curriculum' for the playing learning child.

Playfulness in the curriculum

Despite tensions between the two terms, a number of early years curricula espouse a playful pedagogy as underpinning their curricula (DfE, 2015; Education Scotland, 2020; WG, 2015a). A review into England's Early Years Foundation Stage (EYFS) pedagogy found a number of strengths, including an emphasis on 'age-appropriateness and play in pedagogy' (DfE, 2015: 4). The EYFS framework advocates that each area of learning and development must be applied through purposeful play and a combination of adult-led and child-initiated activities. The framework further states that play is vital for a child's growth, as it teaches them to explore, think about problems and interact with others (DfE, 2017).

Similarly in Wales, the Foundation Phase (FP) framework clearly expresses that children should practise and consolidate their learning through play. In play, they experiment with ideas, take risks, solve issues, and make decisions alone, in small and large groups. Play is also evident in education policy in Scotland, with a prominence that play is a fundamental and integral part of healthy development (Education Scotland, 2020).

However, there are still tensions around playfulness and pedagogy and how it is perceived by adults. UK curricula still continue to prescribe that adults offer planned, purposeful play, somewhat negating the role of free play (Andrews, 2012). McInnes et al., (2011) have researched the use of play frames and play cues, arguing that it is the adult's concept of playful pedagogy and how they facilitate and frame play, which in turn affects how a child perceives play. It is the adults' playful attitudes towards pedagogy that leads to children's playful engagement in the learning environment.

Reflective Question

Is your practice playful and are you a playful practitioner?

Adults' and children's perceptions of play

For historic and cultural reasons, children's perspectives on play are limited. Colliver and Fleer (2016) explain that this is because of romantic, philosophical and developmental psychology perspectives (learning through play) and a lack of belief by adults in children's abilities to report on their own experiences. Drawing on cultural historical theory, Colliver and Fleer report that children aged 2 'are authorities on their own learning' (2016: 1559). Many studies show that practitioners working in the early years 'are not comfortable with play, child-led activities and allowing children choice' (McInnes et al., 2011: 2). According to McInnes et al. (2011), practitioners accept that they have limited knowledge and understanding of play, which therefore explains why they might not be at ease in facilitating children's play.

The relationship and the level of control between adult and child will determine the cues that children use to map activities on a play-work continuum. For children in some settings, there will be clear distinctions between what is play and what is not play, whereas in other settings there will be blurred boundaries. The latter is considered more conducive for learning (McInnes et al., 2011).

Reflective Question

Reflect on your experiences of being with children and think about how they would perceive their experiences with you on a play-work continuum?

Exploring the meaning of play: classical theories

Before discussing classical and contemporary theories, it is important to remember that no one theory is adequately able to explain the importance of play in children's development. Theories are best used as frameworks to better understand play and child development (Hughes, 2010a).

The historical context of play has many parallels with philosophy, economics and sociology – for example, ancient Greek philosophers such as Plato supported children's play and saw it as a contribution to future citizenship and a helpful way of ensuring a creative and artistic society. He believed that 3- to 6-year-olds needed lots of free play. He highly regarded imagination, stories and fantasy for this age group, and believed that through play children would develop individual dispositions and future career talents (Andrews, 2012). Aristotle, who was a student of Plato, introduced the concept of catharsis and the idea that play could be used to let off steam and release surplus energy (Brock et al., 2014).

There are many different theories of play and the 'surplus/excess energy' theory is often described as being one of the classical theories of play that emerged within the nineteenth and early twentieth centuries. British philosopher Herbert Spencer suggested that 'the more highly evolved the animal, the more surplus energy it had' (Brock et al., 2014: 9). In terms of education, the excess energy theory is played out by schools/settings through traditional set 'playtimes' throughout the day, which is believed to help children settle and concentrate on the indoor static tasks (Fisher, 2013).

'Recapitulation' theory is another classical theory which is linked with evolutionary thinking and a belief that children instinctively play and act out primitive behaviours, practise survival skills and build dens (Andrews, 2012). Fisher (2013) describes recapitulation theory in a slightly different way and states that it is play that reflects a child's cultural and personal environment. Anthropology, as discussed in Chapter 5, dovetails well with this theory because it focuses on understanding how culture influences children's interactions with their peers and the environment (Gonen et al., 2019). Understanding children's subcultures, where they have their own ways of thinking and being and views of the world (Montgomery, 2013), is achieved when adults respect, uphold and value a child's subculture.

Another classical theory is the 'practice or preparation' theory, which has many links with education. For example, this theory, which was proposed by Karl Groos in the very early twentieth century, is focused on giving children opportunities to practise developing the skills that will be needed for adulthood (Brock et al., 2014). Fisher (2013) explains that role play is underpinned by the practice/preparation theory whereby children mimic adults, usually with great accuracy – for example, pretending to be mummy or teacher.

Contemporary theories of play

Contemporary theories of play, such as cognitive developmental and arousal modulation theory, were established around the mid to late twentieth century (Brock et al., 2014) and there are many parallels with education, psychology and neuroscience.

Cognitive developmental theorists generally believe that play is an important tool for development and learning, and suggest that play provides opportunities for children to build up mental representations of the world around them, like a cognitive map (Brock et al., 2014). Moreover, they believe that providing children with problem-solving tasks when they are young will help them face and solve more complex problems in adulthood. Piaget and Vygotsky made important contributions to this area – for example, Piaget's concept of assimilation (taking in new information and making it fit with existing structures) and accommodation (adjusting the structures to fit new information) is useful in understanding how children adapt. Piaget believed that assimilation was and should be dominated by play and that children's play can reveal important information about the complexity of a child's thinking (Hughes, 2010a). Play, social interaction and problem solving are all key ingredients of Vygotsky's zone of proximal development (ZPD), states Brock et al. (2014). Vygotsky was interested in signs and systems as psychological tools which enabled children to generate their cognitive map (mental processes/new ways of thinking). The tools will vary from child to child and will depend on their social and cultural contexts. Anthropologists and sociologists would argue that it is vitally important for practitioners to acknowledge and recognise children's cultures and social contexts so they can further understand how they make meaning.

Another contemporary theory of play is the arousal moderation theory, but, as with all theories, there are slightly different propositions put forward – for example, in the 1960s, Daniel Berlyne, Professor of Psychology, developed the arousal modulation theory and suggested that play was an innate feature of the central nervous system which stabilised arousal and kept it at an optimal level (Brock et al., 2014). The level of arousal is determined by the child's boredom or uncertainty; when a child is bored and lacks stimulation, they seek out play opportunities in their environment to achieve the desired arousal level. In contrast, when a child is presented with new stimuli or a new environment and feel confused or unsure, the level of arousal is raised and play is used to reduce and stabilise the level of arousal (Hughes, 2010a).

Similarly, in the early 1970s, psychologist Michael Ellis suggested that children used play to 'increase stimulus and level of arousal' (Brock et al., 2014: 11), but he suggested there was a cycle of creating and reducing uncertainty. For example, children can often be apprehensive about new situations and be faced with uncertainty, but the positive effects of play contribute to reducing the uncertainty; over time, children begin to create new uncertainties for themselves and become very capable of reducing them through play (Hughes, 2010a).

There are various concepts within neuroscience (discussed in Chapter 7) that link well with classical and contemporary theories – for example, plasticity and 'experience-dependent', which is understanding that neural connections are made based upon what a child sees and does when rich play experiences occur (Smidt, 2013). Acknowledging self-regulation and that the prefrontal cortex, which controls and regulates emotions and social behaviour, matures later than other parts of the brain (Potegal and Davidson, 2003) is useful to know about when understanding how children stabilise their arousal through play.

Case Study: A typical day for 5-year-old Bobby

I love going to school because when I get there early I can run around the playground with my friends and chase them. We roar and make lots of noise and hide behind all the grown-ups. When the bell rings, we all run to our spot and line up. When we go into the classroom Miss Jones always lets us choose what to play. I love playing with the sand and choosing the construction with Sarah. Then we do some singing and then sometimes I work with Miss Jones to do some numbers or writing, and sometimes I play. After the tidy-up song we go outside for playtime and I get to see Charlie my big brother and we play games. I'm always hot when I come back in, but then we have a cold drink and do more work with Miss Jones.

The case study above is written from a child's perspective and evidences both classical and contemporary theories. For example, Bobby enjoys free play before school and having the opportunity to play out natural evolutionary behaviours (recapitulation theory), as well as letting off surplus/excess energy during playtime with his brother. Also, Bobby makes clear distinctions between what is play and talks about doing 'work' with Miss Jones, which evidences the cognitive developmental theory.

Reflective question

How important is the role of theory in understanding the concept of play?

Types and stages of play

The earliest and easiest way to categorise play is simply to decide whether or not an activity is play or not play. This has led to taxonomies of play, such as the work of Bob Hughes (see National Playing Fields Association, NPFA, 2000). Hughes (2002) has categorised play into sixteen play types, from symbolic play through to recapitulative play (Andrews, 2012). Prior to Hughes's list, many play workers used the acronym SPICE to categorise types of play.

Table 16.1 Play types

Play type	Definition
Social play	Playing with others; developing social skills
Physical play	Play which develops muscles, motor skills and strength
Intellectual play	Play involving cognitive development
Creative play	Generation of new ideas or things
Emotional play	Therapeutic play; the release of emotions

Adapted from Andrews, 2012: 31.

These types of play should not be viewed in isolation because a play activity such as hide and seek can support physical play, but also intellectual and social play. Hughes's taxonomy greatly broadened the types of observed play and draws upon 'ecological and social understandings' (Andrews, 2012: 32). However, Hughes offers a word of caution in that his taxonomy should not be regarded as the definitive list of all play types (Hughes, 2002). Corinne Hutt also identified three broad types of play: epistemic, ludic and games with rules (Hutt, 1979). Hutt asserted that a child's play behaviour would be adjusted linked to their current experiences and not be age related. Epistemic play is exploratory, ludic play uses past experiences, and games with rules explores social relationships. Heuristic play often involves children discovering things for themselves and was a term used by

Goldschmied and Jackson (1994). It is closely linked to Hutt's epistemic play and Piaget's sensory motor play. It is often associated with treasure baskets and very young children.

Stages of play

In 1932, Mildred Parten classified six stages of play from birth to 6 years, offering a developmental progression from solitary play through to co-operative play. She contended that as children develop, their social skills become more advanced and they move away from solitary play (Parten, 1932).

Table 16.2 Stages of play

Stage of play	Definition
Unoccupied	Not involved in play
Solitary	Plays on their own – no interaction
Onlooker	Not involved with the play – looks on with interest
Parallel	Plays alongside another child, perhaps copying actions and words – no direct social interaction
Associative	Child is interested in social interaction with other children; this overrides the play activity
Co-operative	Child is interested in both social interactions and the activity – is able to handle both domains

Adapted from Andrews, 2012: 33.

As with all stage theories, this is open to critique. Children do not pass through discrete stages in a linear form, but they often engage in these stages at different ages from the ones stated and these stages do not cover all types of play (McInnes and Yuen, 2018). Broadhead et al. (2010) and Smith (2011) argue that children will choose to be either solitary or co-operative depending on their mood, the environment they are in and how familiar they are with the other children present.

Reflective question

Observe the children you work with. What types and stages of play do you see?

Play and child development

The issue of play and its role in development has been considered for many years. Hughes stated that 'a person should not presume to understand children's development without having a complete understanding of children's play' (2010b: xv). Vygotsky indicated that there was a clear link between play and development, arguing that play was the source of development (Andrews, 2012). In terms of developmental domains, play has been linked with physical development, social and emotional development, cognitive development and intellectual development (Crowley, 2017).

Physical play develops muscle strength and motor skills, as defined in the EYFS, where physical development is one of the prime areas, as 'providing opportunities for young children to be active and interactive; and to develop their co-ordination, control, and movement' (DfE, 2017: 8). However, Smith and Thelan (2003) argue that children's developmental systems are interconnected, and physical movement is linked to other developmental domains. An example is crawling: while this is obviously a physical activity, it is linked to cognitive development as the child is remembering and mapping out their space. Positive correlations have been found between play, intellect and cognition, with constructive play positively correlating with intelligence scores (Crowley, 2017). Piaget considered that intelligence arises from action and play and provides the conscious space for exploring concepts (Piaget and Inhelder, 1969). Athey (1990) identified that Piaget postulated that children develop through stages starting with struggle, then practice and finally play. Object play has been of particular interest to researchers in the role of play in cognitive or intellectual development, and this is where researchers have looked at the different objects that children play with and considered the cognitive benefits (Hughes, 2010b). Block play can vary from the very simple stacking to much more complex structures. Playing with blocks facilitates an understanding of measuring, construction, space, area and volume. Block play also links to the development of skills such as visualisation and mental rotation (Caldera et al., 1999; cited in Crowley, 2017).

Play has also been linked with a child's social and emotional development. Play can offer opportunities for the development of social relationships or insights into social patterns (cultures) of society. This social and cultural context of play can influence who and what children play with and their pretend play and behaviour (Andrews, 2012). Pretend play is important for theory of mind development (see Chapter 10), as children take on different roles and negotiate with other children.

However, definitive studies linking play and development have been limited and reviews of such studies have highlighted a number of methodological flaws (see Crowley, 2017: 235). Smith (2010) contends that play should be viewed as useful, but to remember that children benefit from other experiences such as observation, direct instruction and trial and error. This does not devalue play, but instead Smith (2010) argues that play should be valued in its own right.

Case Study: Outdoor play with hollow blocks

Large hollow blocks have been laid outdoors in a circle by the practitioners, in one layer, with a small gap between them and a foam mat in the centre. The intention is for the children to develop their gross motor and loco motor skills (specifically, balancing), sharing and cooperation, by stepping from one block to another. Alfie, Hugo, John, Joel, Lucy and Henry are playing on the blocks. The activity is well within the children's capabilities and at first the children play as the teacher intended. After a short while, Lucy pretends to wobble and 'falls' onto the mat, shouting, 'Look, I can't do it.

I have fallen in the sea. The children make a game of this; there is some rough-and-tumble play as they 'swim' back to the blocks and they 'rescue' each other. The practitioners decide not to intervene and allow the play to unfold. Soon the children are sitting astride the blocks and are pretending to row ashore and back to the safety of the 'land'.

The case study highlights how the play intentions of one activity can change and develop. Here, the main intention was to develop the physical skills of balance and co-ordination. However, as the activity proceeds, the children take ownership and change the learning intention of the activity. The practitioners make the decision not to intervene and, by doing so, they allow the play to unfold in different directions. Now they are able to observe different developmental domains and skills, albeit not what was first intended.

Reflective question

What other developmental domains (apart from physical development) are evident in the children's play in this case study? Make a list and discuss with others.

Importance of outdoor play

Focusing on the importance of outdoor play is significant because children in the twenty-first century tend to have fewer opportunities to play outdoors in the natural environment compared to children three generations ago (Greenwood, 2017; Waller, 2009). Various reasons are put forward, such as increased traffic, concerns about stranger danger, despite the incidents remaining the same over the last thirty years (Waller, 2009), and technological reasons; journalist and author Richard Louv suggests that there is such a thing as 'nature-deficit disorder' where children become disconnected from the natural world. For some children, their early years setting might be the only regular place where they truly experience playing outdoors.

There are many benefits to playing outdoors – for example, children have the opportunity to develop their confidence, discover and explore using their senses, move freely, be active rather than sedentary, problem solve and face new challenges, to name a few. Moreover, there is evidence to suggest that playing outdoors contributes positively to language development (sustained talk) and attention span (Greenwood, 2017). Tovey (2007) argues that the outdoors is unique and can offer children something very different from the indoors, such as whole body experiences, giddy and dizzy play, taking risks, understanding their place within the natural world, and a naturally changing environment that invites curiosity and exploration. In order for children to thrive, they need lots of physical activity and the outdoors can offer this. The recommended UK guidelines for 1 to

5-year-olds is 180 minutes per day, and for children under one year of age, the recommendation is 30 minutes per day (UK Government, 2019).

Attitudes towards outdoor play, risk taking and safety are culturally influenced – for example, practitioners in Sweden may be more comfortable and content with children climbing trees than practitioners in the UK (Waller, 2009). It is thought that children benefit the most when they have practitioners around them who show enjoyment and interest in being outdoors. Children being outside is not enough, suggests Greenwood (2017); it is the experiences and interactions they encounter that make the difference. Practitioners need to have a clear understanding of 'playtime', 'breaktime', 'planned' and 'spontaneous' outdoor play in order for children to have high-quality, worthwhile outdoor experiences. Chapter 20 discusses the outdoor learning environment in more detail.

Case Study: Free-flow access

Mrs Frye loved her job as a nursery teacher. When meeting and welcoming new parents, she would always talk at length about the outdoor space and what it offered young children. However, she often came across parents who were unsure and didn't share the same enthusiasm:

Mrs Frye: So this is our wonderful outdoor space; we go out in all weathers and there is free-flow access from the indoors to the outdoors, which means children can go in and out as they choose.

Nursery parent: Did you say all weathers? Well, I don't think my Jack will be able to decide for himself – he's only 3!

Mrs Frye: Yes, that's right, all weathers; here we have the outdoor clothing such as wellingtons, all-in-one waterproofs, umbrellas and extra jumpers. The children are encouraged to dress themselves and will be developing lots of new skills. We've got plenty of adults around to help. I've been working with 3-year-olds for over thirty years now, and at first some children who are not used to making decisions need time to get used to it, but I find after a few weeks they like it and are very good at it.

Nursery parent: Who will help him get dressed?

Mrs Frye: There are plenty of adults around to help and we encourage lots of independence, and want to give the children lots of opportunities to develop their physical and cognitive development. Look at the children now, getting dressed and helping each other and there are no adults around.

Nursery parent: And they are only 3 years old – it's quite remarkable.

The case study above shows how Mrs Frye's enthusiasm for the outdoors provides the nursery children with lots of rich, exciting opportunities. It also highlights how adults perceive the ability of young children differently and, to some extent, the nursery parent underestimates Jack's capabilities. Therefore, part of Mrs Frye's role is to convince other adults about the importance and value of playing outdoors.

> ## Reflective question
>
> Talk to others about your expectations of a 3-year-old. What do you notice?

Summary of chapter

- Children's perceptions of play are limited and this is mainly due to a lack of belief from adults in a child's ability to report on their experiences.
- There is no one single definition of play and it can be described as a noun, verb or adjective. Playfulness is usually described as a behaviour and an attitude, and is different in nature to play.
- There are many different types of play and different theories of the stages of play.
- Some regard play as essential for development, but research evidence has struggled to prove this. More generally, play is regarded as having a function in development alongside other types of experience.
- Outdoor play is as important as indoor play, and children benefit the most when they have adults around them who enjoy the outdoors and are enthusiastic about what it can offer.

End-of-chapter questions

1. How would you define play and playfulness?
2. What makes an activity play and how does it differ from other activities?
3. How would you reassure an adult who was anxious about children playing outdoors and convince them that playing outdoors is good for children?

Further reading

Ephgrave, A. (2018) *Planning in the Moment with Young Children: A Practical Guide for Early Years Practitioners and Parents*. London: Routledge.

This book explores the concept of planning 'in the moment' and emphasises the critical role of the adult in promoting child-led learning. It supports early years practitioners in having the confidence and insight to work and plan in the moment. It discusses enabling the children to live, learn, play and develop in the here and now.

Ridgway, A., Quiñones, G. and Liang, L. (2015) *Early Childhood Pedagogical Play: A Cultural-Historical Interpretation Using Visual Methodology*. London: Springer.

This book introduces you to cultural historical theory and its relevance to children's play. It includes a chapter on the child's perspective of play, and will extend your knowledge and understanding of sustained shared thinking, affordances and the role of culture in children's play.

White, J. (2020) *Playing and Learning Outdoors: The Practical Guide and Sourcebook for Excellence in Outdoor Provision and Practice with Young Children* (3rd edn). London: Routledge.

This accessible book will provide you with a wealth of practical guidance on how to enact play in settings with young children. The book aims to support high-quality outdoor provision and acts as a source book for practitioners which sets out relevant materials, books and resources that could be used to enhance outdoor learning.

SEVENTEEN

UNDERSTANDING WELL-BEING THROUGH THE DISCIPLINES AND DOMAINS

This chapter will help you to

- develop an interdisciplinary understanding of well-being;
- understand the meaning of well-being in the context of child development;
- develop knowledge and understanding about promoting and supporting children's well-being.

Introduction

Well-being matters because it is a fundamental human right (Soutter et al., 2012) and the importance of promoting and supporting children's well-being is widely acknowledged and accepted (Fraillon, 2004). However, well-being has many meanings, such as happiness, welfare and quality of life (Ryan and Deci, 2001). Roberts (2010) describes well-being in the form of a pyramid, like Maslow's hierarchy of needs, whereby physical well-being is at the base, then followed by communication, then belonging, and boundaries and agency at the top of the pyramid. Lewis (2019) explains the concept by drawing attention to the two overarching dimensions – objective and subjective – as well as highlighting various well-being domains (types) and discourses (see Chapter 6 for a detailed explanation of the meaning of discourses). However, Statham and Chase (2010: 6) state that in general 'there is still limited agreement on what the constituent components of child wellbeing are, or how they should be weighted in terms of importance or priority'. Similarly, Raghavan and Alexandrova (2015: 888) suggest 'there is neither consensus, nor much discussion on what constitutes child well-being'. One explanation for limited agreement and a lack of consensus is that well-being is intertwined with personal values (Gasper, 2010) and this should be considered when reading about well-being. Moreover, the OECD (2011) suggest that the home environment of a child contributes positively or negatively to a child's well-being and there are many interrelating factors that shape well-being and disentangling them is not easy.

This chapter explains the meaning of well-being from different disciplines (as discussed in Part 1 of this book), as well as in the context of child development domains (as discussed in Part 2). Then, adults' and children's perceptions of well-being are briefly explored, with a final discussion on understanding how to support and promote children's well-being.

Exploring the meaning of well-being from different disciplines

Many different theories and explanations of well-being exist, but there is generally a lack of research into understanding the conceptual nature of well-being in the context of education for children under the age of 8 years. Nonetheless, Mashford-Scott et al. (2012), Amerijckx and Humblet (2014) and Raghavan and Alexandrova (2015) have made important contributions to understanding and developing a child well-being discourse.

It is important to note that long-standing discourses of well-being were constructed at a time in history when childhood was not viewed as a distinct life phase, and limited understanding existed about the concept of childhood. A modern understanding of childhood started to emerge towards the end of the fifteenth century (Brockliss and Montgomery, 2013) and for this reason Raghavan and Alexandrova (2015) claim that 'philosophical' discourses of well-being will not straightforwardly extend to children because they were not written with them in mind. Lewis (2019) explores their claim in more detail and demonstrates that many leading theories and discourses of well-being in philosophy and psychology relate to children in some way, particularly when viewed with a positive child development lens, suggesting therefore that a theory of child well-being may not be needed.

Table 17.1 below shows the many different interpretations of well-being and reinforces the point that well-being is a complex concept. You will also notice that there are overlaps with the key words associated with the discourses.

Table 17.1 Relevant well-being discourses and associated key words

Discipline	Discourse	Key words
Psychology	Affect discourse	• Positive and negative emotions
		• Feelings
		• Happiness
		• Subjective well-being
	Life satisfaction discourse	• Cognitive self-evaluations
		• Self-reported measures
		• Happiness
		• Subjective well-being
	Positive psychology (PERMA)	• Positive emotion, Engagement, Relationships,
		• Meaning and accomplishment
Sociology	Community quality of life	• Conditions and factors
		• External indicators – health, education
		• Material resources – income, housing

Discipline	Discourse	Key words
Economics	Capabilities approach	• Individual contexts and flourishing • Interactions and relationships
	Gross Domestic Product (GDP)	• Standard measure for life satisfaction and quality of life • Success of a country • Macro-economic statistics
Anthropology	Hedonic discourse	• Personal experiences • Ethnography • Values • The self
Philosophy	Hedonic/mental states discourse	• Positive and negative emotions • Feelings • Happiness, pleasure and the good life • Subjective well-being
	Eudaimonic/flourishing discourse	• Human functioning and development • Autonomy and authenticity • Self-realisation and fulfilment • Feeling a sense of purpose and meaning to life • Fulfilling potential
	Needs/based objectivist discourse	• Necessary prerequisites – health, education • Meeting someone's needs
Neuroscience	Happiness discourse	• Dopamine • Oxytocin
Education	Objective discourse	• Proxy indicators – school attendance, poverty rates, immunisation rates • Measurable and quantifiable • Concrete noun • External indicators
	Subjective discourse	• Feelings and emotions • Aspirations, likes and dislikes • Not so easy to quantify/measure • Abstract noun • Self-reported measures
	Irreducible construct discourse	• Holistic totality • All-encompassing • Whole child
	Reducible construct discourse	• Well-being domains • Interrelated • Constituent components • Multi-dimensional

Case Study: Reporting on children's well-being

It was the start of the summer term in Vallay Primary School and the school inspection team were about to inspect the standards of the school. The team spent around one week scrutinising various documents, looking at data and talking mainly with staff and parents. The school shortly received the report and the head teacher was somewhat dissatisfied with the comment about children's poor well-being and the evidence used to make the judgement. The school discussed the report as a team, and they were disappointed that the inspection team had not considered the subjective well-being data which had been collected by a member of staff studying for a doctorate in education using an adapted version of Huebner's multidimensional Life Satisfaction Scale (Parkes et al., 2014).

The case study highlights how the objective discourse is privileged, and attendance rates, number of children receiving school meals and number of children with individual learning plans are being used as proxy indicators to report on children's well-being. However, this might not always be a true reflection of a child's well-being as the subjective discourse is being overlooked. When objective and subjective well-being information is used together, it could tell a different story about child well-being.

Reflective question

How would you find out about young children's subjective well-being?

Well-being and child development

Many different well-being domains (also known as 'types') are in use for young children. Despite many domains, adjectives that precede well-being such as 'emotional' well-being, 'social' well-being, 'cognitive' well-being, and so on can be very useful in providing some clarity about the meaning. In 2009, Fauth and Thompson identified four important domains for young children: physical well-being; mental health, emotional and social well-being; cognitive and language development; and school performance and beliefs. However, in 2010 Statham and Chase suggested that there were three important domains for children: emotional well-being; physical well-being; and social well-being. This is a good example showing limited consensus about the domains for children.

Many more domains are in use for children, such as:

- personal/mental/psychological well-being;
- environmental/community/material well-being;

- spiritual well-being;
- intellectual well-being;
- economic well-being;
- present (beings)/future (becomings) well-being.

All domains are relevant to children in some way, but certain contexts might dominate some domains over others. Therefore, in order for children to flourish, grow and develop and reach their potential, a holistic approach towards children's well-being is recommended. This dovetails well with a focus on nurturing children's holistic development, which encompasses physical, social, emotional, creative, spiritual, cognitive and language development (as discussed in Part 2 of this book).

Physical well-being is linked with physical development and is about keeping children healthy and making sure they get exercise; it is about children feeling healthy and well; it also includes children being able to care for themselves personally – for example, washing and dressing. Social well-being is linked with social development and is about building relationships and friendships, and giving children the opportunity to develop a range of social skills, whereas emotional well-being is about feelings, attachment and developing a sense of self, and is linked with emotional development. Creative development is closely linked with cognitive and emotional well-being in that children should be given opportunities to express themselves in multimodal ways. Spiritual development is linked with spiritual well-being and is mainly about beliefs, but is also about existence in the philosophical sense – what does it mean to exist and what should life be like for young children? Cognitive and language development link with cognitive well-being and is about how someone evaluates their life, but in the context of young children the domains suggested by Statham and Chase (2010) – namely, emotional, physical and social well-being – play a very important role in children's cognitive and language development. Dowling (2010) highlights the importance of developing children's confidence when they are young, which is linked to self-concept, self-esteem and self-knowledge, and has a positive impact on future success.

Case Study: Thanks for asking

Don Primary School was situated in a very affluent part of the UK with a very small percentage of children from poorer backgrounds. Harry, aged 7, seemed settled in Year 2 with Mr Gregg (class teacher) and Miss Simpson (teaching assistant), and his ability to read and understand mathematical concepts was excellent. Harry's parents both worked full time, one as a senior civil servant and the other as a chief executive of a large digital company. The staff rarely saw his parents and Harry's nanny was the main contact. Mr Gregg and Miss Simpson were talking about the children's progress about two months into the academic year and they both agreed that Harry was progressing well in certain areas of the curriculum but not in emotional development. They both noticed that while he was immaculately presented, he was very sleepy in the afternoons, a little withdrawn, gazed a

(Continued)

lot and seemed generally unhappy. They talked to him about why he might be sleepy and at first he said he didn't know. Then a few days later, after Harry heard the story of 'Guess How Much I love You', he spoke to Miss Simpson and explained why he was so sleepy. He told her: 'I'm waiting for mummy and mummy to read me a story before I go to bed like they did on holiday, but they never come and I don't see them'. Miss Simpson soon realised that Harry had been waiting up for his parents to read him a story.

The case study above demonstrates how certain aspects of child development are dominated at home, but Harry's emotional well-being is poor compared with his ability to achieve in literacy and numeracy. Even though he is being cared for by his nanny, he desperately seeks love, nurture and attention from his parents. Over time, if his emotional well-being is not nurtured, his ability to achieve well in other areas of the curriculum could be affected.

Reflective question

How can practitioners ensure that the holistic well-being of all children from different backgrounds are supported?

Adults' and children's perceptions of well-being

The majority of research about well-being relates to theoretical discussions and policy discourses, and very little research focuses on understanding well-being from the perspective of professionals who work with children, such as teachers, teaching assistants, health visitors, social workers, to name but a few (Morrow and Mayall, 2009). Education researchers such as Mashford-Scott et al. (2012) write specifically about the young child and suggest that practitioners working in the early years adopt two different discourses of well-being, which is the 'objective' (perceived as a concrete noun and measurable) and the 'subjective' (perceived as an abstract noun and not so easy to measure) discourse. They further claim that the leading discourse is the objective kind 'because it serves to quantify wellbeing; making it more measurable' (Mashford-Scott et al., 2012: 239).

In 2020, Nah et al. conducted a comparative study to find out how practitioners from South Korea and Norway perceived well-being. They found that practitioners from South Korea placed more importance on the cognitive and economic domains, whereas practitioners from Norway perceived the social domain as the most important. In addition, practitioners from Norway placed more emphasis on a child's physical needs, affection and enjoyment, compared with practitioners from South Korea who perceived safety, security and continuity as more important.

Perceptions of well-being from young children under the age of 8 are scarce, but Adams (2012) was keen to find out about children's perceptions of childhood, particularly when a 'childhood in crisis' discourse exists. Adams (2012) reports that 56 7- to 11-year-olds from a deprived town in England perceived childhood to be positive and adulthood to be stressful and boring. These findings are a reminder of how perceptions between children and adults can vary.

Supporting and promoting children's well-being

Respecting children's natural ability to play, giving them agency, listening authentically and giving them project work opportunities are beneficial to children's well-being (OECD, 2006). According to Woolf, play is one of the most important mediums where children can become 'more self-aware, empathetic and motivated as well as becoming more able to manage feelings and develop and deploy social skills' (2013: 28). Play is crucial for supporting children's emotional, social and psychological well-being.

Mashford-Scott et al. (2012) assert that in order to fully support children's well-being, practitioners need to understand a child's first-hand perspective of their subjective experience. Understanding children's subjective experiences is supported by Barblett and Maloney (2010) who state that the meaning of something belongs to the individual. Therefore, proponents who adopt this view value children's perceptions of their experiences, and believe they have valid contributions to make, and should be listened to and respected. Seland et al. set out to explore how 1- to 3-year-olds experience subjective well-being. They found that:

> staff members creating an intersubjective space dominated by high sensitivity and responsivity is also an important factor for toddlers' wellbeing. Wellbeing is expressed in situations where the child is seen, understood and recognized as a subject with their own intentions, needs and preferences... (2015: 70)

The findings from the study by Seland et al. (2015) show that children experience subjective well-being when adults first view children as subjects of their experience in the here and now/present (beings), rather than viewing them as objects of their experience and focusing on the future (becomings). Second, children are more likely to experience subjective well-being when practitioners enact a rights-based pedagogy, but this is an under-researched area.

Roberts (2010) uses the four 'A's acronym to explain how adults can support children's well-being. 'Anchored attention' is remembering that babies need to stay close and thrive on attaching themselves to loved ones, and this can be in the form of physical and emotional attachments. 'Authority' is about being gentle but firm, being fair and consistent, and providing boundaries and routines for children. 'Apprenticeship' is essentially about giving children real opportunities to help – for example, tidying up together and 'real' washing up rather than setting up an activity in a water tray. Roberts (2010) points out that in Western cultures the division of labour between adult and child is far more visible and apprenticeship is less likely. The fourth 'A' is 'Allowing children time and space' ultimately to play, listen and look, and have a space they can call their own. Roberts (2010) states that when children are exposed to the four 'A's, their agency, sense of belonging and communication will flourish.

Case Study: 'Apprentices'

When Mrs Williams joined Redd Primary School as the nursery teacher and leader of play and peda- gogy, she had a vision of children becoming true apprentices and creators of their own space, much to the disagreement of the other teachers and teaching assistants. She identified many opportuni- ties in the provision whereby children would be given responsibilities and meaningful activities. Her first suggestion to the team was to convert part of the staff room to a child-size workable kitchen. At first, there were concerns about safety, cost and need; it took a few months for Mrs Williams to persuade the staff that the kitchen would be beneficial for the children, and would help develop and improve parental partnerships.

The development of the kitchen was unique in that Mrs Williams called upon her contacts at the local university to work with student architects to design the kitchen. The students were able to use a variety of digital technologies to provide visual images of what the kitchen would look like, and the children and students co-designed the kitchen. Children were given opportunities to problem solve, make decisions and work together as a team. The experience was a very positive one for both the students and children, as well as the parents who benefited from getting involved in 'Parent Bake Off', 'Build a baguette day' and 'Soup challenges'. On reflection of the project, one student architect considered setting up a future business of co-designed spaces for children in educational settings. Mrs Williams was keen to engage in future projects to ensure that all children in future years were given similar opportunities to work with the students.

The case study above is an excellent example showing two of the four 'A's acronym by Roberts (2010) and demonstrates how adults can support children's well-being. The children were given a real-life opportunity to become 'Apprentices' in working with the student architects as well as 'Allowing' them to plan their own play space. They were truly able to call this space their own!

Reflective question

What other links can be made with the wider community to enhance children's well-being?

Universal or targeted interventions

Targeted intervention programmes, such as the Student Assist Programme (SAP) and the universal (i.e., whole-school) Social and Emotional Aspects of Learning (SEAL) programme, are interventions that aim to fix or put something right, but the evidence about what they achieve is mixed, and there is dispute over the impact they have in the longer term. Craig (2007) disagrees with the universal explicit teaching of well-being and criticises SEAL for getting children to socially comply with a set of outcomes that outlines the type of person they should become (Craig, 2007). Reports on children's mental health are viewed as over-pessimistic and this has led to an increase in intervention programmes, argues Ecclestone and Hayes (2009a, b). Furthermore, they argue that the debate about therapeutic interventions has largely been uncritical and positions children as vulnerable, needy, weak and fragile (Ecclestone and Hayes, 2009b).

On the other hand, Bartholomew (2007: 27) argues that 'interventions should not be denied to children where there is evidence that they work'. According to Durlak and Weissberg (2013), many studies show improved academic performance as a result of social and emotional learning programmes. In addition, O'Donnell et al. (2014) write very positively about the benefits of intervention programmes in schools, as well as Humphrey et al. (2010) who conducted a study about the SEAL programme. However, the gains started to decline after a few weeks and it was recommended that the SEAL programme should be more intensive and delivered over a longer period of time. Bywater and Sharples (2012: 404) claim that 'choosing a programme that works is not enough to guarantee success; implementing the programme with fidelity takes time and resources, but is necessary to achieve the desired, proven outcome'.

Similarly, Rones and Hoagward (2000; cited in Hallam, 2009) agree that SEAL on its own is not effective. Factors such as consistent implementation of the programme, input from parents/carers, practitioners and peers alongside the integration of SEAL into the day-to-day activities will help to make it more effective. When Coleman (2009) explored the role of well-being in schools, his discussion focused mainly on the limited empirical evidence of the effectiveness of intervention programmes. Many of the programmes have drawn criticism from experts who claim that there is an 'insufficient and inconsistent evidence base' (Ecclestone and Hayes, 2009a; Gillies, 2011; Humphrey et al., 2010: 513; Mayr and Ulich, 1999) between well-being and improved academic performance. Edwards et al. (2015) found that following children's interests is more meaningful to children than intervention programmes aimed at modifying children's behaviour.

A further concern is raised by Clack that schools can often become 'the backdoor for addressing a whole host of societal ills' (2012: 502), which questions the realistic expectation for schools in supporting and improving well-being. Craig strongly feels that 'problems with young people's well-being are the result of an enormous number of social and cultural changes' (2017: 3). Craig (2007), in citing the work of Bradshaw, claims that governments should be targeting and responding to family breakdown, rather than focusing on providing individual lessons on social and emotional skills in schools. Downey and Kelly (1986) claim that too much emphasis is placed on dealing with the symptoms and less focus on dealing with the root causes. Craig's (2009) report suggests that there is little point in teaching universal emotional and social skills to children who do not need it, as they could be utilising their time more effectively.

Experiencing emotions

When practitioners persistently focus on developing positive feelings, there is the argument that this may be disadvantaging children from experiencing a range of emotions more naturally, such as negative emotions, which are needed for healthy well-rounded development (Craig et al., 2007; cited in Watson et al., 2012). Allowing and encouraging children to experience both positive and negative emotions is further supported by Dowling (2010) who states that for children to be able to understand their emotions, they need to experience a range of them. Some argue that 'children need to experience negative emotions and low self-esteem in order to be challenged and motivated to succeed and to develop persistence and resilience' (Watson et al., 2012: 4). Craig (2009) draws upon the work of positive psychologist Professor Martin Seligman to explain the importance of children experiencing a range of emotions. He asserts:

> anxiety, depression, and anger, exist for a purpose: they galvanize you into action to change yourself or your world, and by doing so to terminate the negative emotion. Inevitably, such feelings carry pain but they are an effective 'alarm system' which warns us of danger, loss, and trespass. So artificially trying to protect children from bad feelings will undermine their development, not aid it. (2009: 11)

Manning-Morton (2014) also agrees that experiencing positive and negative feelings play an important part of early learning.

Well-being pedagogy

Very little research has been conducted into the teaching of well-being and there is a view that well-being cannot be taught in the same way as other subjects, such as mathematics and science. According to Morris (2009), well-being has experience at its core and adults should be focused on teaching children how to be well, and in order for them to know what this is like they have to experience it. Essentially, Morris (2009) is arguing for children to be engaged in rich experiences that have meaning and purpose where they can come alive. Moreover, Morris (2009) favours a constructivist pedagogical approach and states that well-being is different from other subjects because it is about being human and about life. For Morris (2009), well-being is conceptualised as something abstract with an unfixed meaning; it is about exploring what it means to exist and bears a resemblance to a eudaimonic discourse of well-being (see Table 17.1). Morris further emphasises the importance of moral education, which closely relates to well-being in the curriculum. He states: 'it is an area to which no clear body of knowledge can be assigned... it extends, like language learning, across every experience children have, both inside school and outside it' (2009: 151). Therefore, supporting and promoting children's well-being is the responsibility of the home environment, wider community and the early childhood education and care setting.

Summary of chapter

- Well-being has many meanings and is described differently within a variety of disciplines.
- Well-being is best understood in the context of holistic development where many domains (types of well-being) are acknowledged and facilitated.
- Perceptions of well-being from the perspective of the adult and child are limited, but in an educational context the objective discourse is usually dominant.
- There are numerous ways of supporting and promoting children's well-being – for example, through targeted and universal programmes, playful pedagogies and giving children rich experiences of life.

End-of-chapter questions

1. What does well-being mean to you?
2. What does well-being look like in a child?
3. What do you think are some of the most effective ways of promoting and supporting children's well-being?

Further reading

Lewis, A. and Rees, L. (2017) 'Understanding well-being in the early years', in K. McInnes, and A. Thomas (eds), *Teaching Early Years: Theory and Practice*. London: SAGE. pp. 65–85.

This chapter is written by an academic and a practitioner, and will help you to further understand the concept of well-being. In order to make links between theories of well-being and practice, two case studies are included, one of which focuses on outdoor child-initiated play and the other which discusses an intervention programme. The chapter also introduces you to understanding how practitioners can assess well-being.

Musgrave, J. (2017) *Supporting Children's Health and Wellbeing*. London: SAGE.

This book will extend your knowledge and understanding of children's contemporary health conditions and how they impact on young children's development. It will provide you with strategies to support children's health and well-being in early childhood education and care settings.

Williams-Brown, Z. and Mander, S. (eds) (2021) *Childhood Well-being and Resilience Influences on Education Outcomes*. London: Routledge.

This book will extend your knowledge and understanding of the strategies used in education, health, and the voluntary and private sectors that promote children's well-being and resilience. A variety of important key topics are examined and the chapters on well-being and outdoor learning and mindfulness for young children will be very useful.

EIGHTEEN

UNDERSTANDING GLOBAL CURRICULA THROUGH THE DISCIPLINES AND DOMAINS

This chapter will help you to

- understand different early years curricula and how they are underpinned by different approaches;
- understand how different early years curricula are enacted in practice;
- compare and contrast how child development domains are facilitated across different early years curricula both nationally and internationally.

Introduction

Across the globe there are a number of different early years curricula, underpinned by different approaches and practices. This chapter will explore some of these different curricula and discuss how child development domains are facilitated within these differing educational curricula. This chapter will start by looking at early years curricula that are underpinned by a developmental psychology approach.

Developmental Psychology Approach within early years curricula

As discussed in Chapters 2 and 8, a developmental psychological approach to child development very much supports a linear progression in terms of development. The child progresses in line with norms of expected behaviour supported by developmental milestones, goals and outcomes. This supports the theory of Piaget who, as discussed in previous chapters, considered child development to unfold in stages (Crowley, 2017). Although there has been criticism of viewing children through a stage-like lens (as argued in Chapter 2), this approach can be seen in education throughout early years curricula in the UK.

England and Wales

Both the 'Early Years Foundation Stage' (EYFS) in England for children aged 0–5 years and the current 'Foundation Phase' (FP) in Wales for children aged 3–7 years (WG, 2015a) have early learning goals or outcomes which the child is required to meet. This can be seen as prioritising a developmental psychology approach to early years education, with a child's development measured in incremental steps.

Within the EYFS and FP, there are seven areas of learning which cover all the developmental domains discussed in this book. The latest revisions to the EYFS which came into force in September 2021, still require practitioners to evaluate children against seventeen early learning goals. Further, alongside the revised EYFS, there is a revised 'Development Matters' non-statutory curriculum document which 'sets out the pathways of children's development in broad ages and stages' (DfE, 2020: 3). Although this document does contend that children's learning is not neat and orderly, there is still an emphasis on using these pathways to assess children's development, the rationale being that assessing children against early learning goals or stages of development allows any developmental delays to be identified early.

Similarly, Wales is embarking upon a new 'Curriculum for Wales' (CfW) starting in September 2022 for learners up to year 6 and some in year 7; then up to year 11 by 2026. This curriculum has six areas of learning and experience which covers all the domains discussed in this book. This new curriculum also has progression steps correlating broadly to the ages of 5, 8, 11, 14 and 16 years (WG, 2020). There is an emphasis throughout the curriculum for more practitioner autonomy and for schools to take ownership of the curriculum design. However, there will be an expectation for practitioners to ensure that all learners progress through the progression steps indicated above. Thus, it can be argued that both England and Wales are still adopting a developmental psychology approach in their early years education.

Scotland

Scotland has the 'Realising Ambition: Being Me' guidance for children up to the age of 3 years (Education Scotland, 2020). This guidance provides information on child development in terms of 'when I am a baby', 'when I am a toddler' and 'when I am a young child' (Education Scotland, 2020: 11). The document emphasises that these should not be seen as rigid lines of progression, but instead that there is a recognition that young children develop at different rates. The guidance draws upon the work of Siraj-Blatchford et al. (2002) who argue that when considering child development there needs to be consideration of the child as an individual, their environment and the socioeconomic culture surrounding them. The guidance goes on to develop themes of Well being; Movement and coordination; Confidence, creativity and curiosity (Education Scotland, 2020). These themes broadly correlate to the domains of Well-being; Physical development (coordination); Creative development; Cognitive development (Curiosity).

Once a child is three, they move on to the 'Curriculum for Excellence' for learners aged 3–18 years. This has experiences and outcomes that the children are expected to meet for eight curriculum areas, covering the development domains discussed in this book (Scottish Government, (2018). The experiences and outcomes are set out in lines of development which describe progress in learning. This resonates with the early learning goals in the EYFS and the FP outcomes in Wales.

Northern Ireland

Northern Ireland has the 'Curricular Guidance for Pre-School Education' (CEA, 2018) and provides a year of non-compulsory pre-school education based on a curriculum that builds on what children learn at home and/or in other settings. It acknowledges that children develop at different rates and attain different goals, but states that all children should have access to a curriculum that allows them to make acceptable academic development and reach their full potential. Within the six pre-school areas of learning (covering the developmental domains) children are assessed through daily observations and progression in learning is underpinned by characteristics and skills.

At the age of 4 years, children enter the 'Foundation Stage' (FS) with non-statutory guidance, 'The Developmental Stages in Learning' to help practitioners track the progress of an individual pupil or a group of pupils (CCEA, 2020). In keeping with the other early years curricula in the UK, the curriculum is divided into seven areas of learning covering the developmental domains (CCEA, 2020).

Reflective Question

Having read about the UK curricula, which do you feel best supports early years development and why?

Sociological Approach within early years curricula

Chapter 3 argued that sociology is important for understanding how child development, behaviour and life chances are influenced by social factors (Barry and Yuill, 2008; Ingleby and Oliver, 2008). Friedrich Froebel (1782–1852) saw family as the first educator in a child's life, thus supporting child development being influenced by social factors.

Froebel's approach to education

Froebel was the inventor of the kindergarten and he believed that women were capable of teaching children – a revolutionary idea at the time. Froebel's key ideas included occupations and gifts (Bruce, 2011a). The occupations were a range of craft like activities such as folding paper and paper weaving. The gifts were sets of wooden blocks and were one of the first of their kind to be used for educational purposes. The first gift was a soft sphere; the second the cube, cylinder and wooden sphere; the third, fourth, fifth and sixth gifts were cubes divided in different ways, with small wooden blocks that could be built into larger ones. Froebel saw the whole child and thought about how the whole child could be developed. This whole-child approach can be seen in the holistic nature of other early years curricula in the UK.

Froebel addressed himself to the physical needs of the child through the forms of life, involving the senses and first-hand experiences (Bruce, 2011a). Forms of beauty were concerned with developing creativity and mathematics. Forms of knowledge addressed thinking and problem-solving. This was an integrated approach to child development and again resonates in the early years curricula seen today.

Froebel was an advocate of learning through play and for him, play was the highest form of learning (Bruce, 2011b). He made a clear distinction between play and work, and he believed play to be child-initiated and work to be fulfilling a task required by an adult. Froebel believed that children should be allowed time to function at the level of development they were at and not to be rushed onto the next stage. This aligns with the philosophy of the FP in Wales, which is a stage, not age-based curriculum. Through observation, Froebel was able to see what children could do and build upon this.

Froebel today

Bruce writes that 'there is an urgent need for Froebel training' to allow for practitioners to function with inspiration and vision (Bruce, 2011b: 64). Further, Froebelian education is now an international movement, promoted through the International Froebel Society. Froebel certificate courses have been re-established at Roehampton University and introduced at Edinburgh University. A critique of Froebel would be a lack of ideas around gender and inequality, and there has been a misinterpretation of the use of his Occupations and Gifts by some, causing the practice to become too rigid. Nevertheless, Froebel's influence lives on in practice, such as reflection, play, observation, use of the outdoors and the importance of family upon a child's development and education.

Reflective Question

To what extent does your setting facilitate children learning about nature, thus supporting Froebel's kindergarten?

Economic Approach within early years curricula

Chapter 4 opened with the argument that economics is bound up with context, political values and beliefs and is very 'influential in determining national and international policies' (Penn, 2014: 149).

Nowhere is this more evident than in the Early Childhood Education (ECE) policies and practices of mainland China.

In mainland China, kindergartens provide education for children aged 3–6 years and can be public, funded by the government or private (Yang and Li, 2019). In 2001, the Ministry of Education of the People's Republic of China devised guidelines for kindergarten education and divided the Early Childhood Curriculum (ECC) into five learning fields: health, language, society, science and art. There was an emphasis that 'children's experiences and individual differences should be recognised and respected; pre-school education should be a collaborative activity that engages teachers, parents as well as communities' (Qi and Melhuish, 2016: 5). This change towards a more child-centred approach proved difficult for some teachers who had been used to a more teacher-centred curriculum.

In 2012, the Ministry of Education of the People's Republic of China issued the non-statutory, 'Early learning and development guidelines: age 3–6' to help ensure consistency across its provision. This document indicates developmental goals for children at different ages (3–4, 4–5 and 5–6 years) with respective guidance across the five learning fields indicated above. This guidance has been disseminated nationwide, but experts have advised that the guidance should not be used to measure children's learning and development, and individual differences should be recognised (Li and Feng, 2013).

Economic implications

As a result of China's one-child policy (in place between 1979–2015) and economic system reform, the number of public pre-school programmes has decreased, while the number of private pre-school programmes has increased rapidly (Qi and Melhuish, 2016). There are few empirical studies in China comparing the education provision between private and public kindergartens, but there are worries that private kindergartens are profit driven or lack financial support and are not able to guarantee basic quality requirements (Qi and Melhuish, 2016).

Some of the publicly funded kindergartens are also too expensive. There has long been criticism that in China the lack of accessible public pre-school services, combined with the lack of affordable and high-quality private services, is causing widespread inequality in early childhood education development (Cai and Feng, 2004). This has resulted in pressure upon the Chinese Government to provide more financial and policy support to the private ECE services (Pang, 2014).

Migration from rural areas to urban areas

Another issue is that of the migration of parents from rural areas to urban areas. In China, migration has become the main cause of family separation. Migrant workers sacrifice family life for a brighter economic future for the rural next-born generation, but their left-behind children are not better off. Children left behind with relatives has resulted in them lagging behind in academic achievements and social and emotional well-being (Hu et al., 2020). In addition, there is a lack of funding from the central government in ECE and a lack of qualified teachers in rural areas, resulting in slow academic progress for children educated in rural kindergartens (Hu et al., 2016).

Case Study: Pre-school education in rural areas

Zhang Wei is 3 years old and lives with his elderly aunt and uncle in the rural Shaanxi Province. Since he was 2 years old, both his parents have migrated to Beijing for work and Zhang Wei is considered a left-behind child. Although his parents regularly send money back home for Zhang Wei's care, it has been nearly a year since he last saw his parents. Zhang Wei attends the local village kindergarten and some of the money his parents send is used for his tuition fees. However, the lack of funding from the government in early childhood education (ECE) services has meant that the kindergarten is not well resourced and the teachers are underpaid, so the quality of education can be poor.

Although there is an ECE curriculum in China that advocates a child-centred approach, the teachers in Zhang Wei's kindergarten still adopt the traditional curriculum of expecting children to achieve proficiency in Chinese and mathematics. This means that the teaching approach is not play-based, but heavily adult-directed teaching. Zhang Wei has become withdrawn and has not wanted to attend the kindergarten, becoming tearful, and he has also reverted to bed wetting. He has asked to go to live with his parents in Beijing; however, private pre-school programmes for children in cities are very expensive and difficult to access without social connections. The potential outlook for Zhang Wei is not good, as research has shown that left-behind children have lower self-esteem, higher rates of loneliness and depression, and their development and academic achievement is not as good as children from non-migrant families.

This case study illustrates how economics can impact a child's development and life chances. Although Zhang Wei's parents felt the need to move to a city to provide financial security for him, the impact upon his well-being has been profound. There are no easy answers here or short-term solutions. Researchers argue that policy-makers need to improve the quality of rural ECE and society needs to make it easier and more affordable for migrant workers to bring their children with them.

Reflective Question

Consider the case study above. How would you help Zhang Wei to adapt to his parents' absence? Make a list and discuss it with your peers.

Anthropological Approach within early years curricula

Chapter 5 states that the discipline of anthropology is broadly about understanding the traditions, habits and views that a group of people, community or society possess and the roles they play in people's lives. This emphasis on traditions and habits can be seen in the Te Whāriki curriculum in New Zealand for children from birth to school entry.

Whāriki means 'woven mat' in Māori and the curriculum is woven from principles, aims and appropriate practice. It is the national curriculum for early childhood education (New Zealand Government, 2016). Underpinning Te Whāriki is the aspiration that all children will 'grow up as competent and confident learners and communicators, healthy in mind, body, and spirit, secure in their sense of belonging and in the knowledge that they make a valued contribution to society' (New Zealand Government, 2016: 7). Te Whāriki recognises the special place of Māori as the indigenous people of Aotearoa, and that there is a shared obligation to protect Māori language. This resonates with the 'Curriculum Cymreig' in the FP in Wales and the requirement for children to learn about the culture of Wales and to learn the Welsh language (ACCAC, 2003).

The Te Whāriki curriculum reflects the holistic way children grow and learn and the wider world of family and community is an integral part of early childhood education (ECE). Through the ECE, children develop a wide range of knowledge, skills and attitudes and these combine to form 'learning dispositions'. These learning dispositions are sometimes described as being 'ready, willing and able to act' (New Zealand Government, 2016: 18).

The curriculum is described in terms of principles and strands, as shown in Table 18.1.

Table 18.1   The Te Whāriki curriculum

4 Principles	5 Strands
Empowerment	Well-being
Holistic development	Belonging
Family and community	Contribution
Relationships	Communication
	Exploration

For each of the five strands of Te Whāriki, there are several learning outcomes for children that are specified, together with related goals for practice. The learning outcomes can be used for curriculum planning and assessing children's progress. This is similar to the FP outcomes and the EYFS learning goals described at the beginning of this chapter. Each strand has three or four goals and each goal has learning outcomes; there are more than 100 across the five strands.

Practitioners develop 'learning stories' to assess and plan for the children's learning. The learning story is written to the child and their family, describing a significant learning event. There is an analysis of the learning along the lines of what is the practitioner learning about the child or what learning did they think was happening. Finally, the learning story can contain an element of future planning, listed as opportunities and possibilities (Lee et al., 2013).

Case Study: Learning stories in action

Noah came into the pre-school setting carrying a photograph, showing him with his dad standing by a telescope. He went on to tell the class that he had gone camping with his dad and they had used the telescope to find stars in the sky. The practitioner in the setting asked Noah if he would like to make his own telescope. Noah readily agreed. Using collage materials and a cardboard tube, Noah enthusiastically spent the day painting and designing his telescope. Once the telescope had dried, Noah asked to go outdoors and to stand on the climbing frame, using his telescope to survey the surrounding area. Noah was able to take his telescope home and his mum reported back that he spent many hours using his telescope in his bedroom at night to look for stars.

What learning is happening?

Design and making is an activity that provides the opportunity for pre-maths skills, pattern designing, hand–eye coordination, colour recognition and problem-solving.

Possibilities

We will continue to keep the collage area well stocked, and provide books and pictures of telescopes. Noah, you might like to create a telescope for a classroom display table all about space. We can look at books about famous telescopes around the world, and learn about different stars and planets in the sky.

Noah focused and concentrated on making his telescope. He thought about the colours he wanted to use and the patterns he wanted to add to his telescope. At our pre-school, we encourage children to be independent thinkers and problem solvers. We encourage free choice and want children to take ownership of their designs. Noah is developing these skills and will be given further opportunities to do so.

This case study is one example of a learning story in action. The pre-school has allowed Noah to set his own learning agenda, building upon his current prevailing interests. The setting has focused upon Noah's learning dispositions and linked to the five curriculum strands illustrated in Table 18.1. By allowing Noah to take ownership of his learning, the setting has empowered him and fostered a good working relationship with him, thus also supporting the principles of the Te Whāriki curriculum.

Reflective Question

Consider the early years curriculum you work with. Can you see a place for learning stores?

Philosophical Approach within early years curricula

In Sweden, the philosophy of the pre-schools is to have a respect for human rights and the fundamental democratic values that Swedish society is built upon (Korpi, 2007). The pre-school environment resembles a family home, and this emphasises the importance that Swedish pre-schools place upon links between them and the home environment of the child. Children have large amounts of unrestricted floor space to play, build and be creative, and attend Swedish pre-schools from the ages of 1–6 years (Lindén, 2018). The pre-schools are publicly funded and complemented by smaller income-related parental fees and offer services from 6am to 7pm. All pre-school meals are free of charge, and the teachers eat for free, as meals are considered part of health education.

The pre-school curriculum

The principles underpinning the early years curriculum in Sweden are norms and values; development and learning; children's influence; cooperation with the home, and cooperation with the school. Each of these principles has goals and guidelines. The guidelines specify the responsibility of pre-school teachers for ensuring that teaching takes place in accordance with the goals set out in the curriculum.

The pre-school curriculum is holistic and has play at its centre (Swedish National Agency for Education, 2019). A child's development and learning should take into account the children's own experiences, needs and what they show an interest in. Children learn through play, social interaction, exploration and creation, but also by observing, conversing and reflecting. Outdoor activities take priority even in freezing weather conditions. Additionally, a midday nap outside and a healthy diet are an integral part of Swedish pre-school programmes (Özar, 2012).

Reflective Question

Do you think early years appears to be 'viewed' differently in the UK? If so, how and why?

Neuroscience Approach within early years curricula

Chapter 7 noted that there is a belief that neuroscience helps educators understand pedagogy – i.e., their methods of teaching and learning in a more scientific way (Tibke, 2019). The HighScope curriculum or approach for early years originated in the USA in the 1960s. It was founded by David Weikart and is a complete system of early childhood education, drawing upon research and brain science (Epstein et al., 2011). In this curriculum, children construct their knowledge and participate in the active learning process (Epstein, 2007).

HighScope originally drew upon the cognitive developmental theory of Piaget and the progressive educational theory of Dewey. Since then, it has been updated, drawing upon ongoing research of children's developmental trajectories and brain research (Goswami, 2002; Shore, 1997). HighScope practitioners are actively involved with the children providing materials, planning activities and talking with them to support and challenge their 'explorations, observations, ideas and thoughts' (Epstein, Johnson and Lafferty, 2011:103).

HighScope in action

HighScope advocates active participatory learning through the following features:

- **Materials** – Open ended, natural, diverse and freely available
- **Manipulation** – Children examine, transform, connect – discoveries through hands on and 'minds on' contact
- **Choice** – Children choose materials and their play partners
- **Child Language and thought** – Children describe what they are doing through verbal and non-verbal communication. They reflect on their actions and adapt their thinking to take on board new learning.
- **Adult Scaffolding** – Adults understand how children reason and support their current level of thinking. They challenge them to move to the next stage, developing knowledge and understanding and creative problem-solving skills. Peer learning is 'highly valued'

(Epstein et al., 2011: 104)

HighScope is unique in that it emphasises the importance of 3- to 5-year-olds planning their activities based upon their own interests and reflecting with adults and peers about what they have learnt. This is similar to the early years curricula in the UK where there is also an emphasis on activities being based upon a child's interests. In HighScope, this is known as 'plan-do-review' (Epstein et al., 2011: 104). The curriculum can be represented as shown in Figure 18.1.

There are eight curriculum areas:

- Approaches to learning.
- Social and emotional development.
- Physical development and health.
- Language, literacy and communication.
- Mathematics.
- Creative arts.
- Science and technology.
- Social studies.

These are comparable with other areas of learning in other early years curricula. There are 58 Key Development Indicators (KDIs) which are based upon the latest research and periodically updated. Child assessment is undertaken through on-going observation, assessed across core content, and programme assessment assesses the delivery methods and their effectiveness.

There are two main criticisms of HighScope, relating to methodology and curriculum content. Criticisms of the daily routine are that there is not enough free play. Group times are initiated by

Figure 18.1 The HighScope curriculum/approach: Hohmann et al. (2008: 6)

adults and critics believe this should be conducted by children. However, alternate criticism is that there is not enough adult-directed teaching (Epstein et al., 2011). Criticisms around curriculum content is that it is too difficult or too time-consuming to use and understand. HighScope has worked to resolve this by having HighScope endorsed trainers who can adapt materials and courses to meet different practitioner backgrounds and abilities.

Case Study: A day in the life of the HighScope Approach

Today in the setting 3-year-old Loren told the teacher about her pet rabbit, Bobtail. She explained that she had watched Bobtail last night and at first he was asleep, then he woke up and had a drink of water. Bobtail then went over to his food bowl, but instead of eating, he picked up the bowl and threw it across the cage. The teacher replied that maybe Bobtail did not like the food in the bowl.

(Continued)

Loren thought about this and then agreed, and added that perhaps she needed to give Bobtail 'nicer' food. The teacher suggested that in the plan-do and review session today, Loren could go and look at some books (plan) on what rabbits like to eat and then make a menu for Bobtail to take home (do); she could share her ideas in the review session and ask other children for their ideas.

Loren did this and went home with a new menu for Bobtail. She reported back the next day that Bobtail had really enjoyed his new foods and she showed a picture she had drawn of him eating this food.

This snapshot of a day in a HighScope setting shows how the teachers take on board children's current interests and give them the time to follow that interest through and incorporate it into the daily routine. Loren is given time to explore her current interest in the rabbit's food and to solve the problem of giving Bobtail nicer food. In terms of the curriculum, this would support health, communication and science (learning about living things).

Reflective Question

What have you observed that is similar or different to this approach?

Summary of chapter

- There are a number of different early years curricula, both nationally and internationally.
- Different curricula support different interdisciplinary approaches to child development and learning.
- Some curricula still assess children against learning outcomes or goals.
- Although different curricula have different areas of learning, they all support the domains of development discussed in Part 2.
- Practitioners are able to train in Froebelian methods in the UK.
- Te Whāriki and the Foundation phase support a bilingual approach.
- Standards in pre-schools in China are variable and there can be cost implications.
- HighScope curriculum is based on many years of research.

End-of-chapter questions

1. What do you feel are the advantages and disadvantages of the different curricula seen throughout this chapter?

2. Which of the curricula discussed in this chapter do you feel most supports your vision of early years education?

3. If you were to design a new curriculum for the early years, what would it look like?

Further reading

Ang, L. (2014) *Early Years Curriculum: The UK Context and Beyond*. Abingdon: Routledge.

This book covers a range of curriculum models from across the world, providing in-depth discussion on key issues and theories. It encourages readers to explore different ways of understanding the curriculum, and to develop a critical understanding of the key issues that shape the way a curriculum is designed.

Blatchford-Siraj, I. and Woodhead, M. (eds) (2009) *Effective Early Childhood Programmes*. Milton Keynes: Open University.

This book cites the argument for the need for effective early childhood education programmes. It covers the research that underpins the HighScope curriculum and discusses the challenges facing early childhood programmes.

Broström, S., Frøkjær, T., Johansson, I. and Sandberg, A. (2014) 'Preschool teachers view on learning in preschool in Sweden and Denmark'. Available at: www.researchgate.net/publication/265520954_ Preschool_teachers'_view_on_learning_in_preschool_in_Sweden_and_Denmark

This research discusses the background to the early years curricula, in both countries and what practitioners' perceptions of how best children learn.

NINETEEN
UNDERSTANDING INCLUSIVITY THROUGH THE DISCIPLINES AND DOMAINS

This chapter will help you to

- develop an understanding of important contemporary topics relating to inclusion, such as social justice, inequalities, special educational needs, children's rights and participation;
- understand how adults can promote and support equitable early childhood practice.

Introduction

Equality is about valuing all children as individuals (Knowles and Mukherji, 2014). This is important because Siraj-Blatchford suggests that even though many early childhood settings appear to be calm, friendly and welcoming places, 'there may be a great deal of underlying inequality, and children disadvantaged in both intentional and unintentional ways' (2014: 194). This chapter explains how children might experience inequality and be disadvantaged in society, and considers how this impacts on their development and life chances. It also discusses the concept of inclusion, models of disability and ways of achieving equitable early childhood practice.

Children's rights and the concept of provision, protection and participation are also discussed, and this chapter is underpinned by the 'evolving capacities' concept which is central to protecting children's rights. The concept rejects the perspective that children follow expected, rigid stages of development which are central to developmental psychology; the concept focuses attention on the capacity of each individual and their uniqueness. Adopting the evolving capacities concept means that practitioners recognise that relationships, opportunities and environments influence a child's capabilities (Willow, 2014), which is more closely aligned with an interdisciplinary approach.

The disciplines and child development domains discussed in Part 1 and Part 2 are integrated throughout this chapter. At times, this chapter draws upon legislation and research specific to Wales, mainly because the regime of truth (i.e., the dominant discourse) that is often portrayed in textbooks for students relates to legislation and policy in England, and this can be somewhat misleading for students studying in other parts of the UK.

Understanding the concept of inclusion

In the past, inclusion often referred to including children with special educational needs (SEN) in mainstream schools, but as time has evolved, inclusion has broadened to mean 'equality of opportunity for all children whatever their gender, ability, ethnicity, culture, faith or socio-economic group' (Borkett, 2019: 151). Moreover, inclusion is about all children having the right 'to have a voice in decisions that affect them' (Borkett, 2019: 155). Borkett (2019) highlights that certain groups of children can be excluded, such as disabled children, those from minority ethnic backgrounds, bilingual children and children from deprived areas.

Being inclusive means valuing all children regardless of their background or personal circumstances, and involves the process of identifying and removing barriers so that all children can participate (Borkett, 2019; Hunt, 2018; Knowles and Mukherji, 2014; Tedam, 2009). However, inclusion, like many other concepts such as quality, childhood, well-being and participation, are often contested and can be difficult to define (Borkett, 2019). According to Tedam (2009), inclusion does not have a fixed definition and Tempriou (2018) explains that inclusion is complex, but essentially it is about removing barriers to participation. Barriers can relate to learning or in society more generally.

Models of disability/inclusion

Models of disability/inclusion are useful in understanding how people and society view others who have different development needs (Hunt, 2018). There are various models of inclusion, such as the medical model, the social model, the affirmation model and the bio-psycho-social model. The medical model focuses on the child's disability/individual impairment and how medical professionals can fix/overcome or develop solutions of support (barriers perceived as internal), whereas the social model focuses on how society and the environment disables a child, which prevents a child from fully participating (barriers perceived as external). The affirmation model focuses on a child's strengths no matter what their disability and sees their impairment as integral to their identity.

The bio-psycho-social model, also called the integrative model, adopts a more holistic view which considers the complex interplay between the biological, environmental and psychological influences that impact a child's experiences. In order to ensure effective provision for a child with special educational needs, their strengths and needs must be considered alongside their condition/impairment (Crutchley, 2018). Adopting the bio-psycho-social model is a good example of how to embed interdisciplinary approaches to your work. For example, disciplines such as neuroscience closely relate to the biological aspect, sociology relates to the environmental aspect and psychology, education and anthropology are closely connected to the psychological aspect of the model.

Inequalities

Justice has been debated for thousands of years – for example, in philosophy, Plato discussed justice by explaining that it was about people living together and enjoying the good life, and everyone being given the opportunity to flourish and fulfil their potential. One way of achieving this is living in a just (equal) society (Knowles and Mukherji, 2014). Therefore, it is important that professionals working with young children understand inequalities.

In order for children to achieve the best out of life and reach their potential, psychologist Maslow suggests that children must have their basic needs met first, such as food, warmth and shelter, before they can move on to higher level needs, such as love, self-esteem and safety, leading to self-actualisation (Knowles and Mukherji, 2014). The Nuffield Foundation state that over half a million children in the UK lack the essentials such as food, shelter and clothing (Oppenheim and Milton, 2021).

The rate of poverty for families with young children under 5 years of age in the UK is high at 36 per cent and is increasing; this rate is higher in England and Wales than it is in Scotland and Northern Ireland (Oppenheim and Milton, 2021). In terms of ethnicity and poverty in the UK, between 2017 and 2020, '71% of children in families of Bangladeshi origin with a young child were living in poverty. In many other minority ethnic groups, over 50% of families were living in poverty' (Oppenheim and Milton, 2021: 5).

Child development and long-term opportunities/life chances

When children experience poverty at a very early age, their long-term opportunities and well-being are likely to be hindered (Oppenheim and Milton, 2021). Bandyopadhyay et al. (2021: 1) explain that the persistent nature of living in poverty 'has a detrimental impact on child health, cognitive and behavioural outcomes'. Moreover, it is known that children who achieve less well in school are those who grow up in poverty and usually experience more mental health difficulties (Bandyopadhyay et al., 2021).

It is important to understand that 'different indicators of socio-economic circumstances predict variation in different aspects of child development' (Joshi et al., 2011: 6). For example, when the Centre for Longitudinal Studies conducted further analysis on the cohort for children in Wales, they found that the age of the mother for their first child, lone motherhood and parental unemployment were predictors of behavioural problems in children at age 7. In terms of maths and reading, circumstances such as low parental education and low incomes were more predictive of poorer outcomes. Other socioeconomic indicators of disadvantage included having multiple older siblings and growing up in families where parents are out of work (Joshi et al., 2011).

The Effective Pre-School, Primary and Secondary Education Project in England found that the home learning environment shapes the GCSE attainment of young people at age 16 and A-level outcomes at ages 17 and 18 – for example, a higher, richer environment where a child is stimulated predicts higher grades at GCSE and higher attainment at A-level (Sammons et al., 2015).

Early intervention is about providing appropriate support to children and their families who are at risk of poorer outcomes. Crutchley and Hunt (2018) suggest that Graham Allen lobbied for an early intervention agenda and culture to improve the life chances of those most disadvantaged. In 2011, the Allen review was published with the core message that intervening early can 'make lasting improvements in the lives of our children, to forestall many persistent social problems and end their transmission from one generation to the next, and to make long-term savings in public spending' (Allen, 2011: vii).

The disciplines implicit in this core message about early intervention from Allen are psychology and sociology (e.g., improving lives and eradicating poverty/societal challenges such as deprivation) and economics (e.g., long-term benefits outweighing the costs). In philosophy, Plato's thinking around the good life and opportunities to flourish are implicit in Allen's further point that intervening early provides children with 'a vital social and emotional foundation which will help to keep them happy, healthy and achieving throughout their lives' (2011: ix).

The importance of children's rights: provision, protection and participation

Children's rights are usually described under the heading of provision, protection and participation. Provision rights broadly relate to standards of living, to education, to culture and the arts, as well as knowledge of the UNCRC. Protection rights usually relate to protection from different kinds of abuse and exploitation, and there are participation rights which are often considered more controversial than protection and provision rights. Participation rights provide opportunities for children to actively and authentically participate in their family and community life, and have a say about matters that affect their lives, but there is often disagreement or controversy over the age at which children can or should participate (Alderson, 2008).

Alderson (2008) suggests the following dyads (child–adult relationship) for the three different kinds of rights:

1. providing adult and the needy child (provision);
2. the protective adult and the victim child (protection);
3. mutual respect between the participating adult and child (participation).

Dyads 1 and 2 describe the adult as 'caretaker' and adopt the view that young children should only be afforded provision and protection rights, whereas 'liberationists' (dyad 3) believe that young should be afforded participation rights and be involved as early as possible in making decisions (Walker, 2011).

Alderson (2008) states that participation is often narrowed down to being two aspects: first being consulted and second making decisions. Adults are mainly in control during participative activities, whereby they select the questions and control how decisions are made: 'the success of participation is seen to depend on the *process* of how far adults allow children to contribute to, influence, and perhaps make decisions, and the *outcome* of how far decisions are acted on – mainly by adults' (Alderson, 2008: 80).

Listening to children can benefit society in numerous ways, such as helping to improve care, services and the community, educating adults about what is important to children, and contributing to a democratic society in which adults and children/young people negotiate with one another (Alderson, 2008). Moss (2007; cited in Borkett, 2019) argues that a democratic space in early childhood settings is characterised by children expressing their views and taking part in decision making.

Alderson (2008) suggests that some of the feelings associated with adults who are in favour of consulting with young children involve optimism, trust and confidence in children's capabilities and strengths, whereas feelings associated with those who are not in favour involve pessimism, doubt, lack of confidence in children's capabilities and a profound concern for their vulnerability.

Case Study: What children think matters...

Mrs Andrews was a newly appointed nursery head teacher and was keen to adopt a strategy from her previous school whereby children were involved in the recruitment process of new staff. It involved candidates spending either a morning or afternoon with the children and then afterwards the children were asked what they liked about the potential new teacher. They were encouraged to place buttons on a range of smiley faces to indicate how the candidate made them feel. On the same day, and on an individual basis, children were shown photographs of the different candidates and they were asked to say which one they liked the best. Essentially, they were asked to vote for their favourite candidate. The majority of Mrs Andrews's team loved this new way of involving children, apart from Miss Hert who disliked the idea and said: 'these children are far too young to understand and get involved in staff recruitment, what's the point... ?' Mrs Andrews explained: 'there are many reasons why we should do this; it shows how we value/position children as important citizens in society, it upholds the UNCRC and respects children's opinions on matters that affect them'.

The case study above demonstrates how young children can become actively involved in the recruitment of early years staff and help adults make decisions about who to select/appoint. However, for this to work successfully, everyone needs to be on board with the concept, and respect children's opinions and believe they have something to offer in the recruitment process, as not everyone will share this belief.

Reflective question

Why do you think Miss Hert dislikes the idea of children getting involved in the recruitment process?

United Nations Convention on the Rights of the Child (UNCRC), 1989

It was not until the latter part of the twentieth century that children were considered to be independent from adults and having rights (Handley, 2009). For example, the UNCRC was adopted in 1989 after a ten-year drafting period, with the UK ratifying the Convention in 1991 (Willow, 2014). The overall aim of the convention is to improve the quality of children's lives (Handley, 2009). It consists of 54 articles which 'cover civil, economic, social and cultural rights' (MacBlain, Dunn and Luke, 2017); articles 2, 3, 6 and 12 are known as the general principles:

- Article 2 – an entitlement to enjoy rights without any form of discrimination.
- Article 3 – best interests of the child in all actions concerning the child.
- Article 6 – right to survival and maximum development.
- Article 12 – right to freely express their view and be heard.

Rights Respecting Schools (UNICEF)

The Rights Respecting Schools Award began in 2004 by UNICEF and is a programme that schools can register for which places a focus on embedding children's rights throughout all aspects of school life. For the programme to be successful, the whole community – parents, governors, children and all staff – need to be fully supportive if it. The programme is aimed at making schools re-evaluate their ethos and embed the principles of the UNCRC. Evidence indicates that children who attend a Rights Respecting School are knowledgeable about their rights and can exercise them; they feel valued and have a good awareness of the rights of others (UNICEF, 2021).

Equality Act 2010

The Equality Act brings together a range of previous laws in an attempt to ban unfair treatment of people and covers nine protected characteristics – age, disability, gender reassignment, marriage and civil partnership, pregnancy and maternity, race, religion and belief, sex and sexual orientation (Knowles and Mukherji, 2014). The Act places an expectation and, more importantly, a requirement on schools to put in place reasonable adjustments to the physical environment, provision/practice, and to offer support services (Crutchley, 2018). As Arnold (2018) states, practitioners need to know about the Equality Act because it also applies to treating parents fairly and respectfully.

Case Study: Feeling welcomed!

Jane and Hayley were really keen to find a high-quality day nursery for their daughter Alice, aged two. Jane worked full-time and Hayley worked part-time, so they were looking for Alice to attend for two-and-half days per week. Finding a high-quality day nursery where Jane and Hayley felt welcomed was really important for two reasons: first, because they were a married same-sex couple and second because Alice has cerebral palsy. In the past, Jane and Hayley had experienced discrimination at antenatal classes mainly from other parents and on occasions from some health professionals. Consequently, they were apprehensive about how they would be accepted by the nursery staff and other parents, and how Alice's needs would be met. They made a few phone calls to different nurseries to arrange a visit and the very short excerpts below are from the initial telephone call with two different day nurseries. Unfortunately, Hayley overheard a discriminatory comment from day nursery 2.

Day nursery 1:

Nursery manager:	Good morning, I'm Mandy, the day nursery manager. How can I help you today?
Hayley:	Hello, I notice from your website that you have spaces available and I was wondering if I could arrange a visit as my wife and I are trying to find a suitable nursery for our daughter who has cerebral palsy.
Nursery manager:	Yes certainly. Would you mind if I asked a few questions so we can make sure that your visit fully matches your needs?
Hayley:	That's fine.
Nursery Manager:	When is it convenient for you and your wife to come and visit? How old is your daughter and what's her name? Does your daughter have any specific needs relating to her cerebral palsy? What does she like doing?

Day nursery 2:

Nursery manager:	Hello, Sunnies.
Hayley:	Hello, I notice from your website that you have spaces available and I was wondering if I could arrange a visit as my wife and I are trying to find a suitable nursery for our daughter Alice who has cerebral palsy.
Nursery manager:	Can I ask when you last looked on the website because we are now full unfortunately. Sorry about that. I do hope you find a nursery suitable for you and Alice. [Overheard by Hayley: 'We can't have another same-sex family attend, look at all the problems it caused with the other families last time and we'd have to make changes to the environment].

The case study above shows how some families and their children are discriminated against by one or more of the protected characteristics – the parents' sexual orientation and the child's disability. It shows how two different day nurseries welcome families and accept or reject diversity.

Reflective question

How do you ensure that children and their families are treated fairly and respectfully and are not discriminated against?

Promoting and supporting equitable early childhood practice

The values, attitudes and beliefs of the adults who work with children can affect their actions and behaviours – for example, the research by Jenson (2009; cited in Knowles and Mukherji, 2014) found that practitioners attach a deficit model rather than a positive focus to certain groups of children, such as those who grow up in poverty, are from minority ethnic families or have special educational needs. Children's self-esteem is more likely to be high when they feel loved, secure and nurtured, and are surrounded by adults who have high and realistic expectations of them (Knowles and Mukherji, 2014) rather than adults who discriminate against them.

It is important to remember that 'the ideas we hold about ourselves make up our "self-concept"and "self-image" and are formed, in part, from the reactions of others around us' (Knowles and Mukherji, 2014: 168). Therefore, it is extremely important that adults are aware of their own beliefs and biases towards certain groups of children in order to help children develop a positive self-concept and self-image. Adults should also pay attention to helping children treat their peers with respect to enable positive self-development.

Practitioners can use the *Index for Inclusion* to evaluate and further understand their provision and take the opportunity to put their ethos, principles and practices under the spotlight (Borkett, 2019). Tedam (2009) states that it is unacceptable for settings to downplay the promotion of diversity when, for example, they have minimal attendance from children from minority ethnic families or disabled children. The aim should be to encourage children 'to appreciate difference as they grow and develop' (2009: 125).

Supporting children with Special Educational Needs (SEN)/Additional Learning Needs (ALN)

The first 'special educational needs' Code of Practice published in 1994 introduced a graduated approach and the statementing process which ensured that children received funding for the most appropriate support and intervention in schools. Then in 2015, the Code of Practice for England was revised for 0- to 25-year-olds whereby the statementing process was replaced with a statutory Education, Health Care (EHC) plan. However, for a child to have an EHC plan, schools need to be able to show that there has been no or little progress made by the child despite the school implementing evidence-based interventions. A related concern about the EHC plan is that they are only available to those 'who have both a disability and a SEN, or who have just a SEN' (Crutchley, 2018: 23); they exclude children with a medical need or disability and no SEN where best practice applies, and this raises concerns about funding arrangements and equitable policy.

As well as the introduction of an EHC plan for the 2015 Code, there was more focus and emphasis on respecting and including the views and wishes of the child as well as the parent, which reflects more emphasis on children's rights than previous codes (Crutchley, 2018).

In Wales, it was decided that the current system for supporting children with Special Educational Needs (SEN) was out-of-date and no longer fit for purpose, and the Welsh Government wanted a system that was more child-centred and less complex. Therefore, they introduced the Additional

Learning Needs and Education Tribunal (Wales) Act 2018 which is the new statutory framework for supporting children and young people with additional learning needs (ALN). ALN replaces SEN in an attempt to break away from the old, outdated systems. The new framework emphasises the importance of children's rights and states:

> the Act requires that the views of children and young people should always be considered as part of the planning process, along with those of their parents. It is imperative that children and young people see the planning process as something which is done with them rather than to them. (WG, 2018a: 7)

The notion of 'done with' rather than 'done to' in the quote above is grounded in the new sociology of childhood discipline. For example, the new movement is about taking children seriously and viewing them as people (Mayall, 2000).

The UK longitudinal millennium cohort study, also known as 'child of the new century' which follows 19,517 children born in 2000–1, reports that children with SEN do less well in school compared to their peers, display more behavioural difficulties and experience bullying (Parsons and Platt, 2018). The key message in supporting children with SEN/ALN is about removing barriers to learning and participation, and considering the affirmation model that focuses on a child's strengths and sees their impairment (e.g., visual, hearing, multi-sensory) as integral to their identity.

Case Study: Removing barriers – positive impacts

When I reflect back on my time in school, I always have happy memories of my nursery teacher communicating with me through Makaton, talking to me face-to-face so I could lip read. I'll never forget the effort the staff went to in providing a visual cue as well as the auditory cue. For example, if the fire alarm bell sounded or it was tidy-up time the teacher would hold up a visual cue card. I loved nursery.

The case study shows that when Sam, who has a hearing impairment, reflects back on his school days, he has very positive memories of how the nursery staff made it possible for him to fully participate. It shows that sensitive and caring staff who make small changes can have lasting positive impacts on a child's experiences.

Reflective question

What small change/s could you make to a child's environment that would make a positive difference to the quality of their life?

Supporting children who speak English as an Additional Language (EAL)

Children who speak English as an additional language (i.e., where English is not their first language) make up around 20 per cent of the school population (NALDIC, 2021). There are a range of helpful strategies that early childhood practitioners can implement for children who are non-verbal (going through a silent phase), such as engage in conversation even if the child doesn't respond, encourage participation in small group work, use the child's first language, accept non-verbal responses, praise minimal effort, encourage a child to repeat words and lastly use role play to reinforce language practice (Clarke, 1992; cited in Ehiyazaryan-White, 2019). Assessing children in their first language and involving parents in the assessment process is worthwhile and should be considered. Having bilingual support staff is vital in ensuring that children and their families feel a sense of belonging, are supported and included (Siraj-Blatchford, 2014).

Supporting Gypsy, Roma and Traveller (GRT) children

Gypsy, Roma and Traveller (GRT) children are one of the lowest achieving groups in education and there are many complex, overlapping factors that contribute to their low achievement (DfE, 2014b). They are often discriminated against and experience inequality (WG, 2018b). But there are many strategies that can be adopted to improve the life chances and opportunities of GRT children, such as having high expectations of all children regardless of their background, a welcoming, inclusive culture, strong engagement and partnerships with parents and the community (DfE, 2014b). Arguably, these are strategies that are effective for all children.

Summary of chapter

- Inclusion means valuing all children regardless of their background or personal circumstances and the bio-psycho-social model of inclusion/disability is interdisciplinary in nature.
- There are a range of socioeconomic factors that can impact on children's outcomes such as living in poverty.
- Children's rights are often described in three ways – provision, protection and participation – and there is often debate over the age at which a child can or should participate.
- For practice to be equitable, practitioners need to acknowledge how their own values and beliefs may impact on their actions and sensitively consider how they can remove barriers to learning and participation.

End-of-chapter questions

1. What does inclusion mean to you, and to what extent has this chapter extended your understanding?

2. How would you ensure that young children have positive life chances?
3. What do you think are some of the most effective ways of promoting and supporting inclusion?

Further reading

Booth, T. and Ainscow, M. (2011) *Index for Inclusion: Developing Learning and Participation in School* (3rd edn). Bristol: Centre for Studies on Inclusive Education (CSIE). See the following link for more information: Index for Inclusion: developing learning and participation in schools (csie.org.uk)

This resource is very useful for helping settings self-reflect and review their cultures, practices and policies to establish if there are any barriers to learning and participation. It focuses on inclusion and provides opportunities for settings to prioritise aspects of practice they want to change and provides a structure for them to evaluate their progress.

Lewis, A., Sarwar, S., Tyrie, J., Waters, J. and Williams, J. (2017) Exploring the extent of enactment of young children's rights in the education system in Wales. *Wales Journal of Education*, 19 (2): 27–50.

This journal article will be useful in understanding how Wales has adopted the UNCRC and stands out from the rest of the UK. The researchers present the findings of a review of readily available empirically based literature that evidences the extent to which young children in Wales (aged 3–7 years) routinely access their rights in education settings.

Siraj-Blatchford, I. and Clarke, P. (2000) *Supporting Identity, Diversity And Language In The Early Years*. Buckingham: Open University Press.

This book will extend your knowledge and understanding of child development specifically to identify development, self-esteem and language acquisition in the context of diversity. Even though it was published in 2000, Chapter 6 is useful as it provides you with guidance about how to assess and evaluate equity and diversity in practice; Chapter 7 provides you with a wide range of resources for use with young children.

TWENTY

UNDERSTANDING HOW SHARED SPACES SUPPORT CHILD DEVELOPMENT AND THE ROLE OF THE ADULT WITHIN THIS

This chapter will help you to

- appreciate the role of the adult in shared spaces;
- develop an interdisciplinary understanding of shared spaces;
- develop an understanding of how shared spaces facilitates child development.

Introduction

Shared spaces in an educational context can be defined as connecting people through maximising collaboration and engagement. It can be a space where children play, explore and learn (Nursery Resources, 2018). Hodgman (2015) also includes space as part of an enabling environment, supporting children's physical and mental well-being. There are a number of different approaches to creating shared spaces between adults and children. These have evolved over time, underpinned with new understandings of child development, and have been influenced by the different approaches discussed in this book towards child development. It can be argued that no environment is neutral and entering any shared space or environment evokes a physical and emotional reaction (Miller et al., 2005). As this chapter explains, children react to the people within, the layout of and the feel of an environment, and how positive, empowering environments can foster and nurture children's holistic development.

Shared Spaces: Classical Theories

Piaget

Chapter 2 described how Piaget, considered to be the grand theorist of developmental psychology, championed ideas of discovery learning (MacBlain, 2018). Here the child is encouraged to make discoveries for themselves through interacting with shared spaces within the learning environment (Crowley, 2017). Readiness to learn is important when the provision of activities within the shared space is appropriate to the child's stage of development. Here the activities will challenge the child, but will not include any activities that the child is not ready for. The practitioner will plan the environment for individual children and small groups rather than the whole class. Piaget (1959) argued that children up to the age of 5 nearly always work alone and are not socially involved with others while playing. He contended that cognitive development occurred through assimilation and accommodation (see Chapter 14) and the practitioner's role was to provide a learning space that supported this. Here the learning environment would include resources that challenge and stimulate thinking, with the practitioner viewed as facilitating learning but not giving direct instruction.

Criticisms of discovery learning include the lack of active transmission of knowledge through interactions with practitioners and peers. Piaget's theory has also been further challenged as he studied child development without observing how children *do* 'interact with their environment, peers and others' (Clare, 2012: 6).

Vygotsky

Vygotsky also saw children as active explorers of their learning spaces. However, in contrast to Piaget, he emphasised the importance of children socially interacting with others to construct their knowledge and understanding. Vygotsky contended that through the zone of proximal development (as discussed in Chapter 2), children are supported to further their knowledge and understanding. Here a child develops higher mental functions not only by interacting with their environment, but through socially interacting with a more knowledgeable other (Ford, 2005). Shared spaces are created so the child can interact with their peers and the adult creates activities that enable the child to cooperate alongside others.

Montessori

As discussed in Chapter 13, Montessori believed that children benefited from being independent learners, which resonates with Piaget's view of the child. She believed that the environment should be prepared according to a child's individual needs and that the child develops in relation to their environment. The learning environment or space should be designed to allow natural learning to occur (Bradley et al., 2011). Montessori contended that the prepared environment affects children's spontaneous learning. Thus, it needed to be organised to promote active learning, resonating with Piaget's theory. The practitioner prepares the environment after careful observation of the child's needs, developmental stage and prior experiences. For Montessori, a favourable environment should have the following characteristics:

- accessible;
- allowing freedom of movement and choice;
- the child to be personally responsible for looking after the environment or space;
- real materials and a natural environment with open-ended activities;
- having beauty and harmony.

(Bradley et al., 2011)

However, a criticism of Montessori was her lack of focus on developing a child's imagination or fantasy play, something she did not think was important for a child's development (Moyles et al., 2002).

Today, evidence of Montessori can be seen through the use of child-sized furniture and resources in settings. The use of large floor spaces and uncluttered areas for children to work and play in links back to Maria Montessori. She also advocated the use of free-flow access between the outdoors and indoors, and viewed the outdoors as an environment or space for purposeful work. This is now commonplace in early years curricula around the UK and internationally. Montessori felt that it was important for children of different ages to play and work together within the shared space to promote good role modelling, and this resonates with Vygotsky's more knowledgeable other (Bradley et al., 2011). Montessori's environment would be kept simple and in neutral colours, and this echoes the Reggio Emilia type of learning space as discussed in Chapter 12.

Contemporary theorists such as Moyles support some aspects of the theoretical approaches detailed above. Moyles's (1989) play spiral theory suggests that children need exploratory or discovery play first (Piaget and Montessori) and then the adult intervenes to guide and direct play (Vygotsky), and finally a return to child-directed exploratory play but with the added skills gained from the adult enhancing this play. Janet Moyles also researched the role of the adult within the learning environment, which will be discussed later in this chapter.

Reflective Question

If you took an audit of your provision, would your shared spaces support more of a Piagetian, Vygotskian or Montessorian approach?

Shared Spaces and the Curriculum

As discussed previously, in terms of early years provision, the ideas of Piaget, Vygotsky and Montessori can be seen in the shared spaces or learning environments on offer. As discussed in Chapter 16, the Early Years Foundation Stage (EYFS) in England and the Foundation Phase (FP) in Wales both espouse a play-based pedagogy. Both curricula are taught through a mixture of adult- and child-led activities and this is reflected in how the learning environment or shared space is set up.

The EYFS *Statutory Framework* (DfE, 2021: 6) clearly states that four principles should shape practice in the early years, including that 'children learn and develop well in enabling environments with teaching and support from adults', whereas the current FP in Wales has three types of provision underpinning the learning environment – the continuous, the enhanced and the focused provision. These are represented in policy documents as a triangle with the continuous provision at the bottom, followed by the enhanced and finally the focused provision at the top. The idea is that the continuous provision is the most used type of provision, and this includes all the everyday classroom resources such as the reading areas, the outdoor play area and the role-play area, etc. Then the enhanced provision includes resources added to the continuous provision usually based on the topics or themes being studied in the setting, but should also include resources based upon children's interests. Both the continuous and enhanced provision facilitate child-led and adult-led activities. The focused, adult-led provision is at the top and this occupies the smallest part of the triangle and should also occupy the smallest part of the provision on offer (Thomas and Lewis, 2016).

There are opportunities within the continuous and enhanced provision for children to be both independent learners (Piaget's theory) and to play and learn alongside their peers and the practitioners (Vygotsky's theory), whereas the focused provision is driven by the adult and is usually linked to specific targets the child needs to meet.

Throughout the rest of the UK, both the Curriculum for Excellence in Scotland and the Foundation Stage in Northern Ireland have play-based pedagogies with a mixture of both child-led and adult-led activities. Further, all early years settings have child-sized furniture, and all espouse the use of the outside as another learning environment and recognise the need for children to have periods of uninterrupted play, as advocated by the theorists at the start of this chapter.

Reflective Question

What is the balance between adult-led and child-led activities within your setting?

Different Approaches to Shared Spaces

Sustained shared thinking (SST) is defined by Siraj-Blatchford et al. (2002) as an approach in which adults and children share the learning space to solve problems by working together using intellectual skills and understanding. Both the child and the adult contribute to the thinking, thus extending the child's existing understanding. This supports the sociological perspective of interactionism, as detailed in Chapter 3.

Brodie (2019) defines SST as 'one of those moments with a child where everything else around you just stops'. She stated that there are key elements to SST as follows:

- Working together so information flows.
- Thinking can be practical or theoretical, but involves deep thinking that leads to solutions or conclusions.

- SST cannot be a short dialogue; extended thinking is needed to ensure that deep level learning takes place and is memorable for the child.

The practitioner's role is to interact with the child and not just to present information but for information to flow between them through dialogue and open-ended questioning. SST encourages key skills such as critical thinking, problem-solving, and curiosity, skills that lead children to be good life-long learners. Brodie (2019) advises observing practitioners who are good at SST to gain an insight into how to do it. She advocates taking time to reflect upon practice in the context of the children and the environment.

Group activities in shared spaces that allow children to play and work in groups can support SST to occur. Examples can include the role-play area or the sand and water tray where children can play together to solve a given problem, either set by the practitioner or one that emerges from the children's own play. Brodie (2019) advocates setting the environment up for provocation and leaving trails of curiosity such as a feather outside with glitter on it. These trails or provocations can be based upon a child's current interests leading to sustained engagement. Cosy corners or peaceful quiet areas are needed for those deep SST conversations to occur.

The home learning environment has a big impact on how prepared children are for SST to take place. In the 2002 Researching Effective Pedagogy in the Early Years study (REPEY) (Siraj-Blatchford et al., 2002), parents' proactive behaviour towards their children's learning was the best basis for SST to occur. Encouraging parents to engage with SST at home with their child can be facilitated through sharing those deep-level conversions they have had with their child in the setting and suggesting ways they can continue this at home.

Case Study: SST in practice

It is half-way through the autumn term and there have been growing issues with the reception-aged children pushing each other and generally being quite rough when it is time to line up on the yard to come in from play and from lunchtime. There have been a number of growing instances and complaints from children and parents. The reception class practitioners have decided to tackle this and adopt a SST approach. They gathered the class in a quiet area of the classroom and they explained the problem. The children were asked to consider a number of scenarios and invited to role-play examples of pushing and shoving in the line and what could potentially happen. Next, the children were asked to work together with practitioners to come up with solutions to the problems. Discussions centred around how would the children feel if they got pushed over and why do people push and how can we stop this? The children came up with a plan of action as to how they could solve this and it was agreed that most of the pushing happened because all the children raced each other to get to line-up first. It was decided that the practitioners would, going forwards, ask children to come to line-up in certain orders such as those whose name starts with a 'S' or those who were wearing trainers that day. It was agreed that this was a fun and fair way as all children would have a turn at being first to line up. It was also agreed that if anyone still pushed, they would have a consequence like missing the next playtime.

This is just one example of how SST can support children to take ownership of a problem and work together to come up with a workable solution. By the children coming up with a solution, they are far more likely to abide by it than an adult imposing this solution upon them.

Reflective Question

How can you provide opportunities to use SST with the children you work with?

The curiosity approach to shared spaces

The curiosity approach in the early years is based on the philosophies of Reggio Emilia, Montessori and Steiner, along with the early years curriculum of New Zealand, Te Whāriki. The aim of this approach is to create calm and tranquil play spaces without bright colours and plastic resources. The environment or shared space is seen as an extension of home and not a preparation for school. Creating spaces that are in neutral colours, calm and tranquil and uncluttered, allows the children to be inquisitive and curious. The curiosity approach aims to develop children's thinking and problem solving by providing authentic resources and a sense of awe and wonder (Hellyn and Bennett, 2017). The focus is on using loose items (such as those found in treasure baskets, discussed later in this chapter) or provocations. The children have to use their imagination and all their senses to engage with the resources, to problem solve and discuss what to do. This resonates with the economic approach to child development discussed in Chapter 4 by wanting young children to gain problem-solving skills needed for the twenty-first century and to create thinkers and doers of the future.

In the moment planning (ITMP)

Another approach to shared spaces or the learning environment is called 'In the moment planning' (ITMP). It is planning a topic spontaneously based on what a child is interested in. Here, activities are planned in the moment and not in advance, which does go against much of the traditional way of setting up the learning environment or shared space. This approach is in tune with Piaget's discovery learning, as it requires an environment that is child-led and not adult-directed. The children get to choose what they would like to play with, the adult observes them and then follows their lead (Cheqdin, 2019). Adults then interact to teach the next step as appropriate for that unique child at that precise moment (Ephgrave, 2017). Ephgrave (2017) provides the following examples of how the shared space or environment should look when adopting an ITMP approach: 'When a child arrives in the setting, *nothing is set out but everything is available and accessible.*' This means that access to the outdoors is readily available and children are encouraged to explore their surroundings and choose what they want to play with. Expectations are shared with the children with regard to tidying up, and the expected behaviours both indoors and outdoors.

The children self-register when they arrive and then choose what they want to play with. There are no focused activities planned by the adult, so the child becomes the focus and not the activity. Parents are asked to say what their child's interests are and practitioners decide on a number of children to focus on each week. These focus children have a learning journey completed by the practitioners, recording any events and next steps. These learning journeys are then shared with the parents.

Reflective Question

Considering the curiosity approach and in the moment planning, what do you think are the advantages and disadvantages of each approach?

The role of the adult within shared spaces

Earlier in the chapter it was stated that Moyles has researched the role of the adult in shared spaces or the learning environment. Moyles et al. (2002: 71) published the *Study of Pedagogical Effectiveness in Early Learning* where they found that practitioners stated they needed to 'promote children's learning through provision of play-based active, hands-on; multisensory… experiences' within a calm, organised environment. The report further argues that 'the environment will reflect children's interests, past experiences, prior learning and current cognitive development; it will also have provision for developing children's construction of ideas and ways of thinking and learning' (2002: 111). The adult is seen as the facilitator of children's learning experiences through a mixture of adult-led and child-led experiences. They need to provide shared spaces and quiet spaces, resources and be available for the children (Moyles and Adams, 2001). In Chapter 15, Jarmen's communication-friendly spaces was mentioned; here the adult creates quiet, uncluttered, bright and airy spaces for children to communicate or sit and think (see: https://elizabethjarman.com/).

The role of the adult can be considered within a neuroscience approach to shared spaces. As discussed throughout this book, brain research has shown that from birth, babies are programmed to recognise human faces (Murray and Andrews, 2000). Babies are born with a need to learn and, as Clare (2012) argues, the way they do this is through interaction with adults. Feeding the brain through experiences and interactions increases brain development. So the role of the adult is crucial in setting up the shared space, observing the children, planning activities and as the co-constructor of knowledge. Babies and young children learn whenever they process input from their senses (Duffy et al., 2006) and from responding to experiences.

Siraj-Blatchford (1999) further advocates that the adults' role in preparing the learning environment or space is to celebrate and embrace children's cultural experiences by including multicultural resources and activities. Children need to see displays that celebrate different cultures and faiths, and take part in activities that reflect different cultures from their own.

Additionally, the adult needs to provide an emotionally safe and secure environment for babies and young children. The key worker system, seen in some settings, recognises this by trying to ensure that the same practitioners work with and care for young children and babies. The importance of continuity of provision is linked to Bowlby's theory of attachment, as discussed in Chapter 11. Traditionally, this may mean adults working in different shared spaces, depending on the age of the children they are responsible for.

The creative environment

Adults also need to consider the creative environment, where babies and young children can express their imagination, originality, take risks and perhaps, most important of all, have fun (Clare, 2012). However, in practice this can be more difficult to achieve. Creativity can often be very adult-directed and dependent upon an outcome as tangible evidence. Clare (2012) advocates that playing in the water and sand tray is creative, albeit not producing an outcome that can be readily evidenced. Children need to be given time and space to produce their own unique creations that are not the product of an adult.

Case Study: Painting Daffodils

Children are painting daffodils as part of a week-long celebration of St David, the patron saint of Wales. The practitioner has set up the painting area to include a vase full of bright yellow daffodils in full bloom. Different children wander over throughout the course of the day to paint their daffodil pictures which will feature as part of a display in the main hall during the Eisteddfod later in the week.

One child, Eva, comes over and spends a long time carefully painting her picture. She uses green and yellow paint to illustrate the daffodils and decides to paint her vase red. The practitioner sits alongside Eva praising her work and telling her that her picture will look fabulous on the display in the hall. The practitioner asks Eva if she has finished, but Eva shakes her head. Instead, she carefully dips her brush into the black paint and then proceeds to cover all of her picture in black paint. Eva looks at the practitioner and claps her hands, saying: 'I have finished now, can we put it up on the wall?' The practitioner smiles and says: 'Not yet, we have to wait for it to dry but then we will.' Eva skips off to wash her hands. The practitioner is true to her word and Eva's daffodil painting goes on the wall with all the others in the hall.

Here the practitioner has realised that the process the children go through is more important than the end product. Eva has invited the adult into her creative space and has felt comfortable enough to share how she wants to represent the daffodils. Eva has been observed covering things over on many other occasions and the practitioners believe she has an enveloping schema (Thomas, 2019). Thus, when she covers her whole painting, the practitioner knows that this is part of Eva's way of constructing knowledge and the practitioner is happy to facilitate this within the painting activity.

When Eva's painting is displayed on the wall, the practitioner includes a note to state that this is Eva's interpretation of the daffodils using her enveloping schema. Here the practitioner has allowed Eva to dictate how she wants to represent the daffodils and has not imposed the way she, as the adult, would expect the daffodils to be painted.

Treasure baskets

Another way to promote creativity within the learning environment or shared space with babies and young children is through treasure baskets. Here they can make connections with their learning through discovering what is inside the basket. Elinor Goldschmied has produced a lot of work around treasure baskets, and Goldschmied and Jackson (1994) state that treasure baskets provide a rich focus for exploring everyday open-ended objects, chosen to stimulate the senses.

Young babies who are not yet mobile can gain autonomy by being able to reach the different items within the basket and explore them. Here the practitioners need to sit back and allow the baby to explore and investigate the objects, without taking over and showing the baby what to do (Clare, 2012). In this way the practitioners can observe the babies closely, see what they prefer to play with, what interests them and use this information to plan future activities that will challenge the environment. Treasure baskets facilitate the sharing of space between adults, babies and young children.

It can be argued that the role of the adult is multifaceted and detailed. Practitioners need time to develop the learning environment or shared space, but to also stand back and observe the children in action and speak with them. Then they can find out what children's interests are and develop the learning spaces accordingly for future use.

Case Study: A day in the life of the adult in a busy nursery setting

I have been working at Tinkerbell's nursery for the past two years. No two days are the same, which I love. I am currently in the baby room in the mornings and the toddler room in the afternoons. One of my roles is to set up the resources for the day and we are really into the curiosity approach and discovery learning. We use lots of treasure baskets with the babies and I love to sit with them and watch them choose the objects and discover how to play with them. We use lots of eye contact and talk with the babies and give them space and time to discover what each object does. I like to make notes, which I share with the parents, and we take lots of photos as we are making a book for each child to take home at the end of the year.

In the toddler room, we adopt the curiosity approach by ensuring that we provide resources that are natural, authentic and represent real life. In our role-play area, the tea set is a bone china one for the children to play with. At first, I was paranoid they would drop it and smash it, but they take really good care of it. They all love to play with it and it is so lovely to see them delicately pouring the 'tea' into the china cups and holding the cups properly to drink from. I think because they know

(Continued)

it is a real tea set and it is fragile, they really take care of it, rather than a plastic one which they know they can drop and it won't break.

We also provide lots of what we call loose parts – things that are open-ended and can be moved around. We have lots of crates and boxes which the children play with in lots of ways, so we are driving their imaginations. I am always amazed at the creative ways they use different objects and, as I said, no two days are the same. I don't think I could work anywhere now that was more rigid in how the learning environment is set up and how the children are expected to use the resources.

Reflective Question

Reflect upon the term 'open-ended resources and loose parts' – do you use enough of this type of resource in your setting?

Summary of chapter

- There are a number of different approaches to shared spaces or learning environments.
- Evidence of past theoretical approaches to shared spaces can be seen in current early years curricula today.
- The role of the adult is crucial in the success of the shared space.
- The shared space is both the indoor and outdoor environment.
- There is a growing awareness of allowing children more autonomy in deciding which resources to play with and how to engage within the shared spaces.
- Different approaches to shared spaces support the different approaches discussed in Part 1 of this book.
- International curricula also adopt different approaches to how the environment or shared space is used.
- Adult interaction with babies and young children within shared spaces facilitates brain development.

End-of-chapter questions

1. What do you see as the adult's role within shared spaces?
2. If you were considering changing how you use the shared space in your setting, which approach would you like to try and why?
3. If you were asked to design a new shared space what would it look like?

Further reading

Ephgrave, A. (2018) *Planning in the Moment with Young Children: A Practical Guide for Early Years Practitioners and Parents*. Abingdon: Routledge.

This book embraces the concept of planning 'in the moment' and emphasises the critical role of the adult in promoting child-led learning within shared spaces.

Gascoyne, S. (2021) *Treasure Baskets and Beyond: Realizing The Potential of Sensory-rich Play*. Milton Keynes: Open University.

This book draws upon observations with children and research into neuroscience to demonstrate the value of sensory play and treasure baskets. It considers how using treasure baskets within shared spaces provides opportunities for problem solving and rich, imaginative and creative play.

Thomas, A. and Boulton, P. (2021) 'Outdoor risky play and schema development in the early years – part 1 and 2': *Smalltalk*, Autumn, 143. Available at: www.earlyyears.wales/cy/node/2325

This covers research into the use of loose parts and risky play in the shared space, and how this can support schema development in young children.

TWENTY ONE
OPPORTUNITIES TO RECAP AND REFLECT (THE CONCLUSION)

This chapter recaps the structure of the book in order to remind you about the purpose of the three parts and what the book achieved, as well as reflecting on the case studies embedded throughout the book. Then the key messages of the book are discussed and the importance of an interdisciplinary approach to understanding child development is summarised. We share two examples of praxis and we also share what we have learnt from writing the book before encouraging you to think about what you have learnt from reading it. Lastly, you are encouraged to revisit the *thoughtful pause* task which we asked you to complete in the introduction.

Recapping the structure of the book

This book was structured in three parts and every chapter had clear objectives to guide you, the reader, in developing your understanding of the holistic nature of child development. Part 1 explained and defined the key concepts and ideas of seven disciplines,[1] thus setting up the theoretical context and background for Part 2 which explained seven child development domains[2] through an interdisciplinary lens. This allowed the reader to build on their understanding from Part 1 and consider child development in a more holistic way. Part 3 synthesised both disciplines and domains and applied them to five contemporary aspects of practice.[3]

The uniqueness of this book is the combination of disciplines, domains and contemporary aspects of practice which take the reader on a journey of knowledge generation and growth, while giving pause for thought and reflection throughout. Through case studies and reflective questions, the reader was able to apply theory to practice and through key questions, the reader was able to reflect upon their own practice and consider if anything needed to change or adapt in the light of

---

[1]Psychology, Sociology, Economics, Anthropology, Philosophy, Neuroscience and Education.

[2]Physical and Growth, Social, Emotional, Creative, Spiritual, Cognitive and Language development.

[3]Play and playfulness, well-being, global curricula, inclusivity and shared spaces.

new knowledge and understanding. Further reading provided at the end of each chapter encourages the reader to explore the topics in more depth. It is hoped that this book will open up debate and discussion, and perhaps a desire for students and professionals to find out more about child development beyond the field of psychology.

Reflecting on the case studies

In total, this book has an impressive 58 case studies, consisting of 22 in Part 1, 21 in Part 2 and 15 in Part 3. As stated in Chapter 1 (the Introduction), the case studies aim to provide opportunities for the reader to develop their understanding of theory and make links to practice and real-life contexts. In order for the reader to gain a more authoritative sense of what something means for a child or a parent, a number of the case studies were written from the perspective of the child or parent.

The case studies in Chapter 2 highlight the importance of respecting one another's views about development and practice, having the confidence to critique principles of developmental psychology, making time to reflect on contemporary understandings of childhood, focusing on a child's strengths and the importance of observation in understanding the detail of behaviour changes. Case studies from Chapter 3 demonstrate how focusing on the individual circumstances of a child and their family can be very helpful in meeting their needs. Chapter 4 case studies help the reader to consider the trade-off between private day nurseries being more competitive and investment in employing high-quality staff. They also help the reader to understand how personal views can impact on interactions with children and their families, the importance of well-trained professionals in supporting families to access a range of services and to understand how some families need support with other family matters, such as budgeting. The case studies in Chapter 5 highlight the ethical dilemmas in assessment and encourage the reader to think about traditions and customs different from their own in order to better understand their cultural self.

Chapter 6 case studies show how two teachers conceptualise children differently in the context of the curriculum and demonstrated the ontological (ways of being) and epistemological (ways of doing) understandings of development from one nursery teacher. In Chapter 7, case studies demonstrate the benefits of professionals working across disciplines and learning from each other, as well as the importance of professionals being creative in promoting and developing children's sensory experiences. Case studies in Chapter 8, the final chapter in Part 1, explain how education is entangled with politics and philosophy, and by engaging in higher order thinking and critical reflection, professionals can articulate and strengthen why they do what they do. Lastly, the case studies point out that practitioners' training, knowledge and understanding about early childhood can impact on children's experiences.

In Part 2, the first case study reinforces the need to view a child's development holistically and to view development as a web rather than a linear sequence or a series of steps. Similarly to Chapter 2, the important role that observation plays in getting to know children is emphasised. Case studies in Chapter 10 highlight the need for practitioners to get the balance right between safety and inclusivity and social development, and, similar to the case study in Chapter 4, acknowledging the impact of our actions on children's self-esteem is important. One of the case studies in Chapter 11 showed how, as children develop, their emotions develop too. Concepts from Bruner, Piaget, Vygotsky and Fowler are drawn out in various case studies in Chapters 12 and 13. Chapter 14 case studies show that when practitioners have informed knowledge of concepts such as schemas, they can support children with their ongoing development. As in Chapters 2 and 8, reflection is highlighted as a tool to address whole-school issues. Chapter 15, which is the final chapter in Part 2, highlights the importance of adults being good role models for children and learning about other cultural expectations from and with children.

Case studies in Part 3 broadly relate to reinforcing messages about theories of play and well-being, the impact of location on development and children's life chances, empowering learners, the important role that children can play in staff recruitment, and understanding how settings discriminate against the protected characteristics. Chapters 19 and 20 demonstrate how children benefit from sensitive, caring, intuitive and knowledgeable practitioners.

Reflecting on the key messages of the book

As a discipline, psychology has much to offer us in understanding children's development from birth to 8 years, but so do other disciplines and this is what we have tried to show in the book. For example, psychology is useful for understanding children's behaviour and how they construct and internalise knowledge, as well as understanding the influencing role of the adult and environment. Sociology helps us become more aware of social factors and how poverty, age, gender, ethnicity and socioeconomic background can influence development, and also life chances. Economics is useful because it can help to predict outcomes for early intervention programmes and help policy-makers shape the direction of services which practitioners implement. Anthropology, on the other hand, helps us understand the habits, values and individual practices of families where we can begin to appreciate the process of how children learn their own culture and that of others. With similar features to anthropology, philosophy helps practitioners tune into the many different ways of living, being, doing and thinking, and how these interact with development. Lastly, neuroscience has lots to offer because it can help practitioners understand brain function for ensuring quality learning experiences, as well as appreciating how experience can shape the brain. Arguably, education is a discipline in its own right, but looks to other disciplines to help further understand the many competing views about knowledge production and curriculum implementation.

However, over time some disciplines and discourses become dominant, and they can influence and shape children's experiences in positive and negative ways. For example, how many of you can remember being rewarded with stickers for positive behaviour or losing privileges for negative behaviour?

This very much resonates with a behaviourist approach, as advocated by psychologist Skinner in the twentieth century. This was certainly evident in our schooling in the 1970s and 1980s, and is still in use today and very much underpinned by psychology. Then there is the importance given to language development (i.e., literacy) and cognitive development (i.e., numeracy) in settings, usually driven by government policy, with less focus on other developmental domains. How often has less time been given to creative activities and opportunities for children to explore what it means to be human at the expense of completing more literacy or number-based tasks to ensure that children meet a milestone or target? We really hope this book challenges some aspects of current practice and allows you to pause, reflect and take a more holistic view of child development. Therefore, praxis is essential in recognising the worth of other disciplines.

The following two examples show how we, as the writers, have understood and applied the philosophical concept of praxis (i.e., theory–action–practice) and discuss two examples from practice – one that relates to young children in a reception class (4- to 5-year-olds) and the other that relates to students in higher education.

The context of the example relating to children in the reception class is about how two teachers transformed a space in the corridor in order to extend the children's environment and enhance their learning and development. The teachers recognised that their main classrooms were busy and somewhat loud places to be, think and do, and felt that the children needed more variety and choice such as a quiet/reflection area. The teachers approached the head teacher and proposed the idea of removing numerous storage cupboards in the nearby corridor to provide an even better learning environment, and with the help of a very supportive head teacher, the space was transformed. Philosophical ideas of living, being, doing and thinking were applied to practice and a quiet/reflective space was developed for the children. Free-flow access was encouraged and the children had autonomy in shifting between the main classroom and the corridor. Playing and being in the corridor meant that children were able to move wider and maintain their friendships from the other reception class. Ideas from psychology about the environment influencing children's development were important, as children now had a quieter place to reflect and relax. The two teachers also took into consideration the socioeconomic and cultural backgrounds of the children, and reflected on the role-play areas they provided and realised that a culturally situated role-play area was needed (i.e., something that the children were more familiar with).

The context of the example relating to students in higher education is about them using sandboxing as a means to reflect upon their recent placements. The ability to reflect in and on practice (Schön, 1983, 1991) is an essential professional skill within the field of education. Students are asked to develop their reflective skills throughout their time at the University of South Wales. The sandboxing technique was developed by Lowenfeld (1967), who recognised that children essentially need to 'play' through their concerns, issues and learning to make sense of their world. Colleagues on the Early Years degree asked students to use small world resources within a sand tray to illustrate how they felt their placements had gone (Pescott and John, 2018). They were asked to think about their feelings at the start of their placement and then again at the end, depicting both as visual imagery within the sand box. After some initial reservations, students embraced this way of reflection. It encouraged students to view their experiences in a different way and facilitated the philosophical ideas of being, doing and thinking, and the sociological view of explaining the social world as being multi-layered. It supported students' metacognition and their creativity, and facilitated a move away from the more formalised academic reflective accounts.

Summary of key messages

- Acknowledge the strengths and weaknesses of different theories in various disciplines and value the contributions they make in helping us understand child development.
- Remember that culture, biology and politics have an important role to play in contextualising children's development.
- Many concepts are often contested, and the meaning is shifting – for example, concepts such as well-being, culture, rights, inclusion and childhood, to name but a few.
- Be more inclusive when thinking about children's development and consider creative and spiritual development.
- Be familiar with the concept of praxis and challenge dominant discourses.

What we (the authors) have learnt from writing this book…

From Amanda Thomas… When I reflect upon my career as an early years teacher, I cannot remember having covered anything on child development within my PGCE and I had to learn on the job. However, having carried out research for this book, I can now see that I was very much following a psychology discourse within the classroom. I used milestones to support me in understanding child development and I relied very little upon any other disciplines to influence my teaching. Now, having researched other disciplines, I can see I would be a very different and more knowledgeable practitioner. I will be using the knowledge gained from writing this book to influence my teaching with my students, and I will urge them to view child development through many different lenses. I will ask them to read this text and hope it will give them pause for thought, and allow them to become more reflective, responsive and knowledgeable future practitioners.

From Alyson Lewis… In writing this book I have reminded myself of the importance of many different disciplines in understanding child development. Rather than favouring one discipline over another, I have developed a stronger understanding and appreciation of the strengths and limitations of key theories and ideas that underpin each discipline. I have enjoyed seeing how they complement each other. When researching for the book, I learnt how some disciplines such as philosophy used to dominate the training of early childhood professionals until the the latter part of the twentieth century, when scientific thinking and the progressive movement started to dominate. I'm still fascinated by the power of dominant discourses such as developmental psychology and their influence on practice, and wonder about future thinking towards child development.

What have you learnt from reading this book?

1. Before reading this book, which discipline do you think best reflected your view of child development the most?
2. Has reading this book changed the way you think about child development and if yes, in what way?
3. Which chapter (relating to disciplines, domains or contemporary aspects) has caused you to really pause and think, and why?
4. How will having read this book lead you to change/adapt your practice/learning environment?
5. How would you best describe this book to someone?

II ━━━━━━━━━━ THOUGHTFUL PAUSE ━━━━━━━━━━

Reflecting back to the exercise we asked you to complete in the Introduction, redo this exercise and reflect on how your knowledge and understanding has changed/improved/refined or been challenged in relation to reading this book about disciplines and child development domains.

• If you could take one message from this book to share with others, what would this be?

REFERENCES

ACCAC (2003) *Developing the Curriculum Cymreig*, Available at: https://hwb.gov.wales/api/storage/8e68e2f5-851f-43b8-af24-9eb38cf62482/developing-the-curriculum-cymreig.pdf (accessed 20 July 2021).

Adams, K. (2012) 'Childhood in crisis? Perceptions of 7–11 year olds on being a child and the implications for education's well-being agenda', *Education, 3–13*, 41 (5): 1–15.

Adams, K., Bull, R. and Maynes, M. (2016) 'Early childhood spirituality in education: towards an understanding of the distinctive features of young children's spirituality', *European Early Childhood Education Research Journal*, 24 (5): 760–74.

Adams, K., Hyde, B. and Woolley, R. (2008) *The Spiritual Dimension of Childhood*. London: Jessica Kingsley.

Ainsfield, E. (1982) 'The onset of social smiling in preterm and full-term infants from two ethnic backgrounds', *Infant Behaviour and Development*, 5 (4): 387–95.

Ainsworth, M.D., Blehar, M., Waters, E. and Wall, S. (1978) *Patterns of Attachment*. Hillsdale, NJ: Erlbaum.

Albon, D. (2011) 'Postmodernism and post-structuralist perspectives on early childhood education', in L. Miller and L. Pound (eds) *Theories and Approaches to Learning in the Early Years*. London: SAGE. pp. 38–52.

Alderson, P. (2008) *Young Children's Rights: Exploring Beliefs, Principles and Practice*. London: Jessica Kingsley.

Alderson, P. (2016) 'The philosophy of critical realism and childhood studies', *Global Studies of Childhood*, 6 (2): 199–210.

Allen, G. (2011) *Early Intervention: The Next Steps*. London: Cabinet Office.

Amerijckx, P. and Humblet, G. (2014) 'Child well-being: What does it mean?', *Children & Society*, 28 (5): 404–15.

Andrews, M. (2012) *Exploring Play for Early Childhood Studies*. London: Learning Matters.

Archer, C. and Siraj, I. (2015) 'Measuring the quality of movement-play in Early Childhood Education settings: Linking movement-play and neuroscience', *European Early Childhood Education Research Journal*, 23 (1): 21–42.

Armstrong, T. (2020) *The Stages of Faith According to James W. Fowler*. Cloverdale, CA: American Institute for Learning and Human Development.

Arnold, L. (2018) 'Working with parents: Principles of engagement', in R. Crutchley (ed.), *Special Needs in the Early Years: Partnership and Participation*. London: SAGE. pp. 25–44.

Asmussen, K., Fischer, F., Drayton, E. and McBride, T. (2020) *Adverse Childhood Experiences: What We Know, What We Don't Know, and What Should Happen Next*. London: Early Intervention Foundation.

Athey, C. (1990) *Extending Thought in Young Children: A Parent–Teacher Partnership*. London: Paul Chapman.

Athey, C. (2007) *Extending Thought in Young Children: A Parent–Teacher Partnership* (2nd edn). London: SAGE.

Bandura, A. (1977) *Social Learning Theory*. Englewood Cliffs, NJ: Prentice-Hall.

Bandura, A. (1989) 'Social cognitive theory', in R. Vasta (ed.), *Annals of Child Development: Vol. 6 – Six Theories of Child Development*. Greenwich, CT: Jai Press. pp. 45–103.

Bandura, A., Ross, D. and Ross, S.A. (1961) 'Transmission of aggression through imitation of aggressive models', *Journal of Abnormal and Social Psychology*, 63: 575–82.

Bandyopadhyay, A., Whiffen, T., Fry, R. and Brophy, S. (2021) *Living in a Safe, Connected Area Improves Life Chances for Children in Poverty in Wales: A Record Linkage Cohort Study*. Wales: Administrative Data Research Wales.

Barbalet, J. (1998) *Emotion, Social Theory, and Social Structure: A Macrosociological Approach*. Cambridge: Cambridge University Press.

Barblett, L. and Maloney, C. (2010) 'Complexities of assessing social and emotional competence and wellbeing in young children', *Australasian Journal of Early Childhood*, 35 (2): 1–6.

Barry, A. and Yuill, C. (2008) *Understanding the Sociology of Health*. London: SAGE.

Bartholomew, R. (2007) 'Well-being in the classroom'. London: The Institute for the Future of the Mind (transcript of keynote seminar).

Bartkowski, J.P., Xu, X. and Bartkowski, S. (2019) 'Mixed blessing: The beneficial and detrimental effects of religion on child development among third-graders', *Religions*, 10 (1): 37.

Bartkowski, J.P., Xu, X. and Levin, M.L. (2008) 'Religion and child development: Evidence from the early childhood longitudinal study', *Social Science Research*, 37: 18–36.

Basford, J. and Bath, C. (2014) 'Playing the assessment game: An English early childhood education perspective', *Early Years*, 34 (2): 119–32.

Bauer, A., Parsonage, M., Knapp, M., Lemmi, V. and Adelaja, B. (2014) *The Costs of Perinatal Mental Health Problems*. London: Centre for Mental Health and London School of Economics.

Benson, P., Roehlkepartain, E. and Rude, S. (2003) 'Spiritual development in childhood and adolescence: Toward a field of inquiry', *Applied Developmental Science*, 7 (3): 205–13.

Bergnehr, D. (2018) 'Children's influence on wellbeing and acculturative stress in refugee families', *International Journal of Qualitative Studies on Health and Well-being*, 13 (1): 1–9.

Bericat, E. (2016) 'The sociology of emotions: Four decades of progress', *Current Sociology*, 64 (3): 491–13.

Berk, L. (2008) *Child Development*. New York: Pearson.

Berkman, L.F. and Kawachi, I. (2000) *Social Epidemiology*. New York: Oxford University Press.

Best, R. (2016) 'Exploring the spiritual in the pedagogy of Friedrich Frobel', 15th International Conference on Children's Spirituality, Spirituality and the Whole Child: Interdisciplinary Approaches. Lincoln, 26–9 July. Lincoln: Bishop Grosseteste University.

Bhat, A., Heathcock, J. and Galloway, J.C. (2005) 'Toy-orientated changes in hand and joint kinematics during the emergence of purposeful reaching', *Infant Behaviour and Development*, 28 (4): 445–65.

Biemiller, A. and Slonim, N. (2001) 'Estimating root word vocabulary growth in normative and advantaged populations: Evidence for a common sequence of vocabulary acquisition', *Journal of Educational Psychology*, 93 (3): 498–520.

Black, M.M., Hutchinson, J.J., Dubowitz, H. and Berenson-Howard, J. (1994) 'Parenting style and developmental status among children with nonorganic failure to thrive', *Journal of Pediatric Psychology*, 19 (6): 689–707.

Blackburn, C., Read, J. and Spencer, N. (2012) *Children with Neurodevelopmental Disabilities*. London: Annual Report of the Chief Medical officer.

Bone, J. (2008) 'Creating relational spaces: Everyday spirituality in early childhood settings', *European Early Childhood Education Research Journal*, 16 (3): 343–56.

Bonetti, S. and Blanden, J. (2020) *Early Years Workforce Qualifications and Children's Outcomes: An Analysis Using Administrative Data*. London: Nuffield Foundation.

Borkett, P. (2019) 'Children, families and English as an additional language', in D. Fitzgerald and H. Maconochie (eds) *Early Childhood Studies*. London: SAGE. pp. 223–39.

Bowlby, J. (1969) *Attachment and Loss: Vol. 1 – Attachment*. New York: Basic Books.

Boyden, J. and Dercon, S. (2012) *Child Development and Economic Development: Lessons and Future Challenges*. Oxford: Young Lives – University of Oxford.

Boyle, C. (2019) 'The community with the bad brain? – Neuroscience as discourse in early childhood intervention', *European Early Childhood Education Research Journal*, 27 (4): 454–67.

Bradley, M., Isaacs, B., Livingston, L., Nasser, D., True, A. and Dillane, M. (2011) 'Maria Montessori in the United Kingdom: 100 years on', in L. Miller and L. Pound (eds), *Theories and Approaches to Learning in the Early Years*. London: SAGE. pp. 71–85.

Brady, G., Lowe, P. and Lauritzen, S. (2015) 'Connecting a sociology of childhood perspective with the study child health, illness and well-being: Introduction', *Sociology of Health & Illness*, 37 (2): 173–83.

Brauer, J., Anwander, A. and Friederici, A.D. (2011) 'Neuroanatomical prerequisites for language functions in the maturing brain', *Cerebral Cortex*, 21: 459–66.

Broadhead, P., Howard, J. and Wood, E. (eds) (2010) *Play and Learning in the Early Years*. London: SAGE.

Brock, A., Jarvis, P. and Olusoga, Y. (2014) *Perspectives on Play: Learning for Life*. London: Routledge.

Brockliss, L. and Montgomery, H. (2013) 'Childhood: A historical approach', in M. Kehily (ed.) *Understanding Childhood: A Cross-disciplinary Approach* (2nd edn). Bristol: The Policy Press. pp. 53–98.

Brodie, K. (2019) 'What is sustained shared thinking? With Kathy Brodie'. Available at: www.famly. co/blog (accessed 14 June 2022).

Bronfenbrenner, U. (1992) 'Ecological systems theory', in R. Vasta (ed.), *Six Theories of Child Development*, London: Jessica Kingsley. pp. 187–249.

Bruce, T. (2011a) *Early Childhood Education* (4th edn). London: Hodder Education.

Bruce, T. (2011b) 'Froebel today', in L. Miller and L. Pound, L. (eds) *Theories and Approaches to Learning in the Early Years*. London: SAGE.

Bruner, J. (1983) *Child's Talk: Learning to Use Language*. Oxford: Oxford University Press.

Bruner, J. (1990) *Acts of Meaning*. Cambridge, MA: Harvard University Press.

Bryce, D., Whitebread, D. and Szues, D. (2014) 'The relationships among executive functions, metacognitive skills and educational achievement in 5 and 7 year-old children', *Metacognition and Learning*, 10: 181–98.

Burns. T., Machado, N. and Corte, U. (2015) 'The sociology of creativity: Part I: Theory: The social mechanisms of innovation and creative developments in selectivity environments', *Human Systems Management*, 35: 179–99.

Bywater, T. and Sharples, J. (2012) 'Effective evidence-based interventions for emotional well-being: Lessons for policy and practice', *Research Papers in Education*, 27 (4): 389–408.

Cai, Y.Q. and Feng, X.X. (2004) 'On the orientation of fair value and its realization in our policy for preschool education', *Education and Economy*, 2: 33–6.

Cameron, C. and Moss, P. (eds) (2020) *Transforming Early Childhood in England: Towards a Democratic Education*. London: UCL Press.

Campbell, T. (2013) 'Ability grouping in primary school may reinforce disadvantage of summer-born children, study finds'. Available at: https://cls.ucl.ac.uk/ability-grouping-in-primary-school-may-reinforce-disadvantage-of-summer-born-children-study-finds/ (accessed 17 March 2021).

Campbell-Barr, V. and Nygard, M. (2014) 'Losing sight of the child? Human capital theory and its role for early childhood education and care policies in Finland and England since the id-1990s', *Contemporary Issues in Early Childhood*, 15 (4): 346–59.

Camras, I.A., Chen, Y., Bakeman, R., Norris, K. and Cain, T.R. (2006) 'Culture, ethnicity and children's facial expressions: A study of European American, mainland Chinese American, and adopted Chinese girls, *Emotion*, 6: 103–14.

Canning, N. (ed.) (2011) *Play and Practice in the Early Years Foundation Stage*. London: SAGE.

Cardwell, M. (1996) *The Complete A–Z Psychology Handbook*. Oxford: Hodder & Stoughton.

Carpendale, J., Lewis, C. and Müller, U. (2018) *The Development of Children's Thinking*. London: SAGE.

CCEA (2014) *Religious Education in Primary Schools: Non-Statutory Guidance Materials*. Belfast: CCEA.

CCEA (2020) *Developmental Stages*. Available at: https://ccea.org.uk/foundation-stage/assessment-and-reporting/developmental-stages (accessed 21 July 2021).

CEA (2018) *Curricular Guidance for Pre-School Education*. Available at: www.education-ni.gov.uk/sites/default/files/publications/education/PreSchool_Guidance_30May18_Web.pdf (accessed 20 July 2021).

Centre for Educational Neuroscience (2020) 'Neuro-hit or neuro-myth?' Available at: www.educational neuroscience.org.uk/resources/neuromyth-or-neurofact/ (accessed 9 February 2020).

Cheqdin (2019) 'A quick guide to in the moment planning'. Available at: https://cheqdin.com/in-the-moment-planning (accessed 22 October 2021).

Child Poverty Action Group (2020) *Child Poverty Facts and Figures*. Available at: https://cpag.org.uk/child-poverty/child-poverty-facts-and-figures (accessed 20 December 2020).

Chomsky, N. (1959) 'Review of B.F. Skinner's verbal behavior language', *Language*, 35, 26–58.

Chomsky, N. (1965) *Aspects of the Theory of Syntax*. Cambridge, MA: MIT Press.

Christensen, D.L., Scheive, L.A, Devine, O. and Drews-Botsch, C. (2014) 'Socioeconomic status, child enrichment factors, and cognitive performance among preschool-age children: results from the follow-up of growth and development experiences study', *Research in Development Disabilities*, 35 (7): 1789–801.

Clack, B. (2012) 'What difference does it make? Philosophical perspectives on the nature of well-being and the role of educational practice', *Research Papers in Education*, 27 (4): 497–512.

Clare, A. (2012) *Creating a Learning Environment for Babies and Toddlers*. London: SAGE.

Clouston, T. (2015) *Challenging Stress, Burnout and Rust-out*. London: Jessica Kingsley.

Cole, P.M. (1986) 'Children's spontaneous control of facial expression', *Child Development*, 57: 1309–21.

Cole, P.M. and Tan, P.Z. (2007) 'Emotional socialization from a cultural perspective', in J.E. Grusec and P.D. Hastings (eds), *Handbook of Socialization: Theory and Research*. New York: Guilford Press. pp. 516–42.

Coleman, J. (2009) 'Well-being in schools: Empirical measure, or politicians' dream?', *Oxford Review of Education*, 35 (3): 281–92.

Collins Dictionary (1992) *Pocket English Dictionary*. Glasgow: HarperCollins.

Colliver, Y. and Fleer, M. (2016) 'I already know what I learned': Young children's perspectives on learning through play', *Early Childhood Development and Care*, 186 (10): 1559–70.

Conger, R. and Donnellan, H. (2007) 'An interactionist perspective on the socioeconomic context of human development', *Annual Review of Psychology*, 58 (1): 175–99.

Craig, C. (2007) 'The potential dangers of a systematic, explicit approach to teaching social and emotional skills (SEAL)'. Scotland: Centre for Confidence and Well-being.

Craig, C. (2009) 'Well-being in schools: The curious case of the tail wagging the dog?' Scotland: Centre for Confidence and Well-being.

Creswell, J.W. (2014) *Educational Research: Planning, Conducting and Evaluating Quantitative and Qualitative Research* (4th edn). Essex: Pearson.

Crowley, K. (2014) *Child Development: A Practical Introduction*. London: SAGE.

Crowley, K. (2017) *Child Development: A Practical Introduction* (2nd edn). London: SAGE.

Crutchley, R. (2018) *Special Needs in the Early Years: Partnership and Participation*. London: SAGE.

Crutchley, R. and Hunt, R. (2018) 'Early intervention and transition', in R. Crutchley (ed.), *Special Needs in the Early Years: Partnership and Participation*. London: SAGE. pp. 114–30.

Csikszentmihalyi, M. (2002) *Flow: The Classic work on How to Achieve Happiness*. London: Rider Books.

Dahlberg, G., Moss, P. and Pence, A. (2007) *Beyond Quality in Early Childhood Education and Care: Postmodern Perspectives* (2nd edn). London: Routledge Falmer.

Damasio, A.R. (1999) *The Feeling of What Happens: Body and Emotion in the Making of Consciousness*. New York: Harcourt Brace.

Danese, A. and McEwen, B.S. (2012) 'Adverse child experience, allostasis, allostatic load, and age-related disease', *Physiology and Behavior*, 106: 29–39.

De Bono, E. (1992a) *Six Thinking Hats for Schools: Resource Book 3*. Melbourne, Vic: Hawker Brownlow Education.

De Bono, E. (1992b) *Six Thinking Hats for Schools: Resource Book 4*. Melbourne, Vic: Hawker Brownlow Education.

De Gioia, K. (2009) 'Parent and staff expectations for continuity of home practices in the child care setting for families with diverse cultural backgrounds', *Australasian Journal of Early Childhood*, 34 (3): 9–17.

de Villiers, J. (2000) *Language and Theory of Mind: What are the Developmental Relationships?* Smith College, Northampton, MA: Philosophy: Faculty Publications.

Dekker, S., Lee, N., Howard Jones, P. and Jolles, J. (2012) 'Neuro-myths in education: Prevalence and predictors of misconceptions among teachers', *Frontiers in Psychology*, 3 (429): 1–8.

Department for Education (DfE) (2011) *National Evaluation of Sure Start Local Programmes: An Economic Perspective*. London: Department for Education.

Department for Education (DfE) (2012) *Statutory Framework for the Early Years Foundation Stage*. London: HMSO.

Department for Education (DfE) (2014a) *The National Curriculum in England: Framework Document*. London: HMSO.

Department for Education (DfE) (2014b) *Gypsy, Roma and Traveller Pupils: Supporting Access to Education – Case Study*. Available at: www.gov.uk (accessed 21 December 2021).

Department for Eduction (DfE) (2015) *Pedagogy in Early Childhood Education and Care (ECEC): An International Comparative Study of Approaches and Policies*. Available at: https://assets.publishing. service.gov.uk/government/uploads/system/uploads/attachment_data/file/445817/RB400_-_ Early_years_pedagogy_and_policy_an_international_study.pdf (accessed July 2021).

Department for Education (DfE) (2017) *Statutory Framework for the Early Years Foundation Stage*. London: DFE.

Department for Education (DfE) (2020) *Development Matters: Non-statutory Curriculum Guidance for the Early Years Foundation Stage*. London: DfE.

Department for Education (DfE) (2021) *Statutory Framework for the Early Years Foundation Stage*. London: DfE.

DeRobertis, E. (2006) 'Deriving a humanistic theory of child development from the works of Carl R. Rogers and Karen Horney', *The Humanistic Psychologist*, 34 (2): 177–99.

DeRobertis, E. (2011) 'Existential–humanistic and dynamic systems approaches to child development in mutual encounter', *The Humanistic Psychologist*, 39: 3–23.

Dickinson, D.K. and Porche, M.V. (2011) 'Relation between language experiences in preschool classrooms and children's kindergarten and fourth-grade language and reading abilities', *Child Development*, 82: 870–86.

Dillon, J.J. (2019) 'Humanistic psychology and the good: A forgotten link', *The Humanistic Psychologist*, 13 (1): 1–13.

Dodge, R., Daly, A., Huyton, J. and Sanders, L. (2012) 'The challenge of defining wellbeing', *International Journal of Wellbeing*, 2 (3): 222–35.

Donaldson, M. (1978) *Children's Minds*. London: Fontana.

Doolittle, P. (2014) 'Complex constructivism: A theoretical model of complexity and cognition', *International Journal of Teaching and Learning in Higher Education*, 26 (3): 485–98.

Dowling, M. (2010) *Young Children's Personal, Social and Emotional Development* (3rd edn). London: SAGE.

Downey, M. and Kelly, A.V. (1986) *Theory and Practice of Education: An Introduction*. London: Harper & Row.

Du, H., Li, X. and Lin, D. (2015) 'Individualism and sociocultural adaptation: Discrimination and social capital as moderators among rural-to-urban migrants in China', *Asian Journal of Social Psychology*, 18: 176–81.

Duffy, A., Chambers, F., Croughan, S. and Stephens, J. (2006) *Working with Babies and Children under Three*. Oxford: Heinemann Education.

Durlak, J. and Weissberg, R. (2013) 'Better evidence-based education social emotional learning' – CASEL. Available at: casel.org (accessed 8 January 2013).

Early Intervention Foundation (2018) 'Realising the potential of early intervention', London: Early Intervention Foundation.

Early Years Education (2012) 'Development matters in the Early Years Foundation Stage' (EYFS). Available at: www.foundationyears.org.uk/files/2012/03/Development-Matters-FINAL-PRINT-AMENDED.pdf (accessed 27 July 2020).

Early Years Healthy Development Review (2021) 'The best start for life: A vision for the 1,001 critical days'. Available at: https://assets.publishing.service.gov.uk/government/uploads/system/uploads/attachment_data/file/973112/The_best_start_for_life_a_vision_for_the_1_001_critical_days.pdf (accessed 26 April 2021).

Eaude, T. (2009) 'Happiness, emotional well-being and mental health – what has children's spirituality to offer?', *International Journal of Children's Spirituality*, 14 (3): 185–96.

Ecclestone, K. and Hayes, D. (2009a) 'Changing the subject: The educational implications of developing emotional well-being', *Oxford Review of Education*, 35 (3): 371–89.

Ecclestone, K. and Hayes, D. (2009b) *The Dangerous Rise of Therapeutic Education*. London: Routledge.

Education Hub (2020) 'The Steiner approach'. Available at: https://theeducationhub.org.nz/the-steiner-approach/ (accessed 22 October 2021)

Education Scotland (2014) *Religious and Moral Education* 3–18. Livingston: Crown copyright.

Education Scotland (2020) *Realising Ambition: Being Me*. Available at: https://education.gov.scot/media/3bjpr3wa/realisingtheambition.pdf (accessed 28 July 2021).

Edwards, C., Gandini. L. and Forman, G. (2012) *The Hundred Languages of Children: The Reggio Emilia Experience in Transformation* (3rd edn). Westport, CT: Praeger.

Edwards, S., Skouteris, H., Cutter-Mackenzie, A., Rutherford, L., O'Conner, M., Mantilla, A., Morris, H. and Elliot, S. (2015) 'Young children learning about well-being and environmental education in the early years: A fund of knowledge approach', *Early Years*, 30 (1): 1–18.

Ehiyazaryan-White, E. (2019) 'Inclusion and participation', in D. Fitzgerald and H. Maconochie (eds), *Early Childhood Studies*. London: SAGE. pp. 149–64.

Ekman, P. and Friesen, W. (1971) 'Constants across cultures in the face and emotion', *Journal of Personality and Social Psychology*, 17 (2): 124–9.

Englebright Fox, J. and Schirrmacher, R. (2015) *Art and Creative Development for Young Children*. Stanford, CA: Cengage Learning.

Ephgrave, A. (2017) 'Planning next steps in the moment'. Available at: https://eyfs.info/articles.html/teaching-and-learning/planning-next-steps-in-the-moment-r217/ (accessed 22 October 2021).

Epstein, A.S. (2007) *Essentials of Active Learning in Preschool: Getting to Know the HighScope Curriculum.* Ypsilanti, MI: HighScope Press.

Epstein, A., Johnson, S. and Lafferty, P. (2011) 'The HighScope approach', in L. Miller and L. Pound, L. (eds) *Theories and Approaches to Learning in the Early Years.* London: SAGE.

Ereaut, G. and Whiting, R. (2008) *What Do We Mean by Wellbeing and Why Might it Matter?* London: DCSF.

Erikson, E.H. (1964) *Insight and Responsibility.* New York: Norton.

Erikson, E.H. (1994) *Identity and the Life Cycle.* New York: Norton.

Fauth, B. and Thompson, M. (2009) *Young Children's Well-being: Indicators and Domains of Development.* London: National Children's Bureau. Highlight no. 252.

Feinstein, L. (2015) *Quantifying the Benefits of Early Intervention in Wales: A Feasibility Study.* Wales: Public Policy Institute for Wales.

Fernyhough, C. and Fradley, E. (2005) 'Private speech on an executive task: Relations with task difficulty and task performance', *Cognitive Development,* 20 (1): 103–20.

Field, F. (2010) *The Foundation Years: Preventing Poor Children Becoming Poor Adults.* London: Cabinet Office.

Fisher, J. (2013) *Starting from the Child* (4th edn). London: SAGE.

Fitzgerald, D. and Maconochie, H. (2019) *Early Childhood Studies.* London: SAGE.

Flanagan, K. (1999) 'Introduction', in K. Flanagan and P.C. Jupp (eds), *Postmodernity, Sociology and Religion.* Basingstoke: Macmillan Press. pp. 1–13.

Flavell, J.H. (1994) 'Cognitive development: Past, present and future', in R.D. Parke, P.A. Ornstein, J.J. Rieser and C. Zahn-Wander (eds), *A Century of Developmental Psychology.* Washington, DC: American Psychological Association. pp. 569–87.

Flavell, J.H., Miller, P.H. and Miller, S.A. (2002) *Cognitive Development* (4th edn). Englewood Cliffs, NJ: Prentice-Hall.

Ford, R. (2005) 'Thinking and cognitive development in young children', in T. Maynard and N. Thomas (eds), *Early Childhood Studies.* London: SAGE.

Ford, R. (2018) 'Young children's cognitive development', in S. Powell and S. Smith (eds), *An Introduction to Early Childhood Studies* (4th edn). London: SAGE. pp. 67–77.

Fowler, J. (1981) *Stages of Faith.* New York: HarperCollins.

Fraillon, J. (2004) *Measuring Student Well-being in the Context of Australian Schooling.* Australia: Ministerial Council on Education.

Gabriel, N. (2017) *The Sociology of Early Childhood: Critical Perspectives.* London: SAGE.

Gallacher, L. and Kehily, M. (2013) 'Childhood: A sociocultural approach', in M. Kehily (ed.), *Understanding Childhood: A Cross-disciplinary Approach* (2nd edn). Bristol: The Policy Press. pp. 211–66.

Gardner, H. (1983) *Frames of Mind: The Theory of Multiple Intelligences.* New York: Basic Books.

Gardner, H. (2000) 'A case against spiritual intelligence', *The International Journal for the Psychology of Religion,* 10 (1): 27–34.

Gasper, D. (2010) 'Understanding the diversity of conceptions of well-being and quality of life', *The Journal of Socio-Economics,* 39 (3): 351–60.

Gauvain, M. (2001) *The Social Context of Cognitive Development*. New York: Guilford Press.

Gerver, R. (2010) *Creating Tomorrow's School Today: Education – Our Children – Their Futures*. London: Continuum.

Gillies, V. (2011) 'Social and emotional pedagogies: Critiquing the new orthodoxy of emotion in classroom behaviour management', *British Journal of Sociology of Education*, 32 (2): 185–202.

Goldfield, E.C. (1989) 'Transition from rocking to crawling: Postural constraints on infant movement', *Developmental Psychology*, 25 (6): 913–19.

Goldschmied, E. and Jackson, S. (1994) *People under Three: Young Children in Day Care*. London: Routledge.

Gonen, M. et al. (2019) 'Examining the association between executive functions and developmental domains of low-income children in the United States and Turkey', *Psychological Reports*, 122 (1): 155–79.

Goodliff, G. (2013) 'Spirituality expressed in creative learning: Young children's imagining play as space for mediating their spirituality', *Early Child Development and Care*, 183 (8): 1054–71.

Goouch, K. (2008) 'Understanding playful pedagogies, play narratives and play spaces', *Early Years*, 28 (1): 93–102.

Gorard, S., Siddiqui, N. and See, B.H. (2015) *Philosophy for Children: Evaluation Report and Executive Summary*. London: Education Endowment Foundation.

Gordon Biddle, K., Garcia Nevarez, A., Roundtree Henderson, W. and Valero-Kerrick, A. (2014) *Early Childhood Education: Becoming a Professional*. London: SAGE.

Goswami, U. (2002) *Blackwell Handbook of Child Cognitive Development*. Malden, MA: Blackwell Publishers.

Goswami, U. (2015) *Children's Cognitive Development and Learning*. York: Cambridge Primary Review Trust.

Goswami, U. (2020) 'What is neuroscience?' Available at: www.thebritishacademy.ac.uk/blog/what-is-neuroscience/ (accessed 9 February 2020).

Grant, C. and Gomez, M.L. (2001) *Campus and Classroom: Making Schooling Multicultural* (2nd edn). Upper Saddle River, NJ: Merrill/Prentice Hall.

Gray, C. and Macblain, S. (2012) *Learning Theories in Childhood*. London: SAGE.

Greenwood, R. (2017) 'Playful learning in natural outdoor environments', in G. Walsh, D. McMillan and C. McGuinness (eds), *Playful Teaching and Learning*. London: SAGE. pp. 116–32.

Griffiths, R. (n.d.) 'Reality check: The spiritual intelligence: Education and training in higher consciousness'. Available at: https://sqi.co/the-spiritual-intelligence-paradigm/ (accessed 22 February 2021).

Hallam, S. (2009) 'An evaluation of the social and emotional aspects of learning (SEAL) programme: Promoting positive behaviour, effective learning and wellbeing in primary school children', *Oxford Review of Education*, 35 (3): 313–30.

Hand, M. (2018) 'On the distinctive educational value of philosophy', *Journal of Philosophy in Schools*, 5 (1): 4–19.

Handley, G. (2009) 'Children's rights to participation', in T. Waller (ed.), *An Introduction to Early Childhood* (2nd edn). London: SAGE. pp. 82–95.

Hart, B. and Risley, T.R. (1995) *Meaningful Differences in the Everyday Experiences of Young American Children*. Baltimore, MD: Brookes.

Hart, T. (2003) *The Secret Spiritual World of Children*. Novato, CA: New World Library.

Harter, S. (2008) 'The developing self', in W. Damon and R.M. Lerner (eds), *Child and Adolescent Development: An Advanced Course*. Hoboken. NJ: Wiley. pp. 216–62.

Hartup, W. (1989) 'Social relationships and their developmental significance', *American Psychologist*, 44 (2): 120–6.

Hartup, W. and Stevens, N. (1997) 'Friendship and adaptation in the life course', *Psychological Bulletin*, 335–70.

Haworth, J. and Hart, G. (2007) *Well-being: Individual, Community and Social Perspectives*. Basingstoke: Palgrave Macmillan.

Hayes, N. (1994) *Foundations of Psychology: An Introductory Text*. London: Routledge.

Hedegaard, M. (2009) 'Children's development from a cultural–historical approach: Children's activity in everyday local settings as foundation for their development', *Mind, Culture, and Activity*, 16 (1): 64–82.

Hefferon, K. and Boniwell, I. (2011) *Positive Psychology: Theory, Research and Applications*. Maidenhead: Open University Press.

Hellyn, L. and Bennett, S. (2017) *The Curiosity Approach*. Birmingham: The Curiosity Approach.

Hirsh-Pasek, K., Adamson, L.B., Bakerman, R., Owen, M.T., Golinkoff, R.M., Pace, A., Suma, K. (2015) 'The contribution of early communication quality to low-income children's language success', *Psychological Science*, 26 (7): 1071–83.

Hobbs, A. (2018) 'Philosophy and the good life', *Journal of Philosophy in Schools*, 5 (1): 20–37.

Hodgman, L. (2015) *Enabling Environments in the Early Years* (2nd edn). London: Practical Pre-School Books.

Hohmann, M., Weikart, D.P. and Epstein, A.S. (2008) *Educating Young Children: Active Learning Practices for Preschool and Child Care Programmes* (3rd edn). Ypsilanti, MI: Highscope Press.

Holme, P. (2007) 'Spirituality: Some disciplinary perspective', in K. Flanagan and P.C. Jupp (eds), *A Sociology of Spirituality*. Farnham: Ashgate Publishing. pp. 23–42.

Howard-Jones, P. (2014) 'Neuroscience and education: Myths and messages', *Nature Reviews Neuroscience*, 15: 1–8.

Howard-Jones, P., Sashank, V., Ansari, D., Butterworth, B., De Smedt, B., Goswami, U., Laurillard, D. and Thomas, M. (2016) 'The principles and practices of educational neuroscience: Comment on Bowers, *Psychological Review*, 123 (5): 620–7.

Hu, B., Roberts, S.K., Leong, S.L. and Guo, H. (2016) 'Challenges to early childhood education in rural China: Lessons from the Hebei province', *Early Child Development and Care*, 186 (5): 815–31.

Hu, B., Wu, H., Winsler, A., Fan, X. and Song, Z. (2020) 'Parent migration and rural preschool children's early academic and social skills trajectories in China: Are "left-behind" children really left behind?', *Early Childhood Research Quarterly*, 51: 317–28.

Hughes, F. (2010a) *Children, Play and Development* (4th edn). London: SAGE.

Hughes, A. (2010b) *Designing Play for the Under 3's: The Treasure Basket and Heuristic Play*. London: David Fulton.

Hughes, B. (2002) *A Playworker's Taxonomy of Play Types* (2nd edn). Ely: Play Education.

Hughes, C., Jaffee, S.R., Happé, F., Taylor, A., Caspi, A. and Moffitt, T.E. (2005) 'Origins of individual differences in theory of the mind: From nature to nurture?', *Child Development*, 76 (2): 356–70.

Humphrey, N., Kalambouka, A., Wigelsworth, M., Lendrum, A., Lennie, C. and Farrell, P. (2010) 'New beginnings: Evaluation of a short social-emotional intervention for primary-aged children', *Educational Psychology*, 30 (5): 513–32.

Hunt, R. (2018) 'Models of SEN provision: The inclusion debate', in R. Crutchley (ed.), *Special Needs in the Early Years: Partnership and Participation*. London: SAGE. pp. 63–79.

Hutt, C. (1979) 'Exploration and play', in B. Sutton-Smith (ed.), *Play and Learning: The Johnson and Johnson Paediatric Round Table*. New York: Gardner Press. pp. 175–94.

Ingleby, E. and Oliver, G. (2008) *Applied Social Science for Early Years*. London: SAGE.

Isaacs, B. (2007) *Bringing the Montessori Approach to Your Early Years Practice*. London: Routledge.

Isaacs, S. (1954) *The Educational Value of the Nursery School*. London: Early Education.

James, A. and Prout, A. (eds) (1997) *Constructing and Reconstructing Childhood: Contemporary Issues in the Sociological Study of Childhood*. London: Routledge-Falmer.

James, S. (2005) 'Language Development in the young child', in T. Maynard and N. Thomas (eds) *Early Childhood Studies*. London: SAGE, pp. 28–38.

Jefferis, B.J., Power, C. and Hertzman, C. (2002) 'Birth weight, childhood socioeconomic environment, and cognitive development in the 1958 British birth cohort study', *BMJ*, 325 (7359): 305.

Johnson, C.N. and Boyatzis, C.J. (2006) 'Cognitive-cultural foundations of spiritual development', in E.C. Roehlkepartain, P.E. King, L. Wagener and P.L. Benson (eds), *The Handbook of Spiritual Development in Childhood and Adolescence*. London: SAGE. pp. 211–23.

Joshi, H., Ketende, S. and Parsons, S. (2011) *Child Development at Age Seven in Wales: Analysis of the Millennium Cohort Study*. Wales: Welsh Government.

Joshi, M.S. and MacLean, M. (1994) 'Indian and English children's understanding of the distinction between real and apparent emotion', *Child Development*, 65: 1372–84.

Justice, L.M., Petscher, Y., Schatschneider, C. and Mashburn, A. (2011) 'Peer effects in preschool classrooms: Is children's language growth associated with their classmates' skills?', *Child Development*, 82: 1768–77.

Kalat, J. (2014) *Biological Psychology* (11th edn). London: Cengage Learning.

Karoly, L. (2016) 'The economic returns to early childhood education', *The Future of Children*, 26 (2): 37–55.

Keller, H. (2013) 'Attachment and culture', *Journal of Cross-Cultural Psychology*, 44 (2): 175–94.

Kerig, P., Ludlow, A. and Wenar, C. (2012) *Developmental Psychopathology: From Infancy through Adolescence* (6th edn.) New York: McGraw-Hill Education.

Khalfaoui, A., Garcia-Carrion, R. and Villardon-Gallego, L. (2020) 'Bridging the gap: engaging Roma and migrant families in early childhood education through trust-based relationships', *European Early Childhood Education Research Journal*, 28 (5): 701–11.

Kimball, M. (2015) 'Cognitive economics', *The Japanese Economic Review*, 66: 167–81.

Kivunja, C. (2015) 'Using De Bono's six thinking hats model to teach critical thinking and problem solving skills essential for success in the 21st century economy', *Creative Education*, 6: 380–91.

Knowles, G. and Mukherji, P. (2014) 'Social inequalities', in P. Mukherji and L. Dryden (eds), *Foundations of Early Childhood: Principles and Practice*. London: SAGE. pp. 161–79.

Kochanska, G. (2001) 'Emotional development in children with different attachment histories: The first three years', *Child Development*, 72 (2): 474–90.

Kohlberg, L. (1963) 'The development of children's orientations towards a moral order. I. Sequence in the development of moral thought', *Vita Humana*, 6 (1–2): 11–33.

Korpi, M. (2007) *The Politics of Pre-School Intentions and Designs Underlying the Emergence*. Stockholm: Ministry of Education and Research.

Kuhn, D. and Franklin, S. (2006) 'The second decade: What develops (and how)'?, in W. Damon and R.M. Lerner (eds), D. Kuhn, and R. Siegler (vol. eds), *Handbook of Child Psychology: Vol. 1. Cognition, Perceptions and Language* (6th edn.) New York: Wiley.

Kuhn, D. and Park, S.H. (2005) 'Epistemological understanding and the development of intellectual values', *International Journal of Educational Research*, 43: 111–24.

Lavelli, M., Carra, C., Rossi, G. and Keller, H. (2019) 'Culture-specific development of early mother–infant emotional co-regulation: Italian, Cameroonian, and West African immigrant dyads', *Developmental Psychology*, 55 (9): 1850–67.

Lee, W., Carr, M., Soutar, B. and Mitchell, L. (2013) *Understanding the Te Whāriki Approach*. London: Routledge.

Levine, L. and Munsch, J. (2016) *Child Development from Infancy to Adolescence: An Active Learning Approach*. London: SAGE.

Levine, R. and New, R. (2008) *Anthropology and Child Development: A Cross-cultural Reader*. Oxford: Blackwell Publishing.

Lewis, A. (2019) 'Examining the concept of well-being and early childhood: Adopting multi-disciplinary perspectives', *Journal of Early Childhood Research*, 17 (4): 294–308.

Li, J.M. and Feng, X.X. (2013) *Interpretation of the 'Early Learning and Development Guideline for Children Age 3–6'*. Beijing: People's Education Press.

Lichtenwalner, J. and Maxwell, J. (1969) 'The relationship of birth order and socio-economic status to the creativity of preschool children', *Child Development*, 40 (4): 1241–7.

Lightfoot, C., Cole, M. and Cole, S. (2013) *The Development of Children* (7th edn). New York: Worth.

Lindén, I. (2018) 'The best interest of the child'. Available at: www.naeyc.org/resources/pubs/yc/jul2018/early-education-in-sweden (accessed 20 July 2021).

Lowenfeld, M. (1967) 'Understanding children's sandplay: Lowenfeld's world technique. London: Dr Margaret Lowenfeld Trust.

Lunn, L. (2015) 'A critical analysis of the role of spirituality within the early years curriculum', *Transformations*, 1: 27–41.

MacBlain, S. (2018) *Learning Theories for Early Years Practice*. London: SAGE.

MacBlain, S., Dunn, J. and Luke, I. (2017) *Contemporary Childhood*. London: SAGE.

MacGregor, A. (1999) *The Evaluation of a New Initiative to Support the Creation of Breakfast Clubs in Greater Glasgow, Stage 1*. Glasgow: Scottish Health Feedback.

MacNaughton, G. (2005) *Doing Foucault in Early Childhood Studies: Applying Poststructural Ideas*. Oxford: Routledge.

Maconochie, H. (2019) 'The brain and children's early development', in D. Fitzgerald and H. Maconochie (eds), *Early Childhood Studies*. London: SAGE. pp. 17–30.

Main, M. and Soloman, J. (1990) 'Procedures for identifying infants as disorganised/disorientated during the Ainsworth Strange Situation', in M.T. Greenberg, D. Cicchetti and E.M. Cummings (eds), *Attachment During the Preschool Years: Theory, Research and Invention*. Chicago: University of Chicago Press. pp. 121–60.

Manning-Morton, J. (ed.) (2014) *Exploring Well-being in the Early Years*. Maidenhead: Open University Press.

Marsh, J. (2018) 'Childhood in a digital age', in S. Powell and S. Smith (eds), *An Introduction to Early Childhood Studies* (4th edn). London: SAGE. pp. 53–63.

Martin, C.D. and Ebrahim, H.B. (2016) 'Teachers' discourses of literacy as social practice in advantaged and disadvantaged early childhood contexts', *South African Journal of Childhood Education*, 6 (2): 1–10.

Mashford-Scott, A., Church, A. and Tayler, C. (2012) 'Seeking children's perspectives on their wellbeing in early childhood settings', *International Journal of Early Childhood*, 44 (3): 231–47.

Maslow, A.H. (1943) 'A theory of human motivation', *Psychological Review*, 50 (4): 370–96.

Maslow, A.H. (1987) *Motivation and Personality* (3rd edn). Delhi: Pearson Education.

Matsumoto, D. (2000) *Culture and Psychology*. Belmont, CA: Wadsworth Publishing.

Mayall, B. (2000) 'The sociology of childhood in relation to children's rights', *The International Journal of Children's Rights*, 8 (3): 243–59.

Mayr, T. and Ulich, M. (1999) 'Children's well-being in day care centres: An exploratory study', *International Journal of Early Years Education*, 7 (3): 229–39.

McDevitt, T.M. and Ford, M.E. (1987) 'Processes in young children's communication functioning and development, in M.E. Ford and D.H. Ford (eds), *Humans as Self-Constructing Systems: Putting the Framework to Work*. Hillsdale, NJ: Erlbaum. pp. 145–75.

McDevitt, T.M. and Ormrod, J.E. (2010) *Child Development and Education*. Upper Saddle River, NJ: Merrill.

McInnes, K. and Yuen, N. (2018) 'Play and playfulness: The foundations of learning and development', in A. Thomas and K. McInnes (eds) *Teaching Early Years: Theory and Practice*. London: SAGE. pp. 47–64.

McInnes, K., Howard, J., Miles, G. and Crowley, K. (2011) 'Differences in practitioners' understanding of play and how this influences pedagogy and children's perceptions of play', *Early Years*, 31 (2): 121–33.

McLellan, R. and Steward, S. (2015) 'Measuring children and young people's wellbeing in the school context', *Cambridge Journal of Education*, 45 (3): 307–32.

McLoyd, V.C., Aikens, N.L. and Burton, L.M. (2006) 'Childhood poverty, policy and practice', in W. Damon, R.M. Lerner, K.A. Renninger and I.E. Sigel (eds), *Handbook of Child Psychology*, Vol. 4. *Child Psychology in Practice* (6th edn.) Hoboken, NJ: Wiley. pp. 700–75.

Meighan, R. (1981) *A Sociology of Educating*. Bath: Holt Education.

Melhuish, E. and Gardiner, J. (2020) *Study of Early Education and Development (SEED): Impact Study on Early Education Use and Child Outcomes up to Age Five Years*. London: Department for Education.

Mercer, J. (2018) *Child Development: Concepts and Theories*. London: SAGE.

Miller, L. and Hevey, D. (2012) *Policy Issues in the Early Years*. London: SAGE.

Miller, L. and Pound, L. (2011) *Theories and Approaches to Learning in the Early Years*. London: SAGE.

Miller, L., Cable, C. and Devereux, J. (2005) *Developing Early Years Practice*. London: David Fulton.

Miller, R. (2002) 'Nourishing the spiritual embryo: The educational vision of Maria Montessori', in J. Miller and N. Yoshiharu (eds) *Nourishing our Wholeness: Perspectives on Spirituality in Education*. Brandon, VT: The Foundation for Educational Renewal. pp. 227–41.

Ministry of Education of the People's Republic of China (2012) 'Early learning and development guidelines for children aged 3 to 6 years'. Available at: www.unicef.cn/sites/unicef.org. china/files/2018-10/2012-national-early-learning-development-guidelines.pdf (accessed 19 July 2021).

Montgomery, H. (2013) 'Childhood: An anthropological approach', in M. Kehily (ed.), *Understanding Childhood: A Cross-disciplinary Approach* (2nd edn). Bristol: Policy Press. pp. 161–209.

Morris, I. (2009) *Teaching Happiness and Well-being in Schools*. London: Continuum.

Morrow, V. and Mayall, B. (2009) 'What is wrong with children's well-being in the UK? Questions of meaning and measurement', *Journal of Social Welfare and Family Law*, 31 (3): 217–29.

Moss, P. (2001) 'The otherness of Reggio', in L. Abbott and C. Nutbrown (eds), *Experiencing Reggio Emilia: Implications for Pre-school Provision*. Maidenhead: Open University Press. pp. 125–37.

Moss, P. and Urban, M. (2020) 'The Organisation for Economic Co-operation and Development's International Early Learning and Child Well-being Study: The scores are in!', *Contemporary Issues in Early Childhood*, 21 (2): 165–71.

Moyles, J. (1989) *Just Playing*. Milton Keynes: Open University Press.

Moyles, J. and Adams, S. (2001) *Statements of Entitlement to Play: A Framework for Playful Teaching*. Maidenhead: Open University Press.

Moyles, J., Adams, S. and Musgrove, A. (2002) *Study of Pedagogical Effectiveness in Early Learning*. Norwich: School of Education, Research and Development Anglia Polytechnic University.

Mukherji, P. and Albon, D. (2018) *Research Methods in Early Childhood: An Introductory Guide*. (3rd edn). London: SAGE.

Murray, L. and Andrews, I. (2000) *The Social Baby*. Richmond: CP Publishing.

Murris, K. (2017) 'Reading two rhizomatic pedagogies diffractively through one another: A Reggio inspired philosophy with children for the postdevelopmental child', *Pedagogy, Culture and Society*, 25 (4): 531–50.

Nah, K., Bjørgen, K., Go, Y. and Yoo, Y. (2020) 'A comparative study of ECEC practitioners' perceptions of children's well-being and their roles in South Korea and Norway', *European Early Childhood Education Research Journal*, 28 (6): 847–63.

NALDIC (2021) Ofsted-removes-National-Lead-for-EAL-EALJ14_Spring2021.pdf. Available at: naldic. org.uk (accessed 21 December 2021).

National Playing Fields Association (NPFA) (2000) *Best Play*. Available at: www.freeplaynetwork.org. uk/pubs/bestplay.pdf (accessed 25 March 2022).

Neaum, S. (2013) *Child Development: For Early Years Students and Practitioners* (2nd edn). London: SAGE.

Neaum, S. (2019) *Child Development for Early Years Students and Practitioners* (4th edn). London: SAGE.

Nelson, K. (2009) 'Narrative practices and folk psychology: A perspective from developmental psychology', *Journal of Consciousness Studies*, 16: 69–93.

New Zealand Government (2016) *Te Whāriki*. Ministry of Education: New Zealand.

Nolan, A., Macfarlane, K. and Cartmel, J. (2013) *Research in Early Childhood*. London: SAGE.

NSPCC (2020) *Child Protection Plan and Register statistics: UK 2015–2019*. London: NSPCC.

Nucci, L.P. and Gingo, M. (2011) 'The development of moral reasoning', in U. Goswani (ed.), *The Wiley-Blackwell Handbook of Childhood Cognitive Development* (2nd edn). Oxford: Wiley-Blackwell. pp. 420–35.

Nursery Resources (2018) 'Creating an enabling environment'. Available at: www.nurseryresources.org/articles/enabling-enviroment/creating-an-enabling-environment/ (accessed 25 October 2021).

Nye, R. and Hay, D. (2006) 'Identifying children's spirituality: How do you start without a starting point?', *British Journal of Religious Education*, 18 (3): 144–54.

Oberski, I. (2011) 'Rudolf Steiner's philosophy of freedom as a basis for spiritual education?', *International Journal of Children's Spirituality*, 16 (1): 5–17.

O'Donnell, G., Deaton, A., Durand, M., Halpern, D. and Layard, R. (2014) *Wellbeing and Policy*. London: Legatum Institute.

OECD (2002) *Reading for Change: Performance and Engagement across Countries. Executive Summary*. Paris: OECD.

OECD (2006) *Starting Strong II: Early Childhood Education and Care*. London: The Children's Society. OECD.

OECD (2011) *How's Life? Measuring Well-being*. Paris: OECD.

Ofsted (2004) *Promoting and Evaluating Pupils' Spiritual, Moral, Social and Cultural Development*. London: HMSO.

O'Leary, Z. (2007) *The Social Science Jargon Buster*. London: SAGE.

Oppenheim, C. and Milton, C. (2021) *Changing Patterns of Poverty in Early Childhood*. London: Nuffield Foundation.

Overall, L. (2007) *Supporting Children's Learning: A Guide for Teaching Assistants*. London: SAGE.

Özar, M. (2012) 'Curriculum of preschool education: Swedish approach', *International Journal of Business and Social Science*, 3 (22): 248–57.

Packer, M. (2017) *Child Development: Understanding a Cultural Perspective*. London: SAGE.

Pang, L.J. (2014) 'The urgent need to optimize the structure of financial investment in early childhood education', *China Education Daily*, 25 May.

Parker, J.G. and Gottman, J.M. (1989) 'Social and emotional development in a relational context: Friendship interaction from early childhood to adolescence', in T.J. Berndt and G.W. Ladd (eds), *Peer Relationships in Child Development*. New York: Wiley. pp. 95–131.

Parkes, A., Sweeting, H. and Wright, D. (2014) *Growing up in Scotland*. Edinburgh: Scottish Government.

Parsons, S. and Platt, L. (2018) SEN-school-life-and-future-aspirations-briefing.pdf. Available at: ucl.ac.uk (accessed 20 December 2021).

Parten, M. (1932) 'Social participation among preschool children', *Journal of Abnormal and Social Psychology*, 27 (3): 243–69.

Pastor, D. (1981) 'The quality of mother–infant attachment and its relationship to toddlers' initial sociability with peers', *Development Psychology*, 17 (3): 326–35.

Paull, G. and Xu, X. (2015) *Childcare Policy Options for Wales*. Cardiff: Public Policy Institute for Wales.

Paull, G., Wilson, C., Melhuish, E. and Gardiner, J. (2020) *Study of Early Education and Development (SEED): Financial Returns to Early Education Spending*. London: DfE.

Pells, K. and Woodhead, M. (2014) *Changing Children's Lives*. Oxford: Young Lives.

Penn, H. (2008) *Understanding Early Childhood: Issues and Controversies* (2nd edn). Maidenhead: Open University Press.

Penn, H. (2010) 'Shaping the future: How human capital arguments about investment in early childhood are being (mis)used in poor countries', in N. Yelland (ed.) *Contemporary Perspectives on Early Childhood Education*. Maidenhead: Open University Press. pp. 49–65.

Penn, H. (2014) *Understanding Early Childhood: Issues and Controversies* (3rd edn). Maidenhead: Open University Press.

Perner, J. (1991) *Understanding the Representational Mind*. Cambridge, MA: MIT Press.

Pescott, C. and John, E. (2018) 'Drawing a line in the sand: Reflective practice using "sandboxing" with HE students'. Available at: www.bera.ac.uk/blog/drawing-a-line-in-the-sand-reflective-practice-using-sandboxing-with-he-students (accessed 28 January 2022).

Philosophy Foundation (2021) 'What is philosophy?'. Available at: www.philosophy-foundation. org/what-is-philosophy (accessed 11 January 2021).

Piaget, J. (1953) *The Origins of Intelligence in the Child* (2nd edn). London: Routledge and Kegan Paul.

Piaget, J. (1959) *Language and Thought of the Child*. London: Routledge.

Piaget, J. (1967) *Six Psychological Studies*. New York: Vintage.

Piaget, J. (1970) *Science of Education and the Psychology of the Child*. Harlow: Longman.

Piaget, J. (1973) *The Child and Reality: Problems of Genetic Psychology*. New York: Grossman.

Piaget, J. (1980) *Six Psychological Studies*. Brighton: Harvester Press.

Piaget, J. and Inhleder, B. (1969) *The Psychology of the Child*. New York: Basic Books.

Potegal, M. and Davidson, R.J. (2003) 'Temper tantrums in young children: 1. Behavioral composition', *Developmental and Behavioral Pediatrics*, 24 (3): 140–7.

Pound, L. (2011) *Influencing Early Childhood Education: Key Figures, Philosophies and Ideas*. Maidenhead: Open University Press.

Pound, L. (2014) 'The historical background of early childhood care and education: influencing factors', in P. Mukherji and L. Dryden (eds), *Foundations of Early Childhood Principles and Practice*. London: SAGE. pp. 143–60.

Qi, X. and Melhuish, E. (2016) 'Early childhood education and care in China: History, current trends and challenges', *Early Years*, 37 (3): 1–17.

Quennerstedt, A. and Quennerstedt, M. (2014) 'Researching children's rights in education: Sociology of childhood encountering educational theory', *British Journal of Sociology of Education*, 35 (1): 115–32.

Raghavan, R. and Alexandrova, A. (2015) 'Toward a theory of child well-being', *Social Indicators Research*, 121 (3): 887–902.

Rinaldi, C. (2013) *Re-imagining Childhood: The Inspiration of Reggio Emelia Principles in South Australia*. Australia: Government of South Australia.

Robbins, B. (2008) 'What is the good life? Positive psychology and the renaissance of humanistic psychology', *The Humanistic Psychologist*, 36 (2): 96–112.

Roberts, R. (2010) *Wellbeing from Birth*. London: SAGE.

Rochat, P. (2009) *Others in Mind–Social Origins of Self-consciousness*. New York: Cambridge University Press.

Rogoff, B. (2003) *The Cultural Nature of Human Development*. New York: Oxford University Press.

Rönnqvist, L. and Hopkins, B. (1998) 'Lateral biases in head-turning and the moro response in the human newborn: Are they both vestibular in origin?', *Developmental Psychbiology*, 33 (4): 339–49.

Rose, J. and McGuire-Sniekus, R. (2016) 'How emotion coaching brings out the best in children', *The Conversation*. Available at: https://theconversation.com/how-emotion-coaching-brings-out-the-best-in-children-60359 (accessed 19 February 2020).

Rothbart, M.K. and Bates, J.E. (2006) 'Temperament', in W. Damon, R.M. Lerner, K.A. Renninger and I.E. Sigel (eds), *Handbook of Child Psychology in Practice* (6th edn.) Hoboken, NJ: Wiley. pp. 99–225.

Royal Society (2011) *Brain Waves Module 2: Neuroscience: Implications for Education and Lifelong Learning*. London: The Royal Society, Science Policy Centre.

Ryan, R. and Deci, E. (2001) 'On happiness and human potentials: A review of research on hedonic and eudaimonic well-being', *Annual Review Psychology*, 52 (1): 141–66.

Saarni, C., Campos, J.J., Camras, L.A. and Witherington, D. (2006) 'Emotional development: Action, communication and understanding', in W. Damon, R.M. Lerner and N. Eisenberg (eds), *Handbook of Child Psychology. Vol 3. Social, Emotional and Personality Development* (6th edn.) Hoboken, NJ: Wiley. pp. 226–99.

Salovey, P. and Mayer, J.D. (1990) 'Emotional intelligence', *Imagination, Cognition and Personality*, 9: 185–211.

Sammons, P., Toth, K. and Sylva, K. (2015) *Pre-school and Early Home Learning Effects on A-level Outcomes: Effective Pre-School, Primary & Secondary Education Project (EPPSE)*. Oxford: University of Oxford.

Sapere (n.d.) *Philosophy for Children, Colleges and Communities*. Available at: www.sapere.org.uk/ (accessed 22 April 2021).

Save the Children (2016) 'The lost boys'. London: Save the Children UK.

Schön, D.A. (1983) *The Reflective Practitioner: How Professionals Think in Action*. London: Temple Smith.

Schön, D.A. (1991) *The Reflective Turn: Case Studies In and On Educational Practice*. New York: Teachers Press.

Schoon, I., Cheng, H. and Jones, E. (2010) 'Resilience in children's development'. Available at: https://cls.ucl.ac.uk/wp-content/uploads/2017/05/04_briefing_web.pdf (accessed 27 August 2020).

Scottish Government (2018) *Curriculum for Excellence*. Available at: https://education.gov.scot/documents/All-experiencesoutcomes18.pdf (accessed 24 September 2020).

Seland, M., Sandseter, B. and Bratterud, A. (2015) 'One-to-three-year-old children's experience of subjective wellbeing in day care', *Contemporary Issues in Early Childhood*, 16 (1): 70–83.

Seligman, M., Ernst, R., Gillham, J., Reivich, K. and Linkins, M. (2009) 'Positive education: positive psychology and classroom interventions', *Oxford Review of Education*, 35 (3): 293–311.

Shaffer, D.R. and Kipp, K. (2010) *Developmental Psychology: Childhood and Adolescence*. Belmont, CA: Wadsworth.

Shanahan, S. (2007) 'Lost and found: The sociological ambivalence toward childhood', *Annual Review of Sociology*, 33: 407–28.

Shonkoff, J.P., Boyce, W.T. and McEwen, B.S. (2009) 'Neuroscience, molecular biology, and the childhood roots of health disparities: Building a new framework for health promotion and disease prevention. *JAMA*, 301 (21): 2252–9.

Shore, R. (1997) *Rethinking the Brain: New Insights into Early Development.* New York: Families and Work Institute.

Siddiqui, N., Gorard, S. and See, B.H. (2017) 'Non-cognitive impacts of philosophy for children, project report'. Durham: School of Education, Durham University. Available at: https://dro.dur.ac.uk/20880/1/20880.pdf?DDD34+DDD29+czwc58+d700tmt (accessed 25 January 2020).

Siegler, R., Saffran, R., Eisenberg, N., DeLoache, J. and Gershoff, E. (2017) *How Children Develop* (5th edn). New York: Worth.

Simmonds, A. (2014) *How Neuroscience is Affecting Education: Report of Teacher and Parent Surveys.* London: Wellcome Trust.

Siraj-Blatchford, I. (1999) 'Early children pedagogy: Practice, principles and research', in P. Mortimore (ed.), *Understanding Pedagogy and its Impact on Learning.* London: Paul Chapman.

Siraj-Blatchford, I. (2014) 'Diversity, inclusion and learning in the early years', in G. Pugh and B. Duffy (eds) *Contemporary Issues in the Early Years* (6th edn). London: SAGE. pp. 181–97.

Siraj-Blatchford, I., Sylva, K., Muttock, S., Gilden, R. and Bell, D. (2002) 'Researching effective pedagogy in the early years' (Research Report RR356). Available at: www.327matters.org/docs/rr356.pdf (accessed 25 October 2021).

Skinner, B.F. (1957) *Verbal Behaviour.* New York: Appleton-Century-Crofts.

Skinner, B.F. (1971) *Beyond Freedom and Dignity.* New York: Knopf.

Smidt, S. (2013) *The Developing Child in the 21st Century: A Global Perspective on Child Development* (2nd edn). London: Routledge.

Smith, K., Tesar, M. and Myers, C. (2016) 'Edu-capitalism and the governing of early childhood education and care in Australia, New Zealand and the United States', *Global Studies of Childhood*, 6 (1): 123–35.

Smith, L.B. and Thelan, E. (2003) 'Development as a dynamic system', *Trends in Cognitive Sciences*, 7 (8): 343–8.

Smith, P.K. (2010) *Children and Play.* Oxford: Wiley-Blackwell.

Smith, P.K. (2011) 'Observational methods in studying play', in A. Pellegrini (ed.), *The Oxford Handbook of Developmental Play.* New York: Oxford University Press. pp. 138–49.

Snarey, J.R. (1985) 'Cross-cultural universality of social-moral development: A critical review of Kohlbergian research', *Psychological Bulletin*, 97: 202–32.

Soler, J. and Miller, L. (2003) 'The struggle for early childhood curricula: A comparison of the English Foundation Stage curriculum, Te Whāriki and Reggio Emilia', *International Journal of Early Years Education*, 11 (1): 57–68.

Soutter, A., O'Steen, B. and Gilmore, A. (2012) 'Wellbeing in the New Zealand curriculum', *Journal of Curriculum Studies*, 44 (1): 111–42.

Sport England (n.d.) *Primary School Physical Literacy Framework.* Available at: https://sportengland-production-files.s3.eu-west-2.amazonaws.com/s3fs-public/physical-siraj-blatchford 1999 understanding pedagogy and its impact on learning literacy-framework.pdf (accessed 28 October 2020).

Sport Wales (n.d.) *Physical Literacy: A Journey Through Life*. Available at: http://physicalliteracy. sportwales.org.uk/en/ (accessed 28 October 2020).

Statham, J. and Chase, E. (2010) *Childhood Wellbeing: A Brief Overview*. Childhood Wellbeing Research Centre.

Steinberg, L. (2001) 'We know some things: Parent–adolescent relationships in retrospect and prospect', *Journal of Research on Adolescence*, 11: 1–19.

Stiglitz, J., Sen, A. and Fitoussi, J. (2009) *Report by the Commission on the Measurement of Economic Performance and Social Progress*. Paris.

Stojanov, K. (2019) 'Children's ideals as a philosophical topic', *Education Theory*, 69 (3): 327–40.

Swedish National Agency for Education (2019) *Curriculum for the Preschool, Lpfö 18*. Available at: www.skolverket.se/publikationsserier/styrdokument/2019/curriculum-for-the-preschool-lpfo-18?id=4049 (accessed 19 July 2021).

Sylva, K., Melhuish, E., Sammons, P., Siraj-Blatchford, I., and Taggart, B. (2004) *The Effective Provision of Pre-School Education (EPPE) Project: Findings from Pre-school to end of Key Stage 1*. London: Department for Education and Skills.

Tassoni, P. (2007) *Child Care and Education* (3rd edn). Edinburgh: Heinemann.

Tedam, P. (2009) 'Understanding diversity', in T. Waller (ed.) *An Introduction to Early Childhood* (2nd edn). London: SAGE. pp. 111–25.

Tempriou, A. (2018) 'Leadership and inclusion: Creating an ethos, culture and provision', in R. Crutchley (ed.) *Special Needs in the Early Years: Partnership and Participation*. London: SAGE. pp. 80–94.

Thelan, E., Corbetta, D., Kamm, K. Spencer, J.P., Schneider, K. and Zernicke, R.E. (1993) 'The transition to reaching: Mapping intention and intrinsic dynamics', *Child Development*, 64 (4): 1058–98.

Thomas, A. (2018) 'Exploring the role of schemas within the Welsh Foundation Phase curriculum' (unpublished doctoral dissertation). Australia: University of South Wales.

Thomas, A. (2019) 'Toolkit to support schemas'. Available at: https://hwb.gov.wales/api/storage/4be12be2-3180-4619-963d-b62c4f252423/Toolkit%20supporting%20schemas.pdf (accessed 21 October 2021).

Thomas, A. and Lewis, A. (2016) *An Introduction to the Foundation Phase*. London: Bloomsbury.

Thurtle, V. (2005) 'The child in society', in J. Taylor and M. Woods (eds) *Early Childhood Studies: An Holistic Introduction*. London: Arnold. pp. 163–84.

Tibke, J. (2019) *Why the Brain Matters*. London: Corwin.

Tickell, C. (2011) *The Early Years: Foundations for Life, Health And Learning*. London: UK Government.

Tomasello, M. and Hermann, E. (2010) 'Ape and human cognition: What's the difference?', *Current Directions in Psychology Science*, 19: 3–8.

Tovey, H. (2007) *Playing Outdoors*. Maidenhead: Open University Press.

Trawick-Smith, J. (2014) *Early Childhood Development: A Multicultural Perspective* (6th edn). London: Pearson Education.

UK Government (2019) 'Physical activity for early years: Birth to 5 years'. Available at: publishing. service.gov.uk (accessed 5 August 2021).

UNICEF (2019) *Children, Food and Nutrition: Growing Well in a Changing World*. New York: UNICEF.

UNICEF (2021) 'Getting started – rights respecting schools award'. Available at: unicef.org.uk (accessed 9 December 2021).

University College London (2021a) 'Millennium cohort study'. Available at: https://cls.ucl.ac.uk/cls-studies/millennium-cohort-study/ (accessed 17 March 2021).

University College London (2021b) 'Being born small doesn't tend to disadvantage IVF babies' cognitive development'. Available at: https://cls.ucl.ac.uk/being-born-small-doesnt-tend-to-disadvantage-ivf-babies-cognitive-development/ (accessed 17 March 2021).

Uprichard, E. (2008) 'Children as "Being and Becomings": Children, childhood and temporality', *Health Education*, 22 (4): 303–13.

van Huizen, T., Plantenga, J. and Dumhs, L. (2019) 'The costs and benefits of investing in universal preschool: Evidence from a Spanish reform', *Child Development*, 90 (3): 386–406.

Van Ryzen, M., Leve, I., Neiderhiser, J., Shaw, D., Natsuaki, M. and Reiss, D. (2015) 'Genetic influences can protect against unresponsive parenting in the prediction of child social competence', *Child Development*, 86: 667–80.

Vygotsky, L. (1978) *Mind in Society: The Development of Higher Mental Processes*. Cambridge, MA: Harvard University Press.

Walker, G. (2011) 'Children's rights: Social justice and exclusion', in P. Jones and G. Walker (eds), *Children's Rights in Practice*. London: SAGE. pp. 32–42.

Walkerdine, V. (2009) 'Developmental psychology and the study of childhood', in M. Kehily (ed.), *An Introduction to Childhood Studies* (2nd edn). London: SAGE. pp. 112–23.

Waller, T. (2009) *An Introduction to Early Childhood* (2nd edn). London: SAGE.

Waller, T. and Davis, G. (2014) *An Introduction to Early Childhood* (3rd edn). London: SAGE.

Wang, Q. and Ross, M. (2007) 'Culture and memory', in S. Kitayama and D. Cohen (eds), *Handbook of Cultural Psychology*. New York: Guilford Press. pp. 645–67.

Watson, D., Emery, C., Baylis, P., Boushel, M. and McInnes, K. (2012) *Children's Social and Emotional Well-being in School: A Critical Perspective*. Bristol: Policy Press.

Wellman, H., Fang, F. and Peterson, C. (2011) 'Sequential progression in a theory-of-mind scale: Longitudinal perspectives,' *Child Development*, 82: 780–92.

Wellman, H.M. (1990) *The Child's Theory of Mind*. Cambridge, MA: MIT.

Welsh Assembly Government (WAG) (2008a) *Creative Development*. Cardiff: WAG.

Welsh Assembly Government (WAG) (2008b) *National Exemplar Framework for Religious Education for 3 to 19-year-olds in Wales*. Cardiff: WAG.

Welsh Assembly Government (WAG) (2009) *Foundation Phase Child Development Assessment Profile*. Available at: https://dera.ioe.ac.uk/3642/1/110517foundassessmenten.pdf (accessed 31 July 2020).

Welsh Government (WG) (2011) *Child Development at Age Seven in Wales: Analysis of the Millennium Cohort Study*. Cardiff: Welsh Government.

Welsh Government (WG) (2015a) *Foundation Phase Framework*. Cardiff: Welsh Government.

Welsh Government (WG) (2015b) *Children and Young People Wellbeing Monitor for Wales 2015*. Cardiff: Welsh Government.

Welsh Government (WG) (2017a) *Foundation Phase Profile Handbook*. Cardiff: Welsh Government.

Welsh Government (WG) (2017b) *Flying Start – Annex Parenting Support Guidance*. Cardiff: Welsh Government.

Welsh Government (2018a) *Additional Learning Needs and Education Tribunal (Wales) Act: Explanatory Memorandum*. Wales: Welsh Government.

Welsh Government (WG) (2018b) *Enabling Gypsies, Roma and Travellers*. Wales: Welsh Government.

Welsh Government (WG) (2020) *Curriculum for Wales*. Available at: https://hwb.gov.wales/curriculum-for-wales (accessed 20 July 2020).

Wethington, H., Pan, L. and Sherry, B. (2013) 'The association of screen time television in the bedroom, and obesity among school-aged youth: 2007 National Survey of Children's Health', *Journal of School Health*, 83 (8): 573–81.

Wharton, A. (2005) *The Sociology of Gender: An Introduction to Theory and Research*. Oxford: Blackwell.

White, J. (2008) *Playing and Learning Outdoors: Making Provision for High Quality Experiences in the Outdoor Environment*. London: Routledge.

White, M. (2009) *Magic Circles* (2nd edn). London: SAGE.

Whitehead, M. (2010) *Physical Literacy: Throughout the Life Course*. Oxford: Routledge.

Wigelsworth, M., Humphrey, N., Kalambouka, A. and Lendrum, A. (2010) 'A review of key issues in the measurement of children's social and emotional skills', *Educational Psychology in Practice: Theory, Research and Practice in Educational Psychology*, 26 (2): 173–86.

Wikipedia (2022) 'Ecological Systems Theory'. Available at: https://en.wikipedia.org/wiki/Ecological_systems_theory. (accessed 18 August 2022).

Willow, C. (2014) 'Upholding children's rights in early years settings', in P. Mukherji and L. Dryden (eds) *Foundations of Early Childhood: Principles and Practice*. London: SAGE. pp. 26–44.

Wimmer, H. and Perner, J. (1983) 'Beliefs about beliefs: Representation and constraining function of wrong beliefs in young children's understanding of deception', *Cognition*, 13 (1): 103–28.

Wood, D., Bruner, J.S. and Ross, G. (1976) 'The role of tutoring in problem solving', *Journal of Child Psychology and Psychiatry*, 17: 89–100.

Wood, E., Payler, J. and Georgeson, J. (2017) 'Conclusion: Key messages and future research', in BERA-TACTYC, *Early Childhood Research Review*. London: BERA. pp. 113–18.

Woodhead, M. (2005) 'Early childhood development: A question of rights', *International Journal of Early Childhood*, 37 (3): 79–98.

Woolf, A. (2013) 'Social and emotional aspects of earning: Teaching and learning or playing and becoming', *Pastoral Care in Education*, 31 (1): 28–42.

Woolfolk, A., Hughes, M. and Walkup, V. (2013) *Psychology in Education* (2nd edn). London: Pearson Education.

Wyse, D. (2020) 'Education: An academic discipline or a field?', British Educational Research Association. Available at: www.bera.ac.uk/blog/education-an-academic-discipline-or-a-field (accessed 2 March 2021).

Yang, W. and Li, H. (2019) *Early Childhood Curriculum in Chinese Societies: Policies, Practices and Prospects*. Oxford: Routledge.

Yeung, W.J. and Pfeiffer, K.M. (2009) 'The black–white test score gap and early home environment', *Social Science Research*, 38 (2): 412–37.

Zilberstein, K. (2006) 'Clarifying core characteristics of attachment disorders: A review of current research and theory', *American Journal of Orthopsychiatry*, 76 (1): 55–64.

Zohar, D. and Marshall, I. (2001) *SQ: Connecting With Our Spiritual Intelligence*. New York: Bloomsbury.

INDEX